The Creativity Mar

NEW WRITING VIEWPOINTS

Series Editor: Graeme Harper, *Oakland University, Rochester, USA*

The overall aim of this series is to publish books which will ultimately inform teaching and research, but whose primary focus is on the analysis of creative writing practice and theory. There will also be books which deal directly with aspects of creative writing knowledge, with issues of genre, form and style, with the nature and experience of creativity, and with the learning of creative writing. They will all have in common a concern with excellence in application and in understanding, with creative writing practitioners and their work, and with informed analysis of creative writing as process as well as completed artefact.

Full details of all the books in this series and of all our other publications can be found on http://www.multilingual-matters.com, or by writing to Multilingual Matters, St Nicholas House, 31–34 High Street, Bristol, BS1 2AW, UK.

The Creativity Market

Creative Writing in the 21st Century

Edited by
Dominique Hecq

MULTILINGUAL MATTERS
Bristol • Buffalo • Toronto

Library of Congress Cataloging in Publication Data
A catalog record for this book is available from the Library of Congress.
The Creativity Market: Creative Writing in the 21st Century/Edited by Dominique Hecq.
New Writing Viewpoints: 8
Includes bibliographical references.
1. Creative writing--Study and teaching. I. Hecq, Dominique.
PE1404.C75 2012
808'.042071–dc232011048975

British Library Cataloguing in Publication Data
A catalogue entry for this book is available from the British Library.

ISBN-13: 978-1-84769-710-3 (hbk)
ISBN-13: 978-1-84769-709-7 (pbk)

Multilingual Matters
UK: St Nicholas House, 31–34 High Street, Bristol, BS1 2AW, UK.
USA: UTP, 2250 Military Road, Tonawanda, NY 14150, USA.
Canada: UTP, 5201 Dufferin Street, North York, Ontario M3H 5T8, Canada.

The policy of Multilingual Matters/Channel View Publications is to use papers that are natural, renewable and recyclable products, made from wood grown in sustainable forests. In the manufacturing process of our books, and to further support our policy, preference is given to printers that have FSC and PEFC Chain of Custody certification. The FSC and/or PEFC logos will appear on those books where full certification has been granted to the printer concerned.

Typeset by The Charlesworth Group.
Printed and bound in Great Britain by the MPG Books Group.

Contents

Contributors

Phillip Edmonds has been active in small press publishing for many years, originally in the 1970s through *Contempa* and, currently, as the publisher of *Wet Ink (the magazine of new writing)*, which was founded in 2005. He has published two collections of short fiction, *Big Boys* and *Don't let me Fall*, and, in 2010, the novella *Leaving Home with Henry* (Australian Scholarly Publishing), which has been well received. Phillip teaches Australian Literature and Creative Writing in the English Department at Adelaide University. He has also taught at the Victorian College of the Arts and Griffith University. His PhD, from Deakin University in 1997, is a study of the contemporary short story in Australia. In 2003, he was a Visiting Fellow in Australian Literature at the University of Madras, under the auspices of the Australia/India Council.

Jeremy Fisher is Senior Lecturer in Writing at The University of New England, Armidale, New South Wales. He was the Executive Director of The Australian Society of Authors, 2004-2009. Jeremy has over 35 year's experience in the Australian publishing industry as editor and publisher. His most recent publications are the novel *Music from another Country* and a story in *Fear Factor: Terror Incognito*. He can be found at: http://drjeremy fisher.blogspot.com/

Mike Harris is a script writer and theatre director. He has had more than 100 scripts, from soap episodes to original plays, performed or broadcast on stage, radio and TV in the United Kingdom, Europe, Russia and Canada. He is also a senior lecturer, working part-time on the MA in Writing at Sheffield Hallam University. His papers on the subject of creative writing and theory have been published in *TEXT, New Writing: the International Journal for the Practice and Theory of Creative Writing* and elsewhere.

Graeme Harper (aka Brooke Biaz) is Professor of Creative Writing and editor of the journal *New Writing: the International Journal for the Practice and Theory of Creative Writing*. He has taught at universities in the United Kingdom, the United States and Australia and is director of the International Centre for Creative Writing Research (ICCWR) and of www.creative-universities.com. His latest creative works are *Camera Phone* (2010) and the forthcoming *A History of Medicine* (2011). His latest critical works are *On Creative Writing* (2010) and the forthcoming *Creative Writing Challenges* (2012).

Dominique Hecq is Associate Professor in Writing at Swinburne University of Technology (Australia) where she is also Discipline and Research Leader. Originally from Belgium, she has a PhD in literature and a background in French and Germanic languages. Widely published in literary studies, creative writing, psychoanalysis and pedagogy, she is also the author of 11 creative books, including *Out of Bounds* (2009). Dominique edits *Bukker Tillibul: the Journal of Writing and Practice-led Research* aimed at postgraduate students. Current research project titles are *Psychoanalysis for the Creative Writer*, *Metaphor and Loss* and *Writing, Madness and Anxiety*. *Stretchmarks of Sun* is forthcoming.

Christopher Lappas is co-founder and director of boutique publishing house, Ilura Press. He is also joint managing editor of the acclaimed creative journal *:Etchings*. Christopher's academic interests include philosophy, psychoanalysis, writing and editing and media arts, and he holds a PhD in Creative Writing. He has been employed as a professional musician, songwriter, photographer and newspaper editor-in-chief. His published works include poetry, interviews, reviews, advertising copy, plays and numerous short stories.

Vahri McKenzie first contributed to this book as a PhD student. She has since been awarded her doctorate and now lectures in Writing at Edith Cowan University. Vahri is also a freelance writer and arts practitioner. She is interested in improvisation, interdisciplinary creative arts and the role of the human body in arts practice. Recent works include 'Complications' in *dotdotdash 7* (short fiction) and performer in *Perth Institute of Sleep Behaviour* (installation by Lisa Carrie Goldberg at the Perth Institute of Contemporary Arts [PICA]). Vahri lives in Western Australia.

Robyn Morris lectures in the English Studies programme at the University of Wollongong, Australia. Her areas of interest include race, whiteness, gender, surveillance and the visualisation of difference. Her focus is contemporary Australian and Canadian women's writing. She has published widely on the work of writers such as Larissa Lai, Joy Kogawa, Hiromi Goto, Evelyn Lau, Lillian Ng, Simone Lazaroo and Hsu-Ming Teo in articles, book chapters, interviews and reviews. She is the editor of *Australasian Canadian Studies* (ACS) and Vice-President of the Association for Canadian Studies in Australia and New Zealand (ACSANZ). Her most recent publications include: 'New Directions in Asian Canadian writing: Larissa Lai's "thinking through" a Contemporary Politics of Identity', *British Journal of Canadian Studies* 25 (1), 2012 (forthcoming); 'Relations of Difference: Asianness, Indigeneity and Whiteness in Simone Lazaroo's Fiction,' *Kunapipi*, Vol 32 (1), 2010 (forthcoming).

Antonia Pont has a long-standing interest in the relationship between making and thinking. Her practice involves the doings of writing/movement/ thought and the thinking of doing in its infinitive form. Given that this almost inevitably leads to encounters with the strangeness of doing-that-*isn't,* she is also committed to a slow mapping of philosophy's attempts to engage with that elegant aporia. Recent projects include a novel called *The Best Thing About Snow,* on-going experiments with enjambment and ephemeral performance-inquiry into the technology we store within our skins. After completing her doctoral studies in deconstruction and the nexus between violence and mourning, she now lectures at Deakin University in Writing and Literary Studies.

Pavlina Radia is an Assistant Professor in English Studies at Nipissing University, Canada. She specialises in American and postcolonial literature, gender studies and critical theory. She is also interested in creative writing and visual arts. She has taught gender studies at the University of Toronto and published articles in international journals, as well as written chapters in books. She is currently working on a book about American modernism and is also co-editing a *Double Dialogues* issue, titled 'The Hunger Artist: Food and the Arts', based on the conference of the same title that she co-organised at the University of Toronto.

Jacques Rancourt was born in Quebec in 1946 and has lived in Paris since 1971. He has a PhD in French Literature from La Sorbonne and has published some 20 books of poetry and artist books, essays and anthologies of contemporary poetry, plus translations from English and Spanish. Since the beginning of the 1980s, he has been Director of the Festival Franco-Anglais de Poésie (which was held in Melbourne in October 2008) and of the poetry translation magazine *La Traductière.* A wide choice of his poems (from 1974–2008) was published in 2010 under the title *Veilleur sans sommeil.* The poem *Les Etoiles du firmament/The Stars in the Firmament* was written for *The Creativity Market* book. It was published in English (John F. Deane's translation) by *Poetry Review* (London, vol. 100-103) in autumn 2010 and in its French original version by the review *Les Ecrits* (Montreal, no. 131) in March 2011.

Professor **Kirpal Singh** obtained his PhD in English from the University of Adelaide, where he was a Colombo Plan Scholar. Until 1991, he taught at the National University of Singapore and was then invited to move to Nanyang Technological University (NTU) to help set up the Bachelor of Arts programme there. For five years he served as Head of the Division of Literature & Drama and initiated several significant programmes. Kirpal Singh has always been an active participant of cultural and literary affairs, whether within the University environment or within the larger public domain. As a writer, critic and scholar, he is among the most powerful voices to emerge from the Asia Pacific region and is constantly sought by international bodies and universities to present papers and sit on various boards. In 1999, he was invited to join the new Singapore Management University, where he coordinates and teaches the Creative Thinking programme. His book *Thinking Hats and Coloured Turbans* (2003) was globally acclaimed. Kirpal Sing is Honorary Member and Global Mentor of the Creative Skills and Training Council for the Asia Pacific and Australia.

Jeff Sparrow is the editor of *Overland* literary journal. He is the co-author of *Radical Melbourne: A Secret History* and *Radical Melbourne 2: The Enemy Within* and the author of *Communism: A Love Story* (shortlisted for the Colin Roderick Award) and *Killing: Misadventures in Violence* (shortlisted for the Melbourne Prize for Literature Best Writing Award).

Eric Tinsay Valles, formerly a journalist and editor, currently teaches English Language and Literature at the National University of Singapore High School of Math and Science. He has been published in Routledge's *New Writing: The International Journal for the Practice and Theory of Creative Writing*, the *Hispanic Culture Review* (George Mason University), the Singapore National Arts Council-published anthology *Reflecting on the Merlion*, the Ethos-published *& Words: Poems Singapore and Beyond*, *Ceriph*, as well as in online journals, *Double Dialogues* (University of Melbourne) and *Bukker Tillibul* (Swinburne University of Technology). He has also been invited to read poetry at the University of Melbourne and at the *Poetry and Voice* conference of the University of Chichester. This year, he won the City Loves Writing competition of the British Council's *Writing the City* website. He draws inspiration from all sorts of music and feeds off great writers (and souls) such as St. Augustine, Geoffrey Chaucer and Flannery O'Connor. Among the places he has called home are Manila, Taipei and Singapore.

Professor **Gerry Turcotte** is President and Vice-Chancellor of St. Mary's University College in Calgary. He was previously the Associate Provost and Executive Dean of the College of Arts & Sciences at the University of Notre Dame, Australia. He is immediate past President of the Australasian Council of Deans of Arts, Social Sciences and Humanities (DASSH) and of the Association for Canadian Studies in Australia and New Zealand (ACSANZ), as well as a former secretary of the International Council for Canadian Studies (ICCS). He is the author and editor of 14 books, including the novel *Flying in Silence*, which was shortlisted for *The Age* Book of the Year in 2001 and *Border Crossings: Words & Images*, which was adapted for performance at the Sydney Opera House. He is also the author of three collections of poetry: *Neighbourhood of Memory* (Dangaroo), *Winterlude* (Brandl & Schlesinger) and *Hauntings: the 'Varuna' Poems* (Five Islands Press). His edited works include *Jack Davis: The Maker of History* (Harper Collins) and *Compr(om)ising Post/colonialisms: Challenging Narratives & Practices*, with Greg Ratcliffe (Dangaroo). His most recent publications include *Peripheral Fear: Transformations of the Gothic in Canadian and Australian Fiction* (Peter Lang) and *Unsettled Remains: Canadian Literature & the Postcolonial Gothic*, co-edited with Cynthia Sugars (Wilfrid Laurier Press), which was shortlisted for the Gabrielle Roy Prize for literary criticism.

Thom Vernon is an American, queer and voluntarily exiled novelist and educator living in Toronto. He has a growing list of publications and critical presentations to his credit. *The Drifts* (Coach House Books, 2010) was called 'magnificent' by the *Globe & Mail*. Other recent articles include: 'The Angel at Our Table: Walter Benjamin, Melancholy and the Art of Brooding', 'Daddies & Papas 2B: The Evolution of Possibilities' and 'Calling All Perverts: International Relations and the Rise of Sexology'. As an actor, Thom's film/television/theatre credits include: *Seinfeld, The Fugitive, Grace Under Fire, General Hospital, A Circle of People: 3 by Chekov* and many others. He is currently researching the exile years of Walter Benjamin in Berlin, Paris and elsewhere. He has a literary novel nearing completion that explores 'absence' in the context of two boys who murder their teacher. In addition to being a passionate arts educator and advocate, Thom teaches creative writing at the University of Toronto School of Continuing Studies. Visit Thom at: thomvernon.com

Jen Webb is Professor of Creative Practice at the University of Canberra and interim Dean of the Faculty of Arts and Design. Jen holds a PhD in cultural theory, focusing on the field of creative production, and a DCA in creative writing. She has published widely in poetry, short fiction and scholarly works. Her most recent book is *Understanding Representation* (Sage, 2009) and she is currently completing a co-authored book on the work of Michel Foucault, a co-authored book on embodiment and a textbook on research for creative writing. Jen is co-editor of the Sage book series, *Understanding Contemporary Culture*, and of the new journal *Axon: Creative Explorations*, an online journal being published out of the University of Canberra. Her current research investigates representations of critical global events and the use of research in, and through, creative practice to generate new knowledge.

Acknowledgements

From its inception, this project has benefited from generous intellectual and material support from a wide range of parties and people. First, I'd like to thank Swinburne University of Technology for a Researcher Development Grant, which enabled some research assistance early on. Especially supportive in that regard have been Carol-Anne Croker and Robert Banagan. I thank Carol-Anne for her enthusiasm and entrepreneurship and Robert Banagan for his honesty and keen eye for detail. I also thank Swinburne for brief periods of study leave that enabled me to attend the 2008 annual conference of the Australasian Association of Writing Programs (AAWP) hosted by the University of Technology (UTS) in Sydney, an occasion that sparked the discussion carried out in this volume, and the 2009 World Conference on Higher Education held at the UNESCO Headquarters in Paris, an event that consolidated the global scope of this book. I thank my colleagues in the Faculty of Higher Education at Lilydale for their support, especially Glenda Ballantyne and Stephen Theiler. My thanks also go to the Writing Group, my PhD students past and present and to our Research Co-ordinator, Nadine White. Members from the AAWP also provided stimulating conversation and moral support. For their early encouragement, Donna Lee Brien, Jeri Kroll and Jen Webb deserve my thanks. Also valuable in this regard have been Ann McCulloch and Paul Monaghan, whose forum, 'Double Dialogues', has provided stimulation over the years. Helen O'Neil, as well as all those who responded to the initial call for papers, have also played, perhaps unwittingly, an important role in convincing me of the worth of the project. I would, of course, especially like to thank the contributors, whose stimulating essays have made this book all I could have hoped for. The presence of all respondents here speaks of their generosity and devotion to critical dialogue that are essential to scholarly enquiry and creative passion. Special thanks to Jacques Rancourt for writing the poem 'The Stars in the Firmament' in French and to John F. Deane for translating it. Thanks also to the series editor, Graeme Harper, and to Anna Roderick and Sarah Williams of Multilingual Matters, who have been unfailingly gracious and efficient in guiding *The Creativity Market* to completion. Finally, I'd like to thank Joan Howard, without whom this book would never have attained the editorial consistency and clarity it now has. On a more personal touch, I am indebted to Luke Murphy and our four boys for putting up with my obsession for this project during the last two years.

In Lieu of a Preface

The Stars in the Firmament

When man had created God
in his own image and likeness
God found himself invited
to continue creation by himself

he created the firmament and the stars in the firmament
and into it slipped the sun and planets

foreseeing Earth already
he made prime matter for Aristotle
and the four elements for Bachelard

he forgot neither yin nor yang
nor the lion's mane
nor the stubbornness of Gilgamesh

he thought up clay and water
and separated the clay from the water

he thought up man and woman
and separated man from woman

then God rested for a moment
he rested and that's when he began to think

so God who's not the last of the half-witted
God remembered he had been created by man

it's an anachronism, he thought,
and he recreated man in his own image and likeness
in his image and dependency

and man found himself invited
to continue creation by himself

to reproduction by scissiparity
he added multiplication by mating
joining the useful to the pleasurable

man then passed on to objects
to tools and representations

he conceived of arrows and their targets
charcoal and sketch

he forgot neither the good nor the beautiful
neither the ugly nor the evil
he did not forget freedom

in this way as he went along
he reinvented God
in his own image at his own risks and perils

since then man attends to his occupations

he creates fishing nets and hexadecimals
cultivates apple trees and secret hopes
abstracts art the way one extracts gold

and as if to slacken off he invents prostheses for himself
one for each limb
thousands for his brain

since that time God rests
he rests on man

Jacques Rancourt (John F. Deane, trans.).

Introduction

Will you be as gods? Gaze in your omphalos. Hello. Linch here. Put me on to Edenville.
Aleph, alpha: nought, nought one.
– James Joyce

He could shuffle & recombine proven en-tertainment formulae into configurations that
allowed the muse of Familiarity to appear cross-dressed as Innovation.
– David Foster Wallace

This book explores the 'creative' component of creative writing in the globalised marketplace. It focuses on creative writing as a subject in universities and beyond academia, with chapters arranged around three organising sub-themes of practice, research and pedagogy, making the point that creative writing is also occurring in, and around, universities throughout Europe, Asia and the United States. It examines the convergence of education, globalisation and economic discourses at the intersection of the university sector and creative industries by foregrounding issues and framing reference points. These issues concern the competing interests at the core of creativity as it appears in the neo-liberal global discourse in which writers are enmeshed. As practitioners, for example, how does one integrate creative freedom, authenticity, responsibility and productivity? The book offers national case studies from the United Kingdom, the United States, Canada, Australia and Singapore that are indicative of the challenges faced by academics, postgraduate students and creative industry professionals. The purpose of the book is to foster a conversation between writers, academics, postgraduate students and education policy-makers, with the additional aim of creating a forum that extends to the other creative arts.

The engaging conceit on which the first epigraph turns is, of course, the notion of the umbilical cord as a long coil of telephone cable linking each of us back to Eden, the ultimate place of creation from nothing, which is a myth that haunts us. In the era of the cordless phone, i-Phone and Cloud, *creativity* itself may, like Eden, be itself a myth, so caught up has it become in global issues raised by national innovation systems arguments. Yet, the myths that our culture holds about creativity influence the ways in which we speak about it. These include the myth that creativity is primarily about a moment of creative insight, one that emerges out of the blue from the unconscious; the myth that creativity is a solitary event; the myth that material concerns interfere with creativity; and the myth that creativity will yield technical innovation and financial returns. Finally, there is the myth that creative writers are masters of their own texts, which brings us full-circle to the meaning of *creativity* in the globalised marketplace, where 'the muse of Familiarity' often appears 'crossed dressed as Innovation' (Wallace, 1999: 235).

The Creativity Market, however, both focuses *and* broadens the international debate by investigating how the creative and expressive arts are positioned within existing 'knowledge economies' (OECD, 1996: 7), particularly the university sector. Key issues revolve around the question that if creativity as a human endeavour is dead, creative mutants nonetheless ceaselessly reappear in discourse. While the discussion focuses on the discipline of creative writing, it is also broader, since it involves creative writing practitioners, academics and postgraduate students, educational managers and theorists, policy experts and those working in the creative industries – those knowledge-intensive industries that rely on creativity as a core attribute and systematise and circulate the intellectual property generated by creative workers. The book allows for a discussion about the nature of creativity by examining the points of contact between theory and practice. *The Creativity Market* differs from other books in that it provides a space where creative workers and educators can engage with the larger theoretical discussions through their craft and reflective practices. The book lays bare the current situation, as experienced at the pointy end of a quantifiable and marketable knowledge economy and the higher education sector. It interrogates both the conservative research cultures and non-creative management practices that hinder the development of creative institutions and proposes new patterns of thought and work.

The essays in this volume are organised so as to facilitate the exchange of views between writers from different countries (Australia, Belgium, Canada, Germany, Singapore, the United Kingdom and the United States) working within the academy and various pockets of the writing industry. The mandate for these exchanges was to enhance an atmosphere of mutually beneficial inquiry. The nature of the relationship between the papers varies somewhat, so that some of the responses pick up and comment directly on the points made in the initial contribution (Hecq, 2008), while others take the initial contribution and develop their insights more fully or in slightly different directions. Ideally, such arrangement will evoke in readers a desire to contribute further, to carry the discussion beyond the covers of the book.

The book arose from challenges attending the attempts of a gathering of writers to establish the focus and boundaries of their work and to find a balance between creativity as connection and self-expression on the one hand, and the exigencies of the publishing industry on the other. There is indeed a strong connection between creative writing and the marketplace, for the role of literary agents, publishers and editors is vital in connecting writers and readers. Further, all writing exists in a specific social and economic context, which comprises the conditions that enable or hinder it. The implications of such context are exciting to some – notably, established writers or emerging writers with an entrepreneurial spirit. However, the situation is daunting for others, as their most profound desires and wills are not driven by the prospect of mere material rewards.

In regard to the creative industries of the past decade, a growing sector of national economies the world over which comprise both for profit and non-profit businesses involved in the creation and diffusion of the arts, cultural myths about creativity are sensitive issues, as these impact on the way creative practitioners define themselves and go about their business. This may even be more of a sensitive issue for creative writers who pursue postgraduate studies in universities, as they have often already established a professional reputation and demonstrated their talent; they now have to prove their commercial potential on top of their academic excellence. Thus, at a time when creativity seems to have become part of advertising rhetoric, we need to redefine the term with a view to paying closer attention to ontological and ethical considerations.

Although recognised before, Richard Florida made the term 'creativity' a catch cry (see, for example, Sternberg, 1988; Landry, 2000). Florida's influential analysis of the ways in which creative individuals both contribute to a nation's economy and re-energise the cities where they live, put forward what has become an international and cross-disciplinary agenda with this statement: 'Any country that doesn't keep building its creative strengths – with broad support for creative activities, and with policies that bring more citizens into the creative sector rather than under-employing them – will fall behind' (Florida, 2002: 12). Yet in the wake of both the European Year of Creativity and of the 2009 financial crisis, the neo-liberal discourse that had been dominating the global marketplace and the University sector since the turn of the millennium seems to have toned down. Research into the nature of creativity has been reinvigorated, and the debate about creativity in the creative industries, which took on a distinct socio-economic ring in the last decade, is currently undergoing a shift towards an understanding of creativity as self-expression and a making of connections (Cunningham, 2009; Sheridan-Rabideau, 2010), indicating a shift from 'knowledge economy' to 'creative economy' and now some new 'creative ecology' (Vaizey, 2011).

The Creativity Market redefines the term *creativity* within the frame of creative writing as both applicable to individual and collective projects. It begins with the work of undoing established and rigidified assumptions about creativity and the market economy to open the debate to new speculative inquiry. In this vein, *The Creativity Market* has three main objectives:

(i)   to examine the convergence of education, globalisation and economic discourses at the intersection of the University sector and creative writing;

(ii) to foster a conversation between writers, academics, creative industry professionals, postgraduate creative writing students and education policy specialists; and

(iii) to tackle the topic of creativity in seeking to identify some of the pedagogical and ethical uncertainties that arise in the discipline of creative writing when artistic, economic and political agendas compete with each other.

It, further, has the potential for application in the framing of practice, research and pedagogy, as well as policy.

The immediate context for this project was the vigorous debate initiated by a paper delivered at the 2008 'Creativity and Uncertainty' conference of the Australasian Associations Writing Programs held at the University of Technology, Sydney (Hecq, 2008), and this volume continues and broadens the conversation. This conversation will offer some knowledge base for creative writing by, first, locating it within the wider international debate and, second, by providing its research 'domain' with a historical genealogy that widens to include 'fields' of theory, such as sociology, psychology, philosophy and politics (Csikszentmihalyi, 1988: 313ff).

At the intersection of creative writing and creativity is the vexed question of defining *creativity* as such. Therefore, this collection does not offer one single definition of the term. However, most authors source from, contextualise and critique two broad sub-groups that are currently circulating in the global discourse: those epitomised by works looking at the creative mind, albeit within a specific socio-political context; and those dealing with management and policy, with direct reference to national economies. It is indeed important to remember that the creative industries sector has increasingly been recognised as sustaining the growth momentum of advanced economies. The creative arts are thus not only relevant to an elite group of artists and connoisseurs, but also make a significant contribution to national economies and local communities, as well as individual lives.

The most recent books looking at this new configuration of creativity and economic activity demonstrate a global preoccupation in the 21st century: the underlying assumption is that by taking on-board new paradigms and ways of doing within business and education, the developed world can avoid the excesses of the market and neo-liberal policies, thus ensuring economically stable and competitive nation states. What is particularly striking is how few of these books actually unpack the concepts of *creativity* and *innovation* to articulate how creative people or the creative industries actually work, or how innovation may simply be an outcome of creative approaches to problem solving. *The Creativity Market* unpacks both of these issues.

At the forefront of research into the creative mind is the work of psychologists such as Scott Barry Kaufman and James C. Kaufman, whose *Psychology of Creative Writing* (2009) looks at multiple aspects of creative writing, including the creative writer as a person, the text itself, the creative process, the writer's development, the link between creative writing and mental illness, the personality traits of comedy and screenwriters and how to teach creative writing. James Kaufman's *Creativity* (2009) complements the above study, as it offers a comprehensive literature review on academic research into creativity during the past half-century and draws on concurrent research carried out with Ronald Beghetto in 'Beyond Big and Little: The Four C Model of Creativity' (Kaufman & Beghetto, 2009).

Although the work of psychologists working on creativity today is exciting, not least because it attempts to break down the false dichotomy between the 'Sciences' and the 'Arts' as creativity research becomes tied to more and more areas of psychology, it is important to have a specific understanding and categorisation of what it means to be creative, even if only to offer the possibility of refusing categorisation and understanding. In the current master discourse, however, despite the push to 'simplify creativity' (Cunningham, 2009: 14), creativity remains linked with *innovation* and, hence, economic return.

One interesting text that looks at creativity in terms of practice, aesthetics, creative energies and processes in their socio-economic contexts is Sternberg's *The Nature of Creativity* (1988). This book offers a comprehensive reviewing of the theories that gave rise to the notion of *creative thinking*, recently made so popular by the work of Richard Florida. Sternberg theorises the concept of creativity by recalling the writings of Howard Gardiner (seven intelligences) and Cszikzentmihalyi (flow theory). The text then very explicitly establishes the usefulness of the theory of creativity as a pedagogical tool for use in education. From the idea of being in the flow to being productive and generative at work and school comes the new jargon-laden term, *creative knowledge environments*.

The notion of creative environments is explored in great detail in Sven Hemlin's (2004) *Creative Knowledge Environments: The Influences on Creativity in Research and Innovation*. In Hemlin's world view, creativity is less about inherent skills brought to an organisation or institution by creative people, but about devising conditions that foster creative thinking and innovative practices. Knowledge is here commodified as *knowledge product*, with outputs in need of being measurable and marketable. Notions of raw innovation, or outcomes of creative thought, become subservient to the development of 'new knowledge products' for a 'new knowledge economy' (Hemlin, 2004: 18). Most of the theorising in this book uses a scientific-industry model to represent the new knowledge economy, by referring to paradigm shifts in the way universities, research institutions and governments position telecommunications, technology and bio-medical research developments. From the micro (individual thinking and/or talent), meso (institutions and companies) to macro (national and international) levels, creativity as a knowledge product is institutionalised and, in turn, globalised.

A more recent addition to a similar world view is *Neo-pragmatism, Communication and the Culture of Creative Democracy* (Swartz et al., 2009), which returns to John Dewey's notion of the 'creative democracy' and re-invigorates the term as a radical activity which purports to ensure community cohesion, solidarity and global citizenship in the face of globalised competition between world economies. It is very much reliant on the power of the communications revolution and global connectivity wrought by the information age. In this light, the creative capital (innovation as output potential) can only be harnessed by recognising the logical progression from 'post-industrial economy' to 'information economy' and 'digital economy' and, finally, from 'knowledge economy' to 'creative economy', in what the book describes as 'knowledge capitalism' (Swartz *et al.,* 2009: 16). The latter is defined as 'not just knowledge management but [...] design and development of "creative institutions", embodying new patterns of work' (Swartz *et al.,* 2009: 17).

Clearly, by the turn of the 21st century, the concepts of creativity and innovation have become conflated, and this is a global phenomenon. In *Creativity and the Global Knowledge Economy*, for example, Peters, Marginson and Murphy, take the discussion a step further. By engaging with leading thinkers in educational policy and market policy, the book positions the creative economy as one in which broader players are necessary (Peters *et al.,* 2009). It defines the space for, and role played by, the expressive arts' and creative arts' practitioners in the development of creative cities and creative capital (Florida, 2004).

It is this connection between creativity, innovation and the new knowledge economy, as well as research and theory, which has seen the rise in recent years of research looking at the education sector. Across the developed world, the rationale for cutting-edge research is to position creative thinking at the heart of education excellence and, in turn, examine how it drives attempts by governments to measure and quantify creativity and innovation, in terms of competitiveness and economic value to the education sector. However, there is a sense that the arts are currently on the verge of assuming far greater significance in both the education sector and the community at large. Not only is there a clear paradigm shift in disciplinary thinking (Haseman & Jaaniste, 2008; Cunningham, 2009; Jaaniste & Cunningham, 2011), but it is already reflected in policy at both national and international levels.

This book conveys a variety of ideas and attitudes in an apprehensible manner, as would be the case in a conversation. The first chapter argues that in the late 20th century and early 21st century, as creativity became more politicised, so its ability to mean something human grew less pronounced. It asks us to pay attention to our vocabulary, for, as suggested above, the term creativity, and indeed often a lay notion of the concept, has lost much of its personal power and even begun to work in reverse to counter the actions and activities of individuals and groups. In Chapter 1, Graeme Harper demonstrates that, in the context of Great Britain, the economic and political worth of creativity has often been immersed in a rhetoric detached from its actual human context, even though new ways of communicating, associating and creating have countered this detachment, including the new 'creative ecology', which is taking us forward presently. Chapter 2 presents creativity as a form of knowledge and mode of knowing inherent in practice-led research and, therefore, argues that in higher degrees, and in creative writing in particular, the marketability, or 'saleability', of the end product shouldn't necessarily factor into the equation. It anticipates the argument put forward by other writers working in the university sector, including doctoral students, which introduces richer ways of thinking about creativity, markets and the creative sector moving into the future.

Thus, in Chapter 3, for instance, 'Creativity and the Marketplace', Jen Webb re-examines some of the key terms that are put to work in discussions of creativity and the marketplace and suggests ways in which writers working in universities might draw on the long history of the creative field to clarify and refine their modes of practices, teaching of practice and understanding of the place of writing in society. In Chapter 4, 'The Publishing Paradigm', on the other hand, Jeremy Fisher uses data from Australian and global publishing, in order to chart the commercial imperatives of publishing and how the impact of those imperatives affects creativity. He reminds us that, for the most part, the process of publishing is a commercial venture, with publishers investing capital in creative works for the purpose of making a profit from the exploitation of those works. In 'As Good As It Gets?', Gerry Turcotte and Robyn Morris then discuss the spurious dichotomy at the interface of creativity and the academic industry, bringing the conversation back to academic and policy circles. In particular, they scrutinise the academic environment where employment, government funding, promotion, enrolments and other factors are dependent upon the question of *value* and how it is captured in a metrics-dominated system. In contradistinction, Jeff Sparrow offers an Australian case study in Chapter 6 to suggest that academic creative writing serves a variety of interests that are rarely publicly acknowledged. He argues that the growth of academic creative writing represents the establishment of a significantly new model of institutional support for writers and the literary arts, in which the most basic questions about social equity and intended outcomes are rarely discussed. Chapter 7, 'Nothing is Free in This Life', takes up the Derridean category of invention, which enables Antonia Pont to ask exactly what it is that the creativity market purports to be able to sell, while, with 'The Ghost in the Machine', Phillip Edmonds refocuses the discussion on the international debate about creativity, as to the nature of the global market for *creative products*. Whereas Pont proposes that deconstruction, through situating writing as that which has no origin which is not already itself a derivation that may help clarify the slippery ethics of the marketing of 'dead traces', Edmonds discusses possible links between the current economic situation and the changing nature of cultural formation, specifically where the industry of creative writing is located with regard to the dichotomy between theory and practice. 'Fighting the War Against Terror' enters the debate from a practitioner's point of view and returns to the main theme of Chapter 2. In it, Mike Harris takes the editor of this book to task by deconstructing the myth of individual creativity and arguing for collaborative models of creation. He examines both problems and paradoxes in creativity, including funding, ethics, politics and aesthetics, by focusing on a case study.

Chapter 10 takes on the challenge of presenting, in dramatic form, an argument. It raises and addresses fundamental questions in the form of a two-act play and, thereby, functions as the creative hinge of the book. As such, it is Christopher Lappas' personal response to the question of creativity, globalisation and commercialisation. Using a two-act structure, it supports the author's argument that creative fiction can convey social, psychological and philosophical ideas as easily as, and often better than, non-fiction. By pondering notions of ethics, authenticity and responsibility, the play proposes that fiction is often more sincere and truthful than non-fiction. From that paradox, a situation is presented in which creative authors find themselves in a hostile creative environment – an environment in which the author is subjugated, commodified and, ultimately, disenfranchised by a consumer-driven audience, – with creativity at stake.

In Chapter 11, Vahri McKenzie voices the concerns of doctoral students. She illustrates the use of the spectrum to reimagine the description and examination of creative writing higher degrees by research. Like Turcotte and Morris, she asks critical questions raised by the global practice of placing creative research within an academic context that increasingly demands quantifiable research outcomes and submits innovative ways of answering these.

Chapter 12, 'Outlying the Point that Tips', takes us to Canada and the United States and argues that the existing lacuna between academia and the corporate world in Canada – be it the publishing market or business in general – is partly a defensive and nostalgic response, based on out-dated assumptions about the value of art and creativity that hamper, rather than instigate, creative ways of thinking about disciplinary boundaries and the riches that lie in their possible intersections. Here, Pavlina Radia reveals that in the age of digital media, the bridges between the academic and business world are not only inevitable, but also essential to cultural development and its sustainability in an era of plenty. This perspective is compounded by Vernon's view, in Chapter 14, that attacks on the arts and humanities in the United States and Canada undermine, not only a social and cultural hunger for recognition, intimacy and authenticity, but also, enormous economic benefits. 'Selling It' offers theoretical and practical connections between the act of creative writing, post-secondary creative writing programmes and the Public Good. It also suggests that authors, if authoring *right*, disturb and displace interests vested in anti-intellectualism, the concentration of wealth and the fetishisation of the Public Good.

Although Chapter 15 focuses on Singapore's attempts to become a creative and innovative nation so as to stay competitive, Eric Tinsay Valles examines the different methods adopted, as well as the reach and limitations of these methods, in terms of putting Singapore on the global map where creativity is concerned. A former journalist, this author looks more closely at Singapore's cultural context, underpinned as it is by some tension between the Singapore-based artists' desire for individuality and state campaigns that are seen to propagate singularity in the creative arts. He shows that, like other East Asian societies, Singapore is keen to learn from the West, while emphasising cross-cultural differences in creative development, suggesting here that the uptake of policy changes is not only dependent upon local cultural factors, but also that attitude to creativity as connection and self-expression ranks very high among them. Kirpal Singh rounds off the discussion, not without irony, by reflecting on how creativity is understood across cultures in an age when globalisation has become the one key determining factor for all of us. He questions the relevance of what seems to be a global commitment to promote and develop a sense of national culture as a way of stimulating the economy and generating innovative responses to national and international markets, as our planet moves, with grim relentless urgency, toward disaster.

Common concerns with the relationship between creativity and the marketplace, practice and theory, research and pedagogy, ethics and motivation run through this group of essays. Though they approach the question of how creativity and the market relate concretely from different perspectives, they reveal telling linkages and pose provocative new ways of thinking and working.

References

Csikszentmihalyi, M. (1988) *Creativity: Flow and the Psychology of Discovery and Invention.* New York, NY: HarperCollins.

Cunningham, S. (2009) The New Creativity is Solving Problems Together, *Australian Financial Review*, 30 November, 14. Online at http://cci.edu.au/publications/the-new-creativity-solving-problems-together

Florida, R. (2004, 2002) *The Rise of the Creative Class: and How it's Transforming Work, Leisure, Community and Everyday Life.* New York, NY: Basic Books.

Haseman, B. and Jaaniste, L. (2008) The Arts and Australia's National Innovation System 1994–2008: Arguments, Recommendations, Challenges, *CHASS Occasional Paper 7*. Online at http://www.chass.org.au/papers/PAP20081101BH.php. Accessed 27 February 2010.

Hecq, D. (2008) Banking on Creativity? [Presentation]. Paper presented at the 13th Conference of the Australian Association of Writing Programs (AAWP), 27–29 November. Sydney, Australia. Online at http://aawp.org.au/files/Hecq_2008.pdf

Hemlin, S. (2004) *Creative Knowledge Environments: the Influences in Research and Innovation.* Camberley: Edward Elgar Publishing.

Jaaniste, L. and Cunningham, S. (2011) Creative Economy Report Card 2011, online document, accessed 16 April 2011. http://cci.edu.au/sites/default/files/dbogg/Creative%20Economy%20report%20card%20March%202011.pdf

Joyce, J. (1969) *Ulysses.* Harmondsworth: Penguin.

Kaufman, J.C. (2009) *Creativity.* New York, NY: Springer.

Kaufman, J.C. and Beghetto, R.A. (2009) Beyond Big and Little: The Four C Model of Creativity. *Review of General Psychology* 13 (1), *1–12*.

Kaufman, S.B. and Kaufman, J. (2009) *The Psychology of Creative Writing.* Cambridge: Cambridge University Press.

Landry, C. (2000) *The Creative City: A Toolkit For Urban Innovators.* London: Comedia/Earthscan.

OECD (1996) *The Knowledge-Based Economy*. Paris: Organization for Economic Cooperation and Development. Online at http://www.oecd.org/dataoecd/51/8/1913021.

Organisation for Economic Co-operation and Development (OECD) (2009) *Assessment of Higher Education Learning Outcomes*, online document, accessed 2 April 2010. http://www.oecd.org/document/51/0,3343,en_2649_35961291_40119475_1_1_1_1,00.html

Peters, M.A., Marginson, S. and Murphy, P. (2009) *Creativity and the Global Knowledge Economy*. Melbourne: Melbourne University Press.

Rothenberg, A. and Hausman, C.R. (eds) (1976) *The Creativity Question*. Durham: Duke University Press.

Sheridan-Rabideau, M. (2010) Creativity Repositioned. *Arts Education Policy Review* 111 (2), 54–58.

Sternberg, R.J. (1988) *The Nature of Creativity*. Cambridge: Cambridge University Press.

Swartz, O., Campbell, K. and Pestana, C. (2009) *Neo-Pragmatism, Communication and the Culture of Creative Democracy*. New York, NY: Peter Lang.

United Nations Educational, Scientific and Cultural Organization (UNESCO) (2009) *Trends in Global Higher Education: Tracking an Academic Revolution*, online document, accessed 2 April 2010. http://unesdoc.unesco.org/images/0018/001831/183168e.pdf.

Vaizey, E. (2011) The Creative Ecology. [Speech]. *Speech given at the State of the Arts*, London, 10 February. Online at http://www.culture.gov.uk/news/ministers_speeches/7834.aspx.

Wallace, D.F. (1999) *Brief Interviews with Hideous Men*. New York, NY: Little, Brown & Co.

Webb, J. and Brien, D.L. (2006) Strategic Directions for Research in Writing: A Wish List. *TEXT* 10 (1). Online at http://www.textjournal.com.au/april06/webbbrien.htm.

1 Creative Writing: The Ghost, the University and the Future

Graeme Harper

Creative Writing Today

The vast majority of creative writers today do not write or distribute their works of creative writing through what would commonly be considered avenues of the creative industries. The majority of creative writers today write beyond the realm of organised industry, their writing being outside of an economic system of direct control and exchange, and *if* they do distribute their works at all, they do so, today, via the internet and in a manner we might broadly call 'free'. This is not said naively, and it is not intended to suggest that economic systems don't impose more general or indirect controls. Nevertheless, in direct terms, creative writers are not required to engage with the creative industries and the choice to do so is, indeed, exactly that: a choice.

It could easily be argued that this has long been the case, with the opportunity for simply writing and printing works having long been present, even if central systems of manufacture and distribution have influenced creative writers as they have influenced other individuals. But the impact of contemporary digital technologies, which have brought about new avenues of personal and personalised exchange, have reduced distribution costs to almost nothing and increased opportunities for distribution a thousand-fold. While there have always been opportunities for the individual creative writer and exchange of works of creative writing, the contemporary world thus recognises and, indeed, encourages immediate interchange between writers, readers, other writers and the wider world.

Why, then, we might wonder, are we frequently still operating in universities, as if creative writing is aligned so closely with a centralised economic system of exchange that we have even sometimes seen the phrase 'of publishable quality' used as an assessment tool to question or confirm the quality of a piece of creative writing submitted for a course of university study? Questioning 'publishability' is absolutely not the same as questioning the quality of creative achievement itself, nor is a focus on portions of the creative industries (e.g. publishing, performance or media industries) the same as a focus on the undertaking of creative writing. Confusing the two fundamentally constitutes what Gilbert Ryle (1951) calls a 'category-mistake' – on which more, later.

Essentially, we need to consider the distinct mismatches (alternatively, misunderstandings or misalignments) that have occurred between our considerable human engagements with creativity and, specifically here, with creative writing and the ways in which creativity has been incorporated or discussed in economic and political systems. Firstly, how have we promoted and advertised human creativity? Secondly, what is the condition of creativity itself? Thirdly, how has creative writing been mapped around universities over time? Finally, on what basis is creativity and higher education currently touted and how does this relate to the current state of play with creative writing?

As it always seems useful to note in any discussion of creative writing, it must also be remarked that creative writing is first and foremost action. That is, creative writing produces completed artefacts, and physical evidence of the making of those artefacts (e.g. other artefacts in the form of drafts, emails, conversations, notes, diaries and doodles), but, most of all, creative writing involves the actions of human beings, human beings doing something – both physical and mental activities. Creative writing actions are primary; the artefacts that emerge are secondary. Creative writing is no different in this to other creative activities: human creativity generally is *mostly* evidenced in human action, regardless of the field of endeavour.

Hubs of Abundance and Illustriousness

Established in February 2008 by Great Britain's Department for Culture, Media and Sport (DCMS), 'Creative Britain: New Talents for the New Economy' was said to acknowledge 'the vital role that the creative industries play in the British economy' (DCMS, 2008: 1) and to highlight 'the need for the UK to invest in *businesses* and *individuals* [my emphasis] in order to ensure that the UK remains globally competitive' (DCMS, 2008: 3). Creative Britain included, in its £70.5 million strategy, 26 'agreed commitments', including 'giving all children a creative education', 'research and innovation' and 'promoting the UK as the world's creative hub' (DCMS, 2008: 76–77). But what is being promoted here by reference to the creative?

In a similar, hub-orientated vein, Dorothy Louise Mackay, in an article wonderfully entitled 'Advertising the Medieval University', quotes a 13th century circular sent out by Charles I, advertising the University of Naples. Here is an extract from that circular:

We have brought here men learned in all branches of scholarship, so that there may come to drink of this university, as from an abundant well, both young and old, the beginners and those who have attained recognition, those wishing to study the trivium and the quadrivium, canon and civil law, as well as theology. Wherefore, let them come, in so far as they are able, to this university, as [they might come] to a great feast which is ornamented by the presence of illustrious guests and which overflows with an abundance and variety of refreshing food. (Mackay, 1932: 516)

Come, the king calls, to 'feast' on this university education. 'Let them come [. . .] to this university [. . .] which overflows with an abundance and variety'. Published, as this circular was, in 1272, who would have thought that the forms of persuasion evident in it would be so familiar here in the 21st century?

There has long been a difference between advertising as 'taking or giving notice of something' and advertising as 'an institutionalised system of commercial information and persuasion', as Raymond Williams (1980: 170) once pointed out. Which, we might wonder, is this example from Charles I? Indeed, what qualities are being promoted to attract these illustrious guests?

As the Creative Britain programme was a declaration of a creative abundance and the need to support and develop such creative abundance in both British corporate bodies and individuals, so Charles I's circular was a declaration of an abundance of learnedness, in the group and in the person, and the opportunities offered to engage with such illustriousness. We are reminded by this that although the language of human communication might have changed over time, many of the human notions that inform our languages have not greatly changed. Seemingly, this can be summarised by saying 'human beings continue to be human beings', but this statement hides as much as it declares.

Essentialist thinking doesn't uncover the connections here (the philosophy, that is, that we have essential human properties, an immutable human essence); rather, the connections are uncovered by a consideration of the varied appearance of common human traits, common human interests and common human issues which underpin our history. Such things as our desire to search out and discover, our human willingness to engage in social interaction, our common human belief in forms of love, our human interest in time and place. Human notions that are either active or latent are revealed by these commonalities. In a minor contribution to such areas of human agreement, the advertising of universities, according to perceived forms or activities of eminence – such advertising appears to be something we have long actively embraced, even if today we see this embrace happening in 21st century ways, using 21st century tools and for prevailing 21st century political, economic and social reasons.

Likewise, consider a second notion (or, more accurately, a set of connected notions) that we humans have endorsed, actively or latently: that is, our communal belief in the human ability (and, often, strong desire) to be imaginative; the relationship between our human imaginations and our sense of what constitutes higher learning; and the frequency of our willingness (and, often, our considerable commitment) to advertising the wonders of the human imagination.

Finally, the ideal and the act of universities engaging with creative writing (as a human pursuit, as something to be learnt and as something to be valued and celebrated), that, too, is a notion we have long approved. While the formal presentation and development of this university engagement with creative writing might have changed over time, what lies beneath this engagement certainly has far longer historical length.

All these notions may be active or latent. In other words, while it might generally be felt that universities should openly encompass the creative, this is not necessarily manifest in all the business of all universities all the time. Similarly, while we might commonly value the imaginative, it is not necessarily the case that all aspects of our lives are considered and deployed in terms of the imaginative. We can analogically consider this in the same way we might consider the constant and significant relationship between day and night.

As many might remember personally, children are sometimes comforted with an adult observation that whatever exists in daylight remains there, benevolently, in the darkness of the night. Thus, the intention of the following traditional folk tale is not to frighten, but, in truth, to familiarise:

> In a dark dark wood,
> there was a dark dark path.
> And up that dark dark path,
> there was a dark dark house.
> And in that dark dark house,
> there was a dark dark stair.
> And up that dark dark stair,
> there was a dark dark room.
> And in that dark dark room,
> there was a dark dark cupboard.
> And in that dark dark cupboard,
> there was a dark dark box.
> And in that dark dark box,
> there was a. . . ghost! (British Council, n.d.)

A common, yet individual, ghost, a representation of something human, yet not immediately ungraspable, often changeable, not fixed in shape or solidified into a temporal or spatial stasis that would, were it said to be so, defy its many forms. This idea of a ghost – and our general idea of a ghost – is that of 'breath' (as the word 'ghost' suggests, in its Latinate origins,[1] and this is the usage to which I will refer here, not to some more manipulated and somewhat modern notion of a spectral entity). The purpose of this folk tale, as with the purpose of the words 'creativity' or 'creative', is to assist us in becoming directly familiar with that which is not directly accessible.

Thus, when we read of a 'Creative Britain', or of 'creative writing', of the 'creative industries' or of a 'creative university', we need not to forget that what the adjective 'creative' is pointing towards is exactly that ghost, that breath, even though the word itself is packaged as political language or as declarations of bodies corporate, as an active practical (a thing being done, or to do) or textual reference. In fact, 'creativity' is more accurately the representative of much more humanity than just these things.

Creativity in Reality

This is not to say, as the concept of the ghost might initially seem to suggest in its modern context, that creativity exists only in some place of its own, within the incorporeal mind, and that the mind is a separately functioning and separately acting entity to the body, to our material (and, indeed, commercial) world. Gilbert Ryle (1951), in *The Concept of Mind*, alerts us to such a suggestion being a 'category-mistake', using a poignant university example:

> A foreigner visiting Oxford or Cambridge for the first time is shown a number of colleges, libraries, playing fields, museums, scientific departments and administrative offices. He then asks 'But where is the University? I have seen where the members of the Colleges live, where the Registrar works, where the scientists experiment and the rest. But I have not yet seen the University in which reside and work the members of your University.' It has then to be explained to him that the University is not another collateral institution, some ulterior counterpart to the colleges, laboratories and offices which he has seen. The University is just the way in which all that he has already seen is organized. When they are seen and when their co-ordination is understood, the University has been seen. (Ryle, 1951: 16)

Ryle contends that 'in opposition to this entire dogma. . . the workings of a person's mind. . . are not. . . a second set of shadowy operations' (Ryle,

1951: 50). Similarly, creativity is not a second set of activities, understandings or operations existing only in one dimension, while another dimension continues alongside it – mind and body, as it were, or creative and non-creative or thoughts and actions. In truth, none of these dualisms are real. Actions, thoughts and results are of the same dimension, not of two or more dimensions.

Ryle suggested the dualistic dogma, with which he disagreed, should be called the 'Ghost in the Machine' (Ryle, 1951: 22). A phrase Arthur Koestler (1968) borrowed, of course, to title his book exploring what he saw as human kind's penchant for self-destruction. I suggest here that Ryle's evaluation of the ghost – which largely focuses on the insubstantial, the mysterious and unobservable – only considers the concept of the ghost in a relatively narrow, at best, early modern way. Here, however, if we consider creativity as a ghost, imbued with a representation of life, mental, physical and emotional, as a holder of physical, as well as mental and emotional activities, then we begin to understand how the concept (and the words connected to it) has been used and is being used. That's the ghost, the breath, to which I refer, which leads me to my primary suggestion:

Creativity cannot be a definition, and the creative cannot be approached successfully via any of our previous or current definitional investigations. Using a definitional approach, we have seen only partial answers to what creativity entails, from the point of view of the disciplines of psychology, textual and cultural studies, educational theory and practice, sociology, ecology and the natural sciences, business studies, philosophy and more. These have resulted, as Ryle's analysis analogically suggests to us, in a fundamental category-mistake.

While such definitional approaches are not entirely worthless, because they provide a safety blanket for contemporary understanding, they do relatively little to elaborate the truth about creativity, though they do quite a bit to fix our sense of creativity in place, according to prevailing cultural, economic or political conditions. We grasp for them when seeking to determine the difference, often between our considerations of the 'original' and the 'unoriginal', for example, and always according to current conditions. In reality, however, creativity is a representation, and creativity, in its distinct representational identity, is a repository, a container for human commonalities. These commonalities exist even if they are not visible at any one time, even if they are not observed, promoted or declared, neither ever fully visible nor ever totally separate from our physical world.

Creativity and Universities

The relationship between creativity and higher education (of which the activity of creative writing is a considerable, historical part) is not often very well-articulated in a discussion of prevailing government policies, prominent contemporary modes of persuasion about the value and importance of creativity or in attempts to define creativity by reference solely to the operations of the mind or to creativity's end results (that is, its outputs or artefacts). But we *can* find, in an investigation of these things, evidence of our many attempts over time to make sense of creativity. We can find evidence, too, of how we similarly associate higher learning with creative capacity – even if we have sometimes (and, certainly, in the contemporary world) used other buzzwords to mean, more or less, creative or creativity; such words as 'innovation', 'invention' and 'entrepreneurial'. These words have certainly found their way into 21st century discussions of the roles and impact of universities on societies and on individuals.

We discover, in these attempts, a sense of how languages of persuasion – whether the advertising of the artefacts and actions of human creativity or the advertising of universities – share similar (sometimes plainly false, sometimes detecting something, but unable to articulate it) notions about creativity, as well as about higher learning, simultaneously, often failing to deal with the tensions suggested by their language and lack of real engagement with the creative or with what higher understanding entails. Nevertheless, higher education's association with creativity and, in the focus here, with creative writing has been a barometer for how definitional approaches have attempted to resolve the issue of what creativity might be.

Mark McGurl writes that: 'creative writing as we know it is the product of a historical moment when traditional concepts of formal education as occasion either for externally imposed mental discipline or the conveyance to the student of standardised matter came under sustained attack' (McGurl, 2009: 82). McGurl's reference is to creative writing as it emerged in American universities, mostly in the 20th century. But, of course, creative writing existed in and around universities long before recent generations had contact with it; long before the historical moment to which McGurl so accurately refers. This longer history of creative writing in the world's universities has seen interactions of many notable kinds, not least in the sometimes difficult communications between the 'creative' and the 'intellectual', or, as some might say, the emotional 'context' of the former and the 'learned' context of the latter:

> In vernacular poetry of the fourteenth century, one often finds a certain tension – or fascination – with the conflicting identities of scholar-cleric

and lover. This can be expressed, on the one hand, as an anxiety about writing love poetry; or on the other, as a tendency to make love poetry into a learned medium. (Huot, 1991: 240)

The 14th century scholar and 14th century creative writer could just as easily be the identities said to be 'in conflict' here in Sylvia Hulot's article, though the author's argument relates to a type of learning common to that period, not necessarily common to our own. However, she also notes that, 'my focus. . . will be not the conflict between amorous *matiere* and clerkly identity but rather their fusion, the elaboration of a poetry at once learned and secular' (Huot, 1991: 241). In other words, she recognises both a specific 14th century instance *and* the general possibility of human creative and critical interaction in the exploration of higher learning.

As the world around us provides immediate stimulus, it is always easy to believe what we see and what we hear is primary. We might call this the *tyranny of the now*, the overwhelming sense that immediacy is the personally significant aspect of our living and all else, all past presences, all reference points bound up in clear evidence or even in hearsay naturally fade behind the immediate. Thus, to address the potential tyranny of the now, let us attempt to be as accurate as possible here about history.

The idea that recent centuries, or the current observable decades, have brought about a paradigmatic shift in relationships between universities, the human imagination and, specifically, higher education's relationships with creative writing, is simply not supported by facts. However, the idea that evolutions and changes, shifts and developments (such as the kind Mark McGurl has reflected upon) are part of an ongoing, and very significant, set of human relationships is accurate. We can ask, then, what is the current condition of those relationships? In particular, in what way has a category-mistake (whether accidental or, dare I suggest, occasionally wilful) shown itself in governmental and institutional declarations about creativity?

Because creative writing is defined by the ghost that is human creativity, it is exceedingly important, in terms of understanding its relationship to formal higher education, to consider how declared formal policies (such as those of governments) on creativity have or haven't supported what the activities of creative writing actually entail.

The Nation State and Creativity

At the 'First Cross-Party Creative Industries Awards Launched with Cross-Party Leader Backing' (British Inspiration Awards, 2010: 1) in Great Britain in March 2010, two years after the launch of the Creative Economy programme and just a few months before a change of government, Gordon

Brown, the then leader of the British Labour Party and, at the time, Prime Minister of Great Britain, declared:

> Britain is a country full of talent. You see it every time you turn on the TV, when you watch a sports event, a film, or flick through the pages of a fashion magazine. You can hear it in our music. And you can feel it in the energy and dynamism of our communities. I am enormously proud of the talented people in this country who, through their creative and entrepreneurial gifts, illuminate their lives and enrich ours. (British Inspiration Awards, 2010: 1)

David Cameron, then Leader of the Conservative Party and soon to become the new Prime Minister, added:

> British design and creativity has led the world for many years, and we should be proud of that heritage. I welcome the opportunity this event brings to celebrate our many creative successes. (British Inspiration Awards, 2010: 2)

'Talent', 'creative and entrepreneurial gifts', 'British design and creativity', 'creative successes': each speaker attempts, here, to advertise and promote the existence of creativity in the British nation, but their rhetoric appears far more connected to 'an institutionalised system of commercial information and persuasion' (Williams, 1980: 170), than it does with 'taking or giving notice of something'. After all, the rhetoric of the 'full' and the 'dynamic', of 'illumination', 'enrichment', 'heritage', 'opportunity' and 'celebration' can hardly be said to be merely taking or giving notice.

Interestingly, neither politician makes an attempt to differentiate one artefactual example of creativity from another, though Gordon Brown highlights the importance of 'fashion' and 'music', and David Cameron highlights British 'design'. Returning to Raymond Williams' comments on advertising–an industry where 'the relationship' with creativity 'is long, rich and textured' (Smith & Yang, 2004: 31)– this highlights an issue. The issue, that is, of how the political rhetoric about creativity might very well not be about what creativity is at all.

Somewhat in contrast to Williams' analysis, Don White (himself engaging in a definitional analysis, this time in the *Fontana Dictionary of Modern Thought*) comments that 'the earliest advertisement extant can be found in the ruins of Ephesus. It is for a brothel. Advertising thinking has not advanced a great deal since then' (White, 1988: 11). Given Raymond Williams' thoughts, White's approach grows even more intriguing when he begins to directly consider creativity:

Creativity, to be noticed by the TV viewer, newspaper or magazine reader, or poster observer, necessarily means instant-attention seeking, resulting in a glibness or lateral cleverness not to be confused with creativity in film, literature or art . . . Concern that such creativity has hidden shallows has resulted in a plethora of self-aggrandizing award festivals, locally and internationally, at which 'creatives' award each other glittering prizes to celebrate the quality of their creative thinking. (White, 1988: 12)

Comparatively, for Williams, advertising is effected by systems and structures (effected, as well as affected), which have changed over time; for White, advertising is affected and effected by the self and, it would seem, not all too positively. So, what is the issue here?

My first suggestion is that White is reacting not to human creativity itself, neither what human creativity is, nor to what it produces. My second suggestion is that White is affronted not by a failure of some individuals to really reach high levels of 'glittering' creative achievement, certainly not by the business and artefacts of advertising, and not either by any suggested creative sector 'shallowness'. I suggest, he is affronted, rather, by a developed (and false) political economy surrounding human creativity and that this is highlighted, made worse and, ultimately, made untenable (certainly for White) by the category-mistake in which the ghost that is human creativity is confused with a manifestation that has very little to do with creativity at all and a great deal to do with the dualism concerned with discussing the material (in this case, preeminent artefacts) and the immaterial (in this case, illustrious thoughts/emotions).

To complete this relatively contemporary, British, political case-study, in a speech entitled 'The Creative Ecology', given at the State of the Arts conference in London on 10th February 2011, Ed Vaizey, British Minister for Culture, Communications and Creative Industries in the government elected in 2010, announced:

I want to take the opportunity today to make the case for the importance of the creative ecology – an alliance between the subsidised and commercial arts; the professional and the voluntary arts; and the arts and the creative industries. . . . I want to argue that arts policy should take this creative ecology into account, in order to see the bigger picture and the wider opportunities. We are a hugely creative nation. (Vaizey, 2011: 1)

The Conservative Party's 'Creative Ecology' thus emerged to replace the previous Labour Party's 'Creative Economy' – advertising British creativity, though whether anything more is said that truly is 'taking or giving notice of something', seems very unlikely. Vaizey does say that we need to 'see the bigger picture and the wider opportunities' and that an 'alliance' is needed and that Britain is 'a hugely creative nation'. Unfortunately, it seems almost certain that he, like those political figures before him, has very little idea of what creativity might actually entail and, equally, how it might thus best be supported.

Creative Writing's Future

Avoiding a fundamental category-mistake and considering the relationship between what creativity is, and the real role that governments could potentially play in supporting human creativity, is the first thing needed to advance the potential of our future engagements with creative writing in and around universities. If political understanding influences institutional understanding – which, frequently, it does – this is undeniably required and required urgently. We often talk of funding for creative writing students, funding for creative writing research, support for a capital infrastructure involving physical spaces and technologies, as well as funding for staffing. All this is dependent on a political (and, indeed, institutional) will.

Recognising that creative writing does not primarily involve the creation of final artefacts is important. Creative writing involves human actions, often many human actions, where artefacts are (sometimes) created that are not completed artefacts, that are not even public artefacts in any fashion, but that sit as evidence of actions (physical and mental/emotion) undertaken by creative writers. Without this recognition, all the rhetoric concerned with what creative writing might contribute to the world will almost entirely focus on the surface of engagement with industries that only partially represent what creative writing is and what creative writers do. There is far more at stake here and far more of human importance than such rhetoric can promote.

Connected with this recognition, it is noted, again, here that the contemporary world, and the technologies of the contemporary world, have allowed (and increasingly allow) creative writers to write and distribute their works and converse with writers readers/audiences; to associate in ways that previously could barely have been imagined. The notion that the future of creative writing, thus, lies in a centralised, industrially distributed system, quite simply makes no sense. It is not the case, and what role universities play in supporting and developing creative writing needs to be considered in light of this 21st century evolution.

Finally, as we humans have long been interested in advertising both creativity and higher learning, it would seem essential that while the future of creative writing in and around universities will be bright in its engagement with individual and communal interests and with common human desires, we need to consider very carefully how we publically promote what creativity is and to question the ways in which it is represented in political and industrial terms. If the way in which we advertise the importance of individual and societal creativity is part of an 'institutionalised system of commercial information and persuasion', then we need to be sure that system is representing these things in the most productive and genuine way. If it isn't, quite simply, we need to change it.

Notes

(1) The word 'ghost' has origins in the Latin word *spiritus*, meaning breath or breathing. Sometimes definitions do reveal underlying truths, sometimes not.

References

British Council (n.d.) Dark Dark Wood. *LearnEnglishKids website*, educational website, accessed 12 March 2011. http://learnenglishkids.britishcouncil.org/en/short-stories/dark-dark-wood

British Inspiration Awards (2010) *The First UK Creative Industries Awards Launched with Cross-Party Backing*, online press release, accessed 22 March 2011. http://www.britishinspirationawards.co.uk/store/bia-pr-20100316.pdf

Department for Culture, Media and Sport (DCMS) (2008) *Creative Britain: New Talents for the New Economy*, online document, accessed 12 March 2011. http://webarchive.nationalarchives.gov.uk/+/http://www.culture.gov.uk/images/publications/CEPFeb2008.pdf

Huot, S. (1991) The daisy and the laurel: Myths of desire and creativity in the poetry of Jean Froissart. *Yale French Studies*, 240–251.

Koestler, A. (1968) *The Ghost in the Machine*. New York, NY: Macmillan

Mackay, D.L. (1932) Advertising a medieval university. *The American Historical Review* 37 (3), 515–516.

McGurl, M. (2009) *The Program Era: Post-War Fiction and the Rise of Creative Writing*. Cambridge: Harvard University Press.

Oxford Dictionary Online, online webpage, accessed 20 March 2011. http://oxforddictionaries.com/view/entry/m_en_gb0979150#m_en_gb0979150

Ryle, G. (1951) *The Concept of Mind*. London: Hutchinson.

Smith, R. and Yang, X. (2004) Toward a general theory of creativity in advertising: examining the role of divergence. *Marketing Theory* 4 (1–2), 31–58.

Vaizey, E. (2011) The Creative Ecology. [Speech]. *Speech made at the State of the Arts*. London, 10 February 2011. Online at http://www.culture.gov.uk/news/ministers_speeches/7834.aspx

White, D. (1988) Advertising. In A. Bullock, O. Stallybrass and S. Trombley (eds) *The Fontana Dictionary of Modern Thought* (2nd edn) (pp. 11–12). London: Fontana.

Williams, R. (1980) Advertising: The magic system. In *Problems in Materialism and Culture*. London: Verso.

2 Banking on Creativity: My Brilliant? Career

Dominique Hecq

The greater one's science, the deeper the sense of mystery.
– Vladimir Nabokov

Three Discourses and One Till

Although globalisation was perceived in the 1980s as a fantastic opportunity to overcome cultural divides, the counter-globalisation movement that emerged at the turn of the 21st century criticised its first phase (political globalisation) and evolutionary phase (economic globalisation) for having made the rich richer and the poor, poorer. We are now in the phase of a third globalisation, one that is concerned with preserving national and local identities, in order to avoid a tremendous process of rationalisation and standardisation (Wolton, 2009). Culturally speaking, this means that we are also in a third phase, with 'the third culture' designating the phenomenon whereby scientists 'communicate directly with the general public' (Lehrer, 2007: 191), a phenomenon increasingly evident in recent press releases (CHASS, 2010). It is, thus, not surprising that in the wake of the worldwide financial crisis, the concept of 'knowledge economy' (OECD, 1996: 9) has given way to 'creative economy' (UNCTAD, 2008; UNESCO, 2010; O'Farrell, 2010), via the work of John Howkins (2001), whereby knowledge, innovation and creativity are now being conflated by dint of their economic potential. This is not a new discourse. Rather, it is a mere variation on what Lacan called the master's discourse (Lacan, 2007[1969–70]: 20), which is informed by capitalist ideologies, dogmas and structural scenarios. What may be new is that economic and scientific paradigms are also being conflated and applied to areas where quantifying, evaluating and cashing in on creativity have become problematic, as is the case in creative arts research. As a writer working in a university, I am confused by what I perceive to be a *discursive crisis*, which is, nonetheless, of economic and political significance for the discipline I teach, that is, creative writing, and not only for myself, but also for the doctoral students I supervise.

In *Proust Was a Neuroscientist*, Lehrer alerts us to the 'serious limitations' of 'the third culture' we are experiencing: 'For one thing, it has failed to bridge the divide between our two existing cultures. . . . Scientists and artists continue to describe the world in incommensurate languages' (Lehrer, 2007: 191). My point is that in the current shift from 'knowledge economy' (OECD, 1996: 9) to 'creative economy' (Howkins, 2001: 7), we witness two epistemological extremes reflexively competing with each other 'between a hard rock and a soft space' (Howard, 2008: 3) for monetary value. With this in mind, and despite my agreeing with Gould (2004) that the science/arts dichotomy is a false one, the question remains: what does this mean for creative writing students and teachers working in corporate universities? (Hecq, 2008b) In particular, if creativity is both a form of knowledge and a mode of knowing, should we be viewing creativity as a revenue stream in writing courses? And, if so, how? By examining policy and education rhetoric, this chapter explores the new discursive crisis around *creativity*, with particular reference to creative writing in higher education as it is deployed in Australian universities at a time when there are overt attempts from the government to embed the arts in higher education research (Ewing, 2010). It suggests that if 'human creativity is the ultimate economic resource' (Florida, 2004: xiii), pedagogical challenges remain when artistic, economic, administrative and political agendas compete with each other (Hecq, 2008b), for I do not think human creativity is really dead, as Graeme Harper provocatively announces in the previous chapter. Perhaps it has just morphed into a myth that serves multiple agendas, including the most uncanny and hidden ones.

The 2009 World Conference on Higher Education held at the UNESCO Headquarters in Paris – at which Denise Bradley (2008) imparted her vision to a global audience – highlighted the complexity of issues facing universities throughout the world in the immediate aftermath of the 2008 global economic crisis. At the conference, the three usual types of stakeholders were represented: governments, institutions and funding bodies. Three main thematic threads ran throughout the conference: internationalisation, regionalisation and globalisation; equity, access and quality; and learning, research and innovation. Although few would question the symbolic importance of the conference, the devil was in the details. For example, a discrepancy between rhetoric and reality was identified. While speakers said again and again that to provide higher education which truly benefits society, governments must ensure four categories: the first three of which are equitable access, international standards of quality and education. Finally, and, perhaps, most critically, graduands must also be professionally and socially relevant to 21st century realities. The message was clear: governments must ensure that their education systems prepare graduates to live and work in a globalised world with equal advantage. Significantly, the final declaration of the conference stressed the importance of *protecting* higher education as a 'public good', particularly in the face of pressure from international trade organisations to define higher education as both a private good *and* a tradable commodity. Whether it is possible to expect a government to ensure this is another story, though one related to the appropriation of the term 'creativity' in the new global capitalist discourse, whereby creativity means creating new products that sell, with products ranging from new objects, new technologies, new pedagogies to new policies.

Thus, tensions exist at all levels between values, aspirations and resources; three factors that impact on both creativity and the market. Still, this is not new. As Sir John Daniels, the president of the Commonwealth of Learning, showed on the last day of the UNESCO conference, a precarious triangular relationship exists between quality, access and cost, as well as between research, teaching and innovation. A suggestion was that this dynamic may be transformed in the future by the effective deployment of information and communication technologies – it was not lost on many attendees that Microsoft and Hewlett Packard were massively represented. Two years on, it is interesting to note that it is precisely this kind of rhetoric that pervades a series of annual Horizon reports disseminated in our universities, which attempt to demonstrate 'the relevance of information and technologies for "Teaching, Learning, or Creative Enquiry"' (Johnson *et al.*, 2011: 12). The conference also highlighted that with conditions in higher education changing rapidly, including greater international mobility for students and academics, the need for shared standards of quality had increased. Although the situation is very different in the United States, we are now otherwise quite familiar with quality assurance schemes and their impending economic significance. Australia trialled the Excellence in Research Australia (ERA) scheme in 2009, with a full roll-out across all university clusters and disciplines in 2010; another round of ERA is scheduled for 2012. Analogous nation-based measurement exercises in the Anglophone world include: the United Kingdom's Research Assessment Exercise (RAE), which has recently been replaced by the Research Excellence Framework (REF); and New Zealand's Performance-Based Research Fund (PBRF). In the Francophone research environment, France leads the way with an equivalent of the British model, which is overseen by the AERES (*Agence d'Evaluation de la Recherche dans l'Enseignement Supérieur*) and affiliated to the H-Index.

Excellence tied to relevance was also discussed at the UNESCO conference in 2009 as an increasingly important agenda item for higher education, with the model of the research university appearing as something of a golden mean for 'world class' institutions, particularly given the positions held by this type of institution in the global rankings of universities. At the stakeholders' panel devoted to institutions, on Wednesday 8 July, the first item on the agenda was 'creativity and innovation'. Yet, issues facing the creative arts were not once mentioned. The dominant theme was really that of *developing partnerships*. Here is exactly the point at which the main thematic track of the 2011 second UNESCO World Conference on Arts Education, hosted by the Government of the Republic of Korea in Seoul, was set. It is in a comparable space and similar discourse that the creative arts are meant to thrive, globally. But what does this means for researchers in the creative arts disciplines in Australian universities?

In the area of research, the calculation of government funding to universities is standardised and based on two criteria: research input (grants and other public or philanthropic funding) and research output (publications). The emphasis on input severely disadvantages the creative arts. There are few grants available for the arts (and humanities) and those available are based on criteria that apply more appropriately to the sciences. Moreover, the sheer monetary size of grants available for the arts is preposterous when compared to those available for the sciences. Thus, with post-ERA 2010 results in the arts and humanities 'not rising to the highest [world] rank has carried with it all the political and, indeed, economic significance that tough times in higher education further embeds' (Harper, 2011: 27). Put bluntly: no funding. As a creative writer, I picture myself in the near future as a failed battery hen: not only are my wings clipped, but my beak is now tied up. This will remain the case, unless a new paradigm emerges, but what guise will it take? As Harper notes in the same article, hinting at the *discursive crisis* announced in my first paragraph, we need to create 'metalanguages for the understanding and assessment of research as not stationary activities but as evolutionary and developmental achievements', in order for the arts, humanities and social sciences to validate and fully realise their 'ability, ambition [and] belief' (Harper, 2011: 27). Ah, I can now see the hen morphing into Klee's *Angelus Novus* and recall how Benjamin interpreted it in 'On the Concept of History':

> Where a chain of events appears before *us, he* sees one single catastrophe, which keeps piling wreckage and hurls at his feet... The angel would like to stay, awaken the dead, and make whole what has been smashed. But a storm is blowing from Paradise and has got caught in his wings: it is so strong that the angel can no longer close them. This storm drives him irresistibly into the future, to which his back is turned, while the pile of debris before him grows towards the sky. What we call progress is *this* storm. (Benjamin, 2003: 392 [*emphasis in original*])

Progress, for Benjamin, also requires learning to see what is behind our back, what we think we are beyond, what we can no longer see distinctly and what is yet out of sight. In other words, we need to be in(ter)ventive (Pope, 2005: 62), by which I mean both 'inventive' and 'interventive' so that creativity is understood as 'both a rehearsal and a refusal of what is familiar and expected, a contribution to and an intervention in the occasion' (Pope, 2005: 64).

The New Creativity Brokers

Human creativity is the ultimate economic recourse.
– Richard Florida

Australian creative industries research is indebted to the Blair Government's experimentation with culture as good business. Since the turn of the 21st century, creativity and economy have been closely connected in Australian policy rhetoric and higher education programmes, including the creative and performing arts. More than a decade of research based on the connection has confirmed the role of arts and creative industries in building a knowledge economy in which significant goods and services industries are built on creativity (Cunningham, 2002; ARC CCi, 2007; Haseman & Jaaniste, 2008; Jaaniste & Cunningham, 2011). Further, consumers appreciate a steadily wider choice of arts-based experiences from film and music on iPods to urban design and tourism.

There is also a new, and welcome, development in policy-making about creativity and the imagination, as recently documented by O'Connor *et al.* (2011). There is a renewed interest in the individual citizen's experience of culture and the quality and nature of that experience. After a decade of work to recognise the economic contribution of the arts to the economy – and the role it has played regarding social inclusion policies for health, welfare and education – policy research seems to be moving to the intrinsic values end of the arts and not its instrumental value in achieving economic and welfare goals (Holden, 2007). Cultural value has been extended beyond the monetary, and words like 'enrichment' and 'self-expression' have been used to stronger effect (Cunningham, 2009). Whether driven by the global financial crisis' impact on the political agenda, or the recognition that non-profit and public sector creativity needed further consideration, it appears that we are at a turning point in cultural policy-making.

The new debate about cultural policy is driven by the recognition that after more than a decade of enthusiastic prediction about the impact of an online world and digital technology, developed economies are seeing the emergence of greater levels of participation and community sophistication in communications areas that are in the heartland of creativity. The idea of the citizen-artist – mashing, writing, composing and editing their own and others work – is now a reality (ACMA, 2010: 10); and audiences for live performance are growing, because the networks of interest in particular productions or artists are growing through online interactivity. The new cultural policy is about exploring the role of national or local governments which help these new actors engage and contribute to a 21st century culture. In Australia, the National government has opened a forum for discussion and contribution about the framework and content of such a policy, which looks at both for-profit and non-profit cultural value and endeavours from the viewpoint of the citizen-consumer.

A re-examination of the relationship between the arts and Australian politics is overdue and looking at the impulses in that debate may be a good starting point. A new arts agenda for the internet age must take risks beyond the political safety net of cultural nationalism. Two years ago, Helen O'Neil, the then Executive Director of the Council for the Humanities, Arts and Social Sciences (CHASS), proposed a new path towards a creative Australia, where the arts would re-invigorate growth and innovation at every level of society.

In the profoundly different world today, where cultural product pervades every waking moment, there is a need for new models that encompass, but go beyond, the nation-building ethos and subsidy driven system that has shaped arts policy since the 1950s and saw Australians beginning to set goals for quality and access. Currently, there is a need for new visionaries in policy and politics, and artists who are prepared to buck the system and push and prod their society to better define and understand itself through the activity of storytelling and the joy and insight that comes through audience participation in outstanding and innovative performances (O'Neil, 2009: 15).

Half a century on from the beginning of public subsidy and philanthropy to build non-profit arts, Australia has developed a confidence in its ability to make work and export it to audiences, readers and viewers in other parts of the world. It has been a fast growth. The arts moved rapidly from a beginning where the Elizabethan Theatre Trust's determination was to ground the performing arts in the traditions of British culture, to a revival of interest in exploring national identity in painting, drama and music. This desire for an expression of a sense of place gave Australian policy-makers a complementary rationale for public support of the arts, alongside a desire to make world-class art (O'Connor et al., 2011).

As Helen O'Neil suggests in the article cited above, policy focus on creativity and the marketplace can look at several alternate policy environments, but this discussion concentrates on Australia's experience and where it connects to the United Kingdom and the United States experience. From a policy standpoint, the artists and creative arts researchers engaged in universities and other research institutions should be aware of both streams of policy debate, because it is likely that education, from pre-school to postgraduate work, will be the arena where the hopes and aspirations of cultural policy are focused and tested (O'Neil, 2009).

The problem for policy-makers in a contemporary democracy is to determine a role in which the state does not dominate and dictate cultural outcomes. As the UNESCO mission statement attests, there is a consensus that the arts should be citizen driven, with provision for minority cultures and diversity within a national cultural framework. An even more difficult problem then emerges – how much to spend on the arts and creativity? The creative arts have honed skills in fund-raising from governments as much as from private philanthropists, but, by its very nature, there will be more new ideas and creative works than investment funds to realise them. There will also be inherent difficulties for risk-averse policy-makers in assessing what is likely to resonate with audiences and receive respect from the creators' peers and successors. Politicians and political systems are not tolerant of failure, but good art-making is based on a degree of experimentation and failure, which is difficult for public investors to understand.

Perhaps it is not surprising that entrepreneurial arts producers and their supporters looked for a new way to prompt public investment in their work and turned to the language of economics and return on investment as a rationale. In 1994, when the then Prime Minister Paul Keating announced Australia's first national cultural policy – *Creative Nation* – he and his government focused on the potential gains to the economy and the concomitant growth generated by a creative nation. From 1997, the Blair Government left older models of arts and cultural funding behind – back in the Keynesian era – with its espousal of Cool Britannia and a major emphasis on creative industries as an engine of growth. Over in the United States, Richard Florida's studies of creative worker clusters prompted a new look at the links between innovation and the arts and allied crafts and professions (Florida, 2004, 2005). In the United Kingdom, there was a national policy to boost the creative industries and, therefore, the arts activity which nourished it. In the United States and Canada, individual cities picked up Florida's work to extend their own view of industry research and development clusters and other collaborations progressing innovation, to include artists, designers, architects and games makers alongside the scientists, IT code writers and engineers who had been the focus of previous industry development. Eleven years after Keating left office, the Rudd Labor Government arrived in power in Australia with some lofty ambitions for its arts policy and picked up the themes embedded in the Creative Nation statement: specific links between economic growth and creativity; training and entrepreneurial development. Two years on, the Gillard government followed suit. However, economic pressures that are both global and national currently seem to put the arts seriously at risk.

Nonetheless, the area has proved a rich one. Growth rates in the creative industries were higher than more traditional areas of the economy; skills were high-end. Before the policy makers' eyes, there was the example of the cinema, music recording, cultural tourism and the fashion and design professions. More reassuring, the area has had a long history with book publishing, as an example, where a traditional manufacturing and creative process has been a wonderful indicator of the economic value of bringing the arts together with goods production for the market. Even better, in the example of book publishing, there has been a strong history of marketing to mass markets (the best sellers and education), together with heritage work leading to long-life products (from history and classics through to the Bible) and a variety of niche and specialist areas from literary novels to children's work. A mix of traditional business and an eye to the future of 'smart' manufacture (Australian Publishers Association, 2009).

This seems like a splendid vision and is mirrored in a timely report on the arts and creative industries (O'Connor *et al.*, 2011) funded by the Australia Council for the Arts, which looks at ways in which the policy relationship between the oft-polarised sectors of arts and creative industries might be re-thought and approached more productively as in(ter)ventive (Pope, 2005: 62). This vision, however, is only splendid in relatively closed circles. It had been anticipated and vigorously critiqued. For example, in their scathing essay, 'Richard Florida and the Arts: A Rescue Fantasy', Hilary Glow and Stella Minahan demonstrate how the political rhetoric of the Rudd Government was out of step with reality, as it is experienced by arts practitioners (Glow & Minahan, 2010). The authors correctly point out that 'there are two issues' at stake:

> The first is that linking creativity to innovation, and the (almost) universal application of the notion of creativity to all manner of commercial activities, means that the arts struggle to position themselves as a distinctive set of creative practices. Second, as the world of business takes up creativity, the arts appear to have developed a rescue fantasy about business management practices.

While Glow and Minahan (2010) relate these two issues to the fantasy whereby 'the adoption of management regimes holds out the promise of increased control and sustainability, while actually delivering stressful and insecure working conditions', they have also put, much more convincingly, what I was trying to articulate in the paper that sparked the present volume (Hecq, 2008b), when I decried that:

> ...creativity is pervasive and its uses multiple. It not only figures in aesthetic theory, but also in managerial programs where it is presented as a resource for problem-solving and successful marketing, in self-help books where its value as a means to psychological well-being and success is highlighted, and in government policies where it is the mainspring of innovation, productivity and business performance.

And, further, that in our corporatised universities, 'the talk is all about innovation... and about prospective economic returns of degrees'.

So how do we begin to redefine creativity at a time when our governments are banking on it and when science is not much clearer on the topic than Freud was in 1928, when, discussing Dostoevsky and Parricide, he bemoaned that 'before the problem of the creative artist analysis must, alas, lay down its arms (Freud, 1928[1927]: 441). Although creativity happens in 'specific social and historical contexts' (Csikszentmihalyi, 1988: 326) or socio-cultural milieus (Sawyer, 2006), it has its own private side, too.

Creativity Broken Down: Inspiration, Constellations and Fingers out of the Till

> *Words are finite organs of the infinite mind.*
> – Ralph Waldo Emerson

> *You cannot... find inspirational value in a text at the same time that you are viewing it as the product of a mechanism of cultural production... If it is to have inspirational value, a work must be allowed to recontextualize much of what you previously thought you knew; it cannot, at least at first, be recontextualized by what you already believe.*
> – Richard Rorty

Though not exclusively confined to the mind, creativity is, nonetheless, one of the mind's capacities. As such, it exceeds the confines of the brain. The mind is not just a myelinated mass of fissures and folds. What science overlooks is that we do not experience the world with a brain whose workings it describes as though human behaviour were merely the product of electrical cells and synaptic spaces. Modern neuroscience itself is now discovering the anatomy underlying rational thought and creativity. Antonio Damasio, a neuroscientist who has done extensive work on the etiology of feeling, for example, has shown that our feelings are embodied and, hence, that the brain generates metaphysical feelings sourced from the body (Damasio, 1999, 2003). Therefore, despite the recent work of neuroscientists (Calvin, 1997; Greenfield, 2004; Jung *et al.*, 2010), psychologists (Runco, 2007; Kaufman, 2009; Kaufman & Beghetto, 2009; Kaufman & Kaufman, 2009) and even physicists (Penrose, 1994; Bohm, 1998) who are leaders in the field of creativity, I reiterate that science is not much clearer on the topic of creativity than Freud was in 1928, for while these scientists *describe* what happens in creative events, they do not *explain* what happens or why it happens. Further, none of these scientists take into account the reality of the unconscious – one of the 'ghosts in the machine' – which Steven Pinker, an advocate of our current 'third culture', dismisses with such scorn in his book, *The Blank Slate: The New Sciences of Human Nature* (2003). Psychoanalysis, at least, offers quite a few clues as to the 'what' and 'why' of creativity. This final section intimates that 'the greater one's science, the deeper the sense of mystery' (Nabokov, 1964), that creativity belongs with 'the infinite mind' (Emerson, 2010), not so much as the self-contained brain. It concludes that creativity should not be seen as only a revenue stream in writing courses.

While in our everyday dealings we often look at encountered objects in terms of their usefulness, namely, as things of possible use, and tend to pay attention to those aspects of objects which serve our needs, artists try to bring out in their work events, situations, things and aspects of things as they are or, at least, as these appear to them. A play of colours, a constellation of shapes, a sequence of sounds or the development of a certain human character may be something of no particular use and, thus, will tend to get overlooked when one is dealing with a master discourse embedded in economics and science which promotes 'knowledge economies' (OECD, 1996: 7) and 'research quality' (Cutler, 2008: 69).

The type of mind I invoke here is one driven by the aesthetic attitude, one that is described in Kant's *Critique of Judgment* as 'purposefulness without purpose' (Kant, 1987: para 42). This seemingly contradictory characterisation brings home the point that in art there is no other purpose to which the aesthetic object is subordinated, but, at the same time, there is a purpose in it, namely, to bring it out well is an ethical premise, whereby 'the artist tends to submerge his or her own subjectivity; the psychological distance between the subject and the object diminishing until, as it were, the artist forgets himself or herself' (Rorty, 1998: 132–33). This brings us into the uncanny territory that creative writing and psychoanalysis share.

Cooking the Books: Creative Writing with Psychoanalysis

There was a mocking smile on the bloated face which seemed to drive me mad.
– Bram Stoker

The conjunction of these two disciplines has excited writers and psychoanalysts at least since Freud published *Creative Writers and Day Dreaming* (1908 [1907]), even though Freud himself had earlier worried that his work read more like fiction than research bearing the 'serious stamp of science' (Freud, 1895: 231). The 20th century saw a further conjunction of the two with Klein, Winnicott and Lacan, to name but a few. And the 21st century is experiencing an acceleration of this conjunction with the publication of Lacan's late seminars where he returns to poetry in order to refashion his theory of human subjectivity. In his seminar on James Joyce (Lacan, 2005 [1975–76]), for example, where Lacan develops his concept of suppletion, suggesting that art may, as in Joyce's case, be a prosthetic device that helps the self cohere, he sparked further debate about the how and why of creativity (Wolf, 2005; Hecq, 2008a; Wulfing, 2008, 2010).

For Lacan, creativity of the writerly sort involves both the ego and the subject. This disjunction foregrounds the question of the relation between writer and text, speaker and utterance. Through a pervasive interest in the connections between the unconscious and language, including poetic diction, Lacan came to rethink subjectivity in poetic terms. A key text, in this respect, is *Lituraterre* (Lacan, 2001[1971]), which presents creativity as an *event*, that is, as a *process* as much as an *effect* and, thereby, a *product* as well. This text anticipates his final theory that creativity is really a question of 'know-how' or *savoir-faire* (Lacan, 2005[1975–76]: 133), which entails a *praxis*, that is, a practice in command of the operative terms of its own agency. In other words, it is a practice that *knows* what it is doing. Ultimately, such a practice knows how its effects can be produced and, thus, leaves aside any recourse to the improvised, intuitive or irrational. Few creative writers would disagree with this, as creative processes, effects and products often evolve from chaotic beginnings that may have momentous 'in(ter)ventive' (Pope, 2005: 62) effects.

The origin of creativity appears chaotic only because on the deepest, indeed, unconscious levels of our imaginative capacities, orderly, single-stranded thinking is replaced by the multi-dimensional, disorderly and infinite circulation of many different impulses. This 'polyphonous structure', as Ehrenzweig put it (Ehrenzweig, 1967: 3), arises from a superimposition of several different strands of thought upon each other. Ehrenzweig also pointed out that artists are obviously able to alternate between rationally determined thinking and the polyphonous structure of unconscious processes, utilising both for their purposes in *new* and *surprising* ways. No wonder, then, that scientists are still racking their brains to crack the creativity mystery. The point is that when scientific paradigms are being applied to areas where quantifying and evaluating creativity seem paramount, little or no attention is being paid to what is new and surprising. This is the case in creative arts research. While I have shown elsewhere that creative writers think and research *differently* (Harper & Kroll, 2012), I maintain with Barnacle (2005) that the creative PhD thesis fulfils an ontological function. I also maintain that it fulfils an ethical function as well (Hecq, 2008b), because in its very event of creation and commitment to new knowledge, writing a PhD entails radical alterity, which means both enacted freedom and respect of the other. It would therefore not be in a doctoral candidate's best interests to determine the future of creative writing by market revenue streams. Here, as on the global stage of higher education, the devil is in the details. This is what enables Kevin Brophy to keep his poise:

> The creative PhD thesis... however, is not always a happy creation. It is still a product and process being shaped by conflicting forces, confused ideas and ongoing debates. Whether it will be the qualities of arguments or the demands of a market that determine the future of the creative PhD we must wait and see. (Brophy, 2009: 159)

To End with the Question Mark

It was Blackwoods, the original publishers of Miles Franklins' proto-feminist novel *My Brilliant? Career* (1901), who removed the question mark from its original title. Even though they removed the question mark from the title, they were unable to obliterate all that it stood for: bitterness, irony, self-doubt, despair. When a film was made with Judy Davis in the role of its heroine, Virago published their edition of the book with a photo of a defiant Davis dominating an otherwise empty landscape, thus cashing in on another art form. Perhaps there is a lesson for creative writing in this story. Perhaps we can, indeed, imagine a *richer* 'in(ter)ventive' (Pope, 2005: 62) way of thinking about *creativity*, markets and the creative sector into the future, as some researchers have started to do by proposing the idea of 'the creative sector' (art, design and media) as a 'complex innovation system', arguing for innovation eco-diversity or market diversity' (ARC CCi, 2007; Cultural Ministers Council, 2008), thus embracing all elements of the innovation cycle, from experimentation to application to diffusion. If this is where the answer is, creative writing will then have to prioritise establishing its own meta-discourse. Otherwise, creative writing will be in the image of neither Klee's 'Angelus Novus', nor the 'riot girl' invoked later in this book, nor indeed a pseudo Judy Davis, but instead, a hen with clipped wings and a tied-up beak. If I am right in suggesting that creativity begins with the question mark, what is the question?

Acknowledgements

'The New Creative Broker' is heavily indebted to private correspondence with Helen O'Neil (2009–2010), who, in turn, acknowledges the work of Demos, particularly, Holden (2007), whose report, 'Publicly-Funded Culture and the Creative Industries', raises many relevant issues. It also draws on Throsby's long-standing work in cultural economics and, particularly, his Currency House Platform Papers (2006). Finally, it draws on the Australian Government's white paper 'Powering Ideas: An Innovation Agenda for the Twenty-first Century'.

References

Australian Communications and Media Authority (ACMA) (2010) *Communications Report 2009–10*, online document, accessed 3 March 2011. http://www.acma.gov.au/webwr/_assets/main/lib311995/2009-10_comms_report-complete.pdf

Australian Government (2009) *Powering Ideas: An Innovation Agenda for the Twenty-first Century*, online document, accessed 8 February 2011. http://www.innovation.gov.au/Innovation/Policy/Documents/PoweringIdeas.pdf

Australian Publishers Association (2009) *2007 Industry Study*. Sydney: Australian Publishers Association.

Australian Research Council (ARC) Centre of Excellence for Creative Industries and Innovation (CCi) (2007) *Annual Report*, online document, accessed 16 April 2011. http://www.chass.org.au/papers/pdf/PAP20071201CC.pdf

Barnacle, R. (2005) Research Education Ontologies: Exploring Doctoral Becoming. *Higher Education Research and Development* 24 (2), 179–88.

Benjamin, W. (2003) On the Concept of History. In H. Eiland and M.W. Jennings (eds), E. Jephcott *et al.* (trans.), *Walter Benjamin: Selected Writings, Volume 4, 1938–1940* (*pp.* 288–98). Cambridge, MA: Belknap Press.

Bohm, D. (1998) *On Creativity*. London: Routledge.

Bradley, D. (2008) *Review of Australian Higher Education*, online document, accessed 31 January 2011. http://www.deewr.gov.au/Highereducation/Review/Pages/Reviewof AustralianHigherEducationReport.aspx

Brophy, K. (2009) *Patterns of Creativity: Investigations into the Sources of Creativity*. Amsterdam: Rodopi.

Calvin, W.H. (1997) *How Brains Think: Evolving Intelligence, Then and Now*. London: Weidenfeld and Nicolson.

Council for the Humanities, Arts and Social Sciences (CHASS) (2010) *A Strategic Break-through in Building Public Support for Research and Science*, online media release, accessed 8 February 2011. http://www.chass.org.au/media/MED20100209HO.php

Csikszentmihalyi, M. (1988) *Creativity: Flow and the Psychology of Discovery and Invention*. New York, NY: Harper Collins.

Cultural Ministers Council (2008) *Building a Creative Innovation Economy: Opportunities For the Australian and New Zealand Creative Sectors in the Digital Environment*, online document, accessed 16 April 2011. http://www.cmc.gov.au/__data/assets/pdf_file/0006/85596/Building_a_Creative_Innovation_Economy.pdf

Cunningham, S. (2002) From Cultural to Creative Industries: Theory, Industry, and Policy Implications. *Media International Australia Incorporating Culture and Policy: Quarterly Journal of Media Research and Resources*, 54–65.

Cunningham, S. (2009) The New Creativity is Solving Problems Together. *Australian Financial Review*, 30 November, online document, accessed 16 May 2010. http://cci.edu.au/publications/the-new-creativity-solving-problems-together

Cutler & Company Pty Ltd (2008) *Venturous Australia - Building Strength in Innovation (The Cutler Report)*. Canberra: Australian Government Department of Innovation, Industry, Science and Research, online document, accessed 10 January 2011. http://www.innovation.gov.au/Innovation/Policy/Documents/NISReport.pdf

Damasio, A (2003) *Looking for Spinoza*. London: Vintage.

Damasio, A. (1999) *The Feeling of What Happens*. New York, NY: Harvest.

Ehrenzweig, A. (1967) *The Hidden Order of Art*. London: Paladin.

Emerson, R. W. (2010) *Nature*. Boston: Mobi Classics, p. 112.

Ewing, R. (2010) *The Arts and Australian Education: Realising Potential*. Camberwell: Australian Council for Educational Research (ACER), online document, accessed 27 February 2011. http://www.acer.edu.au/documents/AER-58.pdf

Florida, R. (2004) *The Rise of the Creative Class*. New York, NY: Routledge.

Florida, R. (2005) *Cities and the 'Creative Class'*. New York, NY: Routledge.

Franklin, M (1980) *My Brilliant Career*. London: Virago.

Freud, S. (1895) *Studies on Hysteria* (Penguin Freud Library, Vol. 3). Harmandsworth: Penguin.

Freud, S. (1908) *Creative Writers and Day-Dreaming* (Penguin Freud Library, Vol. 14). Harmandsworth: Penguin (original work published 1907).

Freud, S. (1928) *Dostoevsky and Parricide* (Penguin Freud Library, Vol. 14). Harmandsworth: Penguin (original work published 1927).

Glow, H. and Minahan, S. (2010) Richard Florida and the Arts: a Rescue Fantasy. *Meanjin* 69 (3), online article, accessed 23 February 2011. http://meanjin.com.au/editions/volume-69-number-3-2010/article/newsreel-essay-richard-florida-and-the-arts-a-rescue-fantasy/

Gould, S.J. (2004) *The Hedgehog, The Fox and the Magister's Pox: Mending and Minding the Misconceived Gap between Science and the Humanities*. London: Vintage.

Greenfield, S. (2004) *Tomorrow's People: How 21st Century Technology is Changing the Way we Think*. London: Allen Lane.

Harper, G. (2011) Speaking the Lingo: Case of the ERA. *The Australian*, 16 February, online document, accessed 27 February 2011. http://www.theaustralian.com.au/higher-education/opinion-analysis/speaking-the-lingo-case-of-the-era/story-e6frgcko-1226006547582

Harper, G. and Kroll, J. (2012) *Research Methods in Creative Writing*. New York & London: Palgrave.

Haseman, B. and Jaaniste, L. (2008) The Arts and Australia's National Innovation System 1994–2008: Arguments, Recommendations, Challenges. *CHASS*, Occasional Paper 7, online article, accessed http://www.chass.org.au/papers/PAP20081101BH.php. Accessed 27 February 2010.

Hecq, D. (2008a) Writing the Unconscious: Psychoanalysis for the Creative Writer. *TEXT* 12 (2), online article, accessed http://www.textjournal.com.au/oct08/hecq.htm. Accessed 27 February 2010.

Hecq, D. (2008b) Banking on Creativity? [Presentation]. *Paper presented at the 13ᵗʰ Conference of the Australian Association of Writing Programs (AAWP)*, 27–29 November. Sydney, Australia. Online at http://aawp.org.au/files/Hecq_2008.pdf

Holden, J. (2007) *Publicly-Funded Culture and the Creative Industries*. London: Demos. Online at http://www.demos.co.uk/files/Publicly_Funded_Culture_and_the_Creative_Industries.pdf?1240939425

Howard, J. (2008) Between a Hard Rock and a Soft Space: Design, Creative Practice and Innovation. *Council for the Humanities, Arts and Social Sciences (CHASS)* Occasional Paper 5, online article, accessed 31 January 2011. http://www.chass.org.au/papers/pdf/PAP20080521JH.pdf

Howkins, J. (2001) *The Creative Economy: How People Make Money from Ideas*. Harmondsworth: Penguin.

Jaaniste, L. and Cunningham, S. (2011) *Creative Economy Report Card 2011*, online document, accessed 16 April 2011. http://cci.edu.au/sites/default/files/dbogg/Creative%20Economy%20report%20card%20March%202011.pdf

Johnson, L., Smith, R., Willis, H., Levine, A. and Haywood, K. (2011) *The 2011 Horizon Report*. Austin: The New Media Consortium. Online at http://net.educause.edu/ir/library/pdf/HR2011.pdf

Jung, R., Segall, J., Bockholt, J., Flores, R., Smith, S. Chavez, R. and Haien, R. (2010) Neuroanatomy of Creativity. *Human Brain Mapping* 31 (3), 398–409.

Kant, I. (1987) *Critique of Judgment* (W.S. Pluhar, trans.). Indianapolis, IN: Hackett Publishing Company.

Kaufman, J.C. (2009) *Creativity*. New York, NY: Springer.

Kaufman, J.C. and Beghetto, R.A. (2009) Beyond Big and Little: The Four C Model of Creativity. *Review of General Psychology* 13(1), 1–12.

Kaufman, J.C. and Kaufman, S.B. (2009) *The Psychology of Creative Writing*. Cambridge: Cambridge University Press.

Lacan, J. (2001) Lituraterre. In J.A. Miller (ed.) *Autres Ecrits* (pp. 11–20). Paris: Seuil (original work published 1971).

Lacan, J. (2005) *Le séminaire: Livre XXIII. Le sinthome*. J.A. Miller (ed.) Paris: Seuil (original work published 1975–6).

Lacan, J. (2007) *The Other Side of Psychoanalysis*. R. Grigg (trans.) New York, NY: Norton (original work published 1969–70).

Lehrer, J. (2007) *Proust Was a Neuroscientist*. New York & Boston, NY: Houghton Miflin.

Nabokov, V. (1964) Interview with Alvin Toffler, *Playboy* 3, online document, accessed 17 February 2011. http://lib.ru/NABOKOW/Inter03.txt

O'Connor, J., Cunningham, S. and Jaaniste, L. (2011) *Arts and Creative Industries. A Historical Overview; and an Australian Conversation*, online document, accessed 8 February 2011. http://www.australiacouncil.gov.au/__data/assets/pdf_file/0005/86180/Arts_and_creative_industries_FINAL_Feb_2011.pdf

O'Farrell, L. (2010) *The Second World Conference on Arts Education Final Report*. UNESCO, online document, accessed 17 February 2011. http://portal.unesco.org/culture/en/files/41171/128628564452nd_World_Conference_on_Arts_Education_-_Final_Report.

pdf/2nd%2BWorld%2BConference%2Bon%2BArts%2BEducation%2B-%2BFinal%2BReport.pdf

O'Neil, H. (2009) Ratbags at the Gates. *Griffith Review* (edn 23). Online at http://www.griffith.edu.au/griffithreview/campaign/ed23/ONeil_ed23.pdf

OECD (1996) *The Knowledge-Based Economy.* Paris: Organization for Economic Co-operation and Development. Online at http://www.oecd.org/dataoecd/51/8/1913021.pdf

Penrose, R. (1994) *Shadows of the Mind.* Oxford: Oxford University Press.

Pinker, S. (2003) *The Blank Slate.* New York, NY: Penguin.

Pope, R. (2005) *Creativity: Theory, History, Practice.* New York, NY: Routledge.

Rorty, R. (1998) *Achieving Our Country.* Cambridge, MA: Harvard University Press.

Runco, M. (2007) *Creativity: Theories and Themes, Research, Development and Practice.* Burlington, MA: Elsevier Academic Press.

Sawyer, W.K. (2006) *Explaining Creativity: The Science of Human Innovation.* Oxford: Oxford University Press.

Throsby, D. (2006) *Does Australia Need a Cultural Policy.* Redfern: Currency House Platform Papers.

UNCTAD (2008) *Creative Economy Report*, online document, accessed 16 April 2011. http://www.unctad.org/en/docs/ditc20082cer_en.pdf

UNESCO (2009) *The 2009 World Conference on Higher Education: The New Dynamics of Higher Education and Research for Societal Change and Development.* [Conference]. UNESCO Headquarters, Paris. Online at http://www.unesco.org/en/the-2009-world-conference-on-higher-education/about-the-conference/

UNESCO (2010) Seoul Agenda: Goals for the Development of Arts Education. Outcome of *UNESCO's Second World Conference on Arts Education*, online document, accessed 17 February 2011. http://portal.unesco.org/culture/en/files/41117/12798106085Seoul_Agenda_Goals_for_the_Development_of_Arts_Education.pdf/Seoul%2BAgenda_Goals%2Bfor%2Bthe%2BDevelopment%2Bof%2BArts%2BEducation.pdf

Wolf, B. (ed.) (2005) *Psychoanalytical Notebooks No. 13: Lacan with Joyce.* London: London Circle of the ESP.

Wolton, D. (2009) Globalisation and Cultural Diversity. [Lecture]. *Lecture presented at The University of Melbourne*, 7 May. Melbourne.

Wulfing, N. (ed.) (2008) *Psychoanalytical Notebooks No. 19: Ordinary Psychosis.* London: London Circle of the ESP.

Wulfing, N. (ed.) (2010) *Psychoanalytical Notebooks No. 20: Object A and the Semblant.* London: London Circle of the ESP.

3 Creativity and the Marketplace
Jen Webb

Introduction

Creativity is, as many essays and books announce, a vexed topic. 'The concept of creativity has traditionally proved an elusive one to pin down,' writes Anna Craft (2001: 13); it is 'a mystery, not to say a paradox,' writes Margaret Boden (2004: 1); and the title of H.B. Parkhurst's influential essay of 1999, 'Confusion, Lack of Consensus, and the Definition of Creativity as a Construct', speaks to the difficulties theorists identify in attempting to delimit and define this concept. Despite millennia of discussion about inspiration and centuries of research into creativity – particularly since the middle of the 20th century (see Runco, 2004) – the word is used, as are other evaluative terms such as 'excellence', as though its meaning were self-evident. This is despite the fact that the connotations for such terms spiral wildly out of reach and the denotations frequently remain either obscure or circular. Excellence, for instance, is defined by the Webster's English Dictionary as 'the quality of being excellent', while 'creative' is 'the quality of creating'. Definitions of this nature leave us no further ahead, particularly in an essay that attempts to trace and analyse the connections between the concept of creativity and the values and practices of the marketplace.

I do not intend to attempt yet another definition, but following Mihaly Csikszentmihalyi, to focus on *where* creativity emerges, rather than on *what* it might be. Creativity, he writes, 'exists only in specific social and historical contexts' (1988: 326), so it is more usefully investigated through an analysis of those contexts, their properties and their effects, than through attempts to pin down particular characteristics of creativity. This paper focuses precisely on the *where* – albeit, a metaphorical where – by drawing attention to the agora as the site in which the interests of both the marketplace and the creative community can find accommodation. To lay out the ground for this, I first examine some of the key terms that are put to work in discussions of creativity and the marketplace and suggest ways in which we might draw on the long history of the creative field to clarify and refine our modes of practice, our teaching of practice and our understanding of the place of our practice in society.

Delimiting the Construct

Perhaps in consequence of the murky nature of most formal definitions of 'creativity', researchers and commentators have come up with a plethora of definitions of their own. As noted above, I do not intend to offer yet another. Still, it is necessary that I set out how I perceive the boundaries around creativity, as I use the term in this essay. My approach takes up the concept from two perspectives – one that addresses the generation of works of art and a second that addresses the generation of knowledge. The literature of science is productive for both perspectives: Albert Einstein, for example, could be writing as an artist when he states, 'To raise new questions, new problems, to regard old problems from a new angle, requires creative imagination and marks real advances in science' (cited Csikszentmihalyi, 1992: 20). As Csikszentmihalyi shows in his account of 20th-century science, this association of creativity with the formulation of an important question, and the appropriation of creative imagination, is one that runs through the literature of science. For many writers in this field, it is creativity that is key to the generation of 'real advances'. The raising of a question, a new way of looking at the world – these are how both new art and new knowledge typically emerge.

The key to such 'real advances' – whether in science or in art – may appear to be simply chance or intuition. An observation is made, an insight gleaned, because the artist (or scientist) was lucky enough to be in the right place at the right time, or because the artist (or scientist) is fortunate to have particular intuitive capacity. But just as the ancient world dryly reminded us that 'fortune favours the bold',[1] so, too, I suggest that creative success is the result not of luck, but of preparedness. Generally speaking, a creative act or a creative advance in knowledge, thought or application is not simply chanced upon by a lucky person. Rather, they are 'chanced upon' by a person whose mind and body are trained; a person who possesses an attitude of attention and a capacity to focus and reflect; a person with sufficient literacy in their field to know that they have spotted something new. So we can say that creativity is, first, an attribute of thinking and acting that is based on perception, conceptual thinking and self-reflexivity; and, next, that it is 'the ability to come up with ideas or artefacts that are new, surprising and valuable' (Boden, 2004: 1) – that offer a contribution to knowledge, to society or to culture.

The inclusion of 'contribution' needs a little attention in the context of this essay. A contribution, in the dictionary definition, is something that 'adds to a larger whole'. This definition does not, however, identify what constitutes the larger whole. It may be that a contribution adds to the larger whole of a discipline; it may be an addition to the larger whole of society or its culture; it may be an addition to the larger whole of the market. Scholars tend to perceive contributions as being additions to knowledge, and artists tend to perceive contributions as additions to our cultural capital, the aesthetic 'bank' of a society. Each of these identifies a contribution as an object or act that is directed outward – toward society at large or toward the greater good. But this is not the perception at the heart of capitalism, which values individual striving for individual gain over collective action or the public good.[2] Though capitalist discourse may claim that public good comes from individual efforts, the heart of capitalism is individual effort directed toward individual gain (or good). It is not concerned with reciprocal relations or contributions to general wellbeing, but to the amassing of personal profit. Contemporary writers on creativity and capitalism might disagree with me here, since in much of the literature it is clear that they marry the logic of capitalism with the logic of creativity, identifying each as contributing to the larger whole. These writers have argued enthusiastically not only that creativity can be exploited for economic purposes, but also that it is central to market concerns that effect a public good: contribution to the market becomes a contribution to the self, because the creative worker is able to generate an income. Creative activity becomes a contribution to society in the form of the provision of goods and services and the building of a stronger economy.

Creativity and Economic Value

One of the best known of this group of writers is Richard Florida, who simultaneously celebrates and delimits creativity:

> I define the highest order of creative work as producing new forms or designs that are readily transferable and widely useful – such as designing a product that can be widely made, sold and used; coming up with a theorem or strategy that can be applied in many cases; or composing music that can be performed again and again. People at the core of the Creative Class engage in this work regularly; it's what they are paid to do. (Florida, 2002: 69)

Those of us who have invested in the creative arts side of the field of creative production are likely to squirm at this definition. Vera Zolberg points out that the romantic notion 'that art is the spontaneous expression of its creator, that it should eschew playing any social role, or fulfilling any social function, and exist for its own sake alone' (Zolberg, 1990: 11) still has considerable traction in the creative and wider community. As early as 1771, there was a clearly articulated hierarchy of value, with 'literature' placed far above 'commerce' (Prickett, 1981: 64),[3] and the Romantic discourse, which is marked by an opposition between art and money, continues to cast a long shadow. However, this is a view that Florida, an economist, manifestly does not hold.

His first example, of 'the highest order of creative work', is at odds with the values of the field of creative production. New forms and designs may have great aesthetic appeal, but if their production is driven by market imperatives, as is the case for Florida, then they do not fit comfortably with the values of the arts field – expressivity, disinterestedness, autonomy (with respect to the market). Nor do they necessarily fit with generally accepted definitions of creativity – the raising of new questions, the interrogation of established ways of seeing and thinking, the contribution of what is both novel and valuable in terms beyond those of money. Florida's second two examples of high-order creative work are about production in maths and music. In both cases, their value, for Florida, is in their utility: they 'can be applied in many cases'; they 'can be performed again and again'. This seems to overlook the issue of novelty or the possibility that they might initiate a new paradigm, instead, for Florida, they remain firmly in the realm of commodity objects, rather than 'advances' in science or arts and rather than exploratory or expressive acts.

What Florida identifies as 'the highest order of creative work' is, for many artists, in fact, the lowest order: commercial work, produced for a pre-established market. In Pierre Bourdieu's terminology, it is heteronomous production – work that is not free, with respect to social or economic imperatives, art that is 'doubly suspect, being both commercial and popular' (Bourdieu, 1993: 50) and Florida, in fact, makes this evident. The work involved here is not art for art's sake, but is something the creative practitioners 'are paid to do'. It is art for a purpose: heteronomous production. It is art that is fully invested in the social fabric of its time, and those principles of organisation, as is clear in Florida's central thesis, that, for him, creativity is about class structure: 'as with other classes, the defining basis of this new class is economic. . . . The Creative Class derives its identity from its members' roles as purveyors of creativity' (Florida, 2002: xiii).

This unabashed association of creative practice with economic systems is narrow, I would argue, because it ignores or excludes much of the work that is done in the creative field and by creative practitioners. It excludes those practitioners who might 'engage in this work regularly', but whose outputs are not transferable, but unique; whose outputs are not 'applied in many cases', but are ephemeral, site specific, not generalisable. And it excludes a vast proportion of the creative community: those who are not 'paid to do' it, who, in fact, may spend both time and money to perform their practice and who follow the advice of David Throsby (Throsby & Hollister, 2003) and 'don't give up [their] day jobs'. For Florida, it seems, such artists are not part of the creative community, because they do not and could not, make their living from their artwork.

But for the same reason that Florida's view of creativity is unpalatably narrow, so, too, it is (for many in the creative community) unpalatably broad, because it focuses on the economy, rather than on creative expression. Florida catches in the net of his definition of creative people 'roughly 30 percent of the entire U.S. workforce' (Florida, 2002: 74), including those working in the creative industries, sciences, technology, engineering and the economy. Consequently, he suggests, 'the creative individual is the new mainstream' (Florida, 2002: 6). This is a significant issue: the notion not only that creativity is part of the mainstream, but also that this is a new way of understanding creativity.

It certainly can seem new, to those of us brought up in the romantic tradition, but, in fact, alienated creative production is an anomaly in history. Art, as such, or creativity, more generally, has only had a few centuries of 'special' status. Zolberg points out that, '[e]xcept briefly, mainly during the Periclean Age [461–429 BCE], when art came to be considered a value in its own right, on the whole, art was not distinguished from craft, nor artists from artisans' (Zolberg, 1990: 9–10). Up to and throughout the Middle Ages, workers performing functions we would now see as 'creative' – painters, sculptors, musicians – were considered just workers, artisans and not artists (Williams, 1981: 59). They worked not (primarily) because of inspiration, but because it was their job; as is the case for the workers in Florida's Creative Class, it was what they were 'paid to do', by the church, by patrons, by the court.

It was not until the Renaissance that artists began the long work of alienating themselves from the broad economic field and from the ordinariness of workers in the general economy. Zolberg identifies this happening first with one branch of musicians, who segregated their practice out from other music forms – the artisanal, the sacred or the demotic – and established music as part of the curriculum of the medieval European university. They were followed by the visual and plastic artists who, by drawing on Platonism, were able to establish a theoretical basis for their practice that allowed them to break away from the guild structure and to exchange the traditional artisanal identity for the more prestigious identity of artist and scholar. They began the moves that led to the disinterested, transcendent genius of modern discourse. During the 17th and 18th centuries, with the development of philology and rhetoric, the language arts also managed to become worthy of scholarly attention, though it is perhaps worth noting that it was critical, rather than creative, writing that had its place in the university.

What we see in Florida's thesis is something of a return to the traditional function of creative practice: the making of an object for exchange, rather than for personal expression; a preference for high production values over high expressive values; and the integration of creative work within the broad economy. This goes against the romantic discourse of the autonomous artist, the charismatic 'free' agent (who, of course, existed more in the discourse than in lived experience). As Pierre Bourdieu points out, artists do not spring fully formed from Zeus' brow, but are 'created' out of social formations (Bourdieu, 1996: 167), just as they themselves 'create', not out of magic or through the intervention of the Muses, but as a result of cultural influences, personal disposition and training. Still, the fantasy of charisma or 'magic' in the world of art continues to influence the discourse, despite the increasing significance of the creative industries and the obvious (and necessary) relationship between art and money, creative production and a market.

The Market in History

Given this context, it may be time for those of us at the autonomous end of the arts spectrum to accept that there is something to be said for the market, or for the idea of market; to examine the extent to which the market may afford fresh ways of thinking about creativity and creative practice; and to consider how we might best prepare students in creative disciplines to function across the competing imperatives of art and the economy. The market is, after all, as much a part of human history as is innovation, art or creativity. As Karl Polanyi writes, 'No society could, naturally, live for any length of time unless it possessed an economy of some sort' (1957: 43), but, like 'creativity' or 'excellence', the word 'economy' is defined in vague or circular terms. It often presents as a thing-in-itself, but, as Marshall Sahlins points out in his *Stone Age Economics* (2004 [1972]), economy is more a participle than a noun:

> . . .even to speak of *'the* economy' of a primitive society [and, by extension, of any society] is an exercise in unreality. Structurally, 'the economy' does not exist. Rather than a distinct and specialized organization, 'economy' is something that generalized social groups and relations . . . *do*. Economy is a function of the society rather than a structure. (Sahlins, 2004: 76)

In this, Sahlins is in accord with conventional understandings of the economy and, particularly, of contemporary capitalism. While 'capitalism' is now so thoroughly embedded in Western culture that it barely needs definition – in fact, the word 'has become a synonym for the market economy', as Richard Grassby writes (1999: 3) – it is 'a function rather than a structure' and a system of ideas, practices, attitudes and values, rather than a material form. Max Weber famously refers to it as a 'spirit' or 'ethos', as he writes in his influential work *The Protestant Ethic and the Spirit of Capitalism* (2003 [1904–1905]):

> This philosophy of avarice appears to be the ideal of the honest man of recognized credit, and above all the idea of a duty of the individual toward the increase of his capital, which is assumed as an end in itself. Truly what is preached here is not simply a means of making one's way in the world, but a peculiar ethic. (Weber, 2003: 51)

'Avarice' is a harsh term, but, still, most commentators agree that capitalism is about private ownership and self-interest, as expressed within the public sphere (Grassby, 1999: 45). It places the individual, rather than the community, at the heart of society, and it rewards production for economic exchange, rather than production for the disinterested pursuit of knowledge or (for example) art's sake. But, of course, the individual is just one element of the wider organism known as society, and, so, the public and private cannot be distinctly separated. Similarly, exchange is not something separate from society, but a part of it. Markets are socially embedded, and while, as a result, they differ radically in different historical epochs and in different cultural contexts, they share the property of being places for exchange and, hence, relationships.[4] One of the best places to observe and reflect on the connection between the marketplace and relationships is that early arrangement – the agora, or forum or basilica. The term refers to a public space where buyers and sellers could meet, and it had a transparent commitment not just to trade, but also to civic and political functions, to significant social encounters (Merrill, 1977: 308). The agora seems to have started its life not as a commercial site, but as 'a political, military and religious assembly point' (Cetina, 2006: 554). Although marketplaces have existed across history and cultures, it is the ancient Athenian agora that sets the standard for its role as a public space. It was here that citizens of Athens (a category that did not include women or slaves) met to discuss important issues and to come to decisions about civic action. This was the heart of the community, the political, commercial and philosophical centre and the seat of justice. Every public thing that happened was debated and evaluated in the agora: here was made possible the rich political engagement, the public dialogue and debate that formed the basis of contemporary understandings of free speech, democracy and human being. This is not to say that the agora was a place of concord; for Hannah Arendt, it was, rather, a place of 'incessant discourse' (1968: 27), where plurality of opinion ruled over mere rational argument. This is significant to current understandings of the agora, because, as Arendt writes, debate 'constitutes the very essence of political life' (1983: 241), and opinions provide the ground on which politics can play out.

That agora has gone, now. The only markets that replicate those of the ancient or the medieval worlds are quaint replicas or places for hobby rather than conventional commerce: farmers markets, craft markets. Economic exchange takes place on a huge – a global – scale and can no longer be confined to the narrow walls of the local market. Similarly, the notion that democracy provides an effective space for civil intercourse or full political engagement fails to convince; a vote once every three or four years for a pre-selected candidate hardly constitutes the taking of a political position. The agora relied on members of the community understanding themselves as citizens, fully engaged in the politics and social functions. Television and other forms of media have replaced the agora and provide a contemporary version of that simultaneously public/private space. So, though the agora in its ideal Athenian form is lost to history, we still have public spaces for conversation, communication, debate and exchange: new agora, sites in which it is possible to recapture something of the logic of the marketplace of ideas; the civic space for politics and polity.

The Agora in the Present

The 'new agora' is a term applied quite liberally in contemporary writings. For Zygmunt Bauman (2004), television affords a new version of the public/private space: a sort of Oprah-agora. For Habermas, 'new agora' is conveniently applied to European coffeehouses (Habermas, 1992), since they combine economic and social-informational exchange. The term is used for museums, because they offer public spaces where citizens can meet (Einsiedel & Einsiedel, 2004: 73); it is used for shopping malls and airports (Kohn, 2004: 57). Howard Rheingold speaks of the 'electronic agora' (1994: 19), and Hénaff and Strong name the new media a virtual public space (2001: 221). Architects, new media producers, IT engineers, public policy writers, political theorists, museum specialists, city planners and economists all look back to the agora as a metaphorical space and analogue for contemporary practice. Why not artists, too? Why not, particularly, writers? Writing is an art form that works with the same materials used in politics and argument.

Taking this as a foundation point, I would like to move, in the remainder of this essay, to how creative practice – and, particularly, creative writing – might be accommodated in tertiary education to generate creativity and innovation. I have suggested that the Richard Florida version of creative practice is limited by its focus on economic outputs; though this is an important aspect of the broad creative field, many teachers and students in creative disciplines are far more committed to the expressive, than the marketable, mode of practice. Moreover, a focus on economic generation is, *pace* Florida, likely to limit creative activity that operates according to the model of the field of art ('art for art's sake'). As analysts have shown, creative practice is as much about finding problems as it is about solving them. A creative output may eventually prove to offer social or economic utility, but is unlikely to offer the quick solutions or easy application of knowledge to a problem that is of most benefit to government and economic sectors. This is not to overlook the social and economic utility of all practice, but to suggest that, for many of us, creativity is more than production for a market and it is more than simple novelty. Though we can agree that there is a 'continuous creation of unforeseeable novelty', for art-oriented creativity we need, in addition, knowledge, practice, craft and attention and the act of 'turning thought upon itself in order that it may seize this ability and catch this impulse' (Bergson, 1946: 91, 94).

Teaching, Creativity and the Marketplace

As teachers in creative disciplines in tertiary institutions, there are several pedagogical and methodological paths we might take to support our students in becoming highly creative practitioners. One is the traditional university approach of a lot of theory and a wee bit of practice, designed to produce informed consumers of creative goods. Another is the art school approach, which involves a lot of practice and a wee bit of theory, designed to produce informed practitioners. A third, and much more recent, approach is that found in schools of creative or cultural industries, which are often seen to be in direct competition with the former two modes, although it actually began more as a Florida-esque move, focused on commercial media, rather than on art practice. Stuart Cunningham, an Australian guru of creative industries, notes that: '[t]he "cultural industries" was a term invented to embrace the commercial industry sectors (principally film, television, book publishing and music) which also delivered fundamental popular culture to a national population' (Cunningham, 2004: 106).

This is a long way from the domain of creative practice as it is experienced in studios or in art schools. We may produce commercially successful work (if we're lucky!), but this is not the object of our practice. Rather, the objects of practice tend to be: to find a way to express a certain something; to tell a story; to test or explore form; to resolve a formal, conceptual or expressive problem; in short, to *find out*. For many of us, it is first about 'original thought', which may be manifested in what research agencies call 'blue-sky thinking', an approach that is utterly divorced from the utility or applicability of any possible outcomes, but is committed to the demonstrably novel, reflective and skillfully accomplished. This cannot be accomplished under the aegis of the market or within the creative industries dicta:

> ...the market is accepted more and more as a legitimate means of legitimation. ... Audience ratings impose the sales model on cultural products. But it is important to know that, historically, all of the cultural productions that I consider (and I'm not alone here, at least I hope not) the highest human products – math, poetry, literature, philosophy – were all produced against market imperatives. (Bourdieu, 1998: 27)

Much as I am drawing a line between creative arts and creative industries, so, too, Cunningham seems eager to introduce a distinction, writing:

> For *Knowledge Nation* [the 2001 Australian Labor Party policy], the creative industries are coterminous with the arts. The result of this conflation is that recommendations for advancing the creative industries are residual at best, being lumped in with some afterthought recompense for universities' humanities and social sciences rather than upfront in the document as the sector that will deliver the content essential for next generation ICT sector growth. (Cunningham, 2004: 109)

Cunningham is writing about the Australian context, but the terminology and concept of the creative industries are borrowed from the United Kingdom – products of Tony Blair's New Labour – which perceived cultural industries as the mechanism to bring into being the 'Cool Britannia' his government promised (Hartley, 2005: 225). In both Britain and Australia, the focus is the generation of intellectual property, typically on an industrial scale. Cunningham's point is that it is not feasible to collapse the two sets of practices: the creative industries do not offer an alternative to the traditional art school or traditional humanities department. John Hartley and Michael Keane also make this evident when they describe the tension, for creative industries, as being 'between individual imagination and industrial scale' (Hartley & Keane, 2006: 260). But neither the art school nor the humanities department engages conventionally with the problem of industrial scale, rather, like both the Romantic movement and conventional capitalism – two radically opposed ideologies with remarkably similar discourses in, at least, this respect – they are committed to the individual.

All three approaches – training in the humanities, arts and industry – are important elements in higher education, and I do not intend to throw babies out with bathwater. But I do want to suggest that there may be a fourth way that offers the benefits of the other three, while nimbly avoiding their limitations. Economist Richard Caves points out that 'University-based creative training blends in another element – giving the aspiring artist general training that provides backup for the highly risky investment in artistic training' (Caves, 2000: 25). This we already find to varying degrees in creative writing programmes across the university sector, in courses designed to:

- draw from the humanities, offering training in the literary and cultural traditions and contexts;
- draw from the art schools, offering training in craft and expression; and
- draw from the creative industries, offering training in professionalism and public responsibility.

The significance of this blend is that it allows teachers, students and graduates a space in which to consider what we do when we make creative work as professionals, and what we do when we employ the processes of creative thinking and practice to generate objects of benefit to ourselves as practitioners (the private sector) and to society more broadly (the public sector). It is always worth remembering that art is not only a matter of personal expression, but also a matter of public communication and public identity. Where the creative industries are bound by the logic of the market-place *qua* profitability, creative arts are, in the best of cases, committed to the logic of the marketplace *qua* agora: that is, the simultaneously public/private space for social, intellectual and political encounters, for debate, for the rich messy life of the society as a whole. Creative objects, in general, and novels, in particular, can create public spaces – spaces for conversation, discussion, argument, reflection and exchange.

Conclusion

Of course, the mass media creates such spaces too. But in its need to cater to a mass audience – its 'industrial scale' – it necessarily crafts a public space that is reductive, that requires conformity to a central line of thinking. Although, as was also true of Greek orators in the ancient agora, the mass media institutions seek to appeal to, or woo, their audiences, like the ancient Greek agora, it is not a space of genuine democracy. In Athens, only property owning men could truly participate in the civic and political life – a highly elitist form of the commons. In the mass media, only a limited range of stories and perspectives are offered, and the commons thus created is one that is given, or determined, rather than the outcome of open debate. It is true that an artwork, too, is 'given' to its consumers, but they engage with it in a direct and individual way and (in an ideal situation) are able to argue with it, debate, discuss and negotiate. It affords a commons, an agora, in a way that is not possible to the mass media because it does not – indeed, it cannot – demand conformity to one way of thinking.

This is particularly the case for creative writing, which comes to its audience in a language already committed to conversation – words – and makes use of reading, that so-democratic technique. It allows (encourages, demands) an ongoing engagement between reader and text, reader and reader, a space where, in the words of Fred See (1994: 345), the 'exhausted' (the story that resolves itself) is 'inexhaustible' (because we keep returning to it, keep discussing it, keep finding something new to say). Reading is an extraordinary capability, one that opens worlds through words and one that is at the heart of civic and political encounter. A 'good book' – a text that is thoughtful or polemic, insightful or interrogative, that shifts perspective, that breaks with the popular and the general – such a book can create a space for public/private interaction that is the hallmark of the agora. Such a book can generate creative thinking by posing questions that had, perhaps, not previously occurred to the readers of the book. It can generate creativity, too, by shifting the terms of reference for fiction.[5] Finally, because it operates within the marketplace, but according to the rules of the field of creative production, it can model, for students, a way of being, first, creative; then, professional; and then, socially engaged.

Notes

(1) 'Audaces fortuna iuvat' is Virgil's phrasing from the *Aeneid* (10.284). Cicero uses it in his *Tusculan Questions* (2.4.11), Ovid in the *Fasti* (2.782), Livy in *Macedonian War* (37.37.4) and it appears in many other places in ancient literature.

(2) Adam Smith acknowledged that the foundation for individual action was self-interest, but insisted that the mass of individual striving would add up to the public good: 'By pursuing his own interest he frequently promotes that of the society more effectually than when he really intends to promote it' (Smith, 1909: 352).

(3) Bertrand Russell writes: 'the romantic outlook, partly because it is aristocratic, and partly because it prefers passion to calculation, has a vehement contempt for commerce and finance' (Russell, 2004: 622).

(4) One of the earliest forms of exchange is what is called 'silent trade'. This involved the use of known (and, often, sacred) locations where people from one group would

place piles of goods and then withdraw; people from another group would arrive, collect the goods they wanted, and leave other goods behind, to be collected in their turn by the first group. In this form of exchange, Marshall Sahlins writes, 'good relations are maintained by preventing any relations' (2004: 201), though since they do seem to have been governed by reciprocity (giving and receiving), it seems they do involve some sort of relationship.

(5) See Milan Kundera's *The Curtain* (2006) for a discussion of creative generation in fictional works.

References

Arendt, H. (1983) *Between Past and Future*. New York, NY: Penguin Books.

Arendt, H. (1968) *Men in Dark Times*. New York, NY: Harcourt, Brace & World.

Bauman, Z. (2004) Liquid sociality. In N. Gane (ed.) *The Future of Social Theory* (pp. 17–46). London: Continuum.

Bergson, H. (1946) *The Creative Mind: An Introduction to Metaphysics*. New York, NY: Citadel Press.

Boden, M. (2004) *The Creative Mind: Myths and Mechanisms* (2nd edn). London: Routledge.

Bourdieu, P. (1993) *The Field of Cultural Production*. Cambridge: Polity.

Bourdieu, P. (1996) *The Rules of Art: Genesis and Structure of the Literary Field* (S. Emanuel, trans.). Cambridge: Polity Press.

Bourdieu, P. (1998) *On Television and Journalism* (P.P. Ferguson, trans.). London: Pluto.

Caves, R.E. (2000) *Creative Industries: Contracts Between Art and Commerce*. Cambridge, MA: Harvard University Press.

Cetina, K.K. (2006) The market. *Theory Culture Society* 23 (2–3), 551–56.

Marcus Tullius Cicero 1839 [c45BCE] *The Tusculan Questions* (trans George Alexander Otis), Boston: James B Dow.

Craft, A. (2001) An Analysis of Research and Literature on Creativity in Education, *Qualifications and Curriculum Authority*, online document, accessed 9 August 2009. http://www.euvonal.hu/images/creativity_report.pdf

Csikszentmihalyi, M. (1988) Society, culture and person: A systems view of creativity. In R.J. Sternberg (ed.) *The Nature of Creativity: Contemporary Psychological Perspectives* (pp. 325–39). Cambridge & New York, NY: Cambridge University Press.

Csikszentmihalyi, M. (1992) Motivation and creativity. In R.S. Albert (ed.) *Genius and Eminence*, (2nd edn) (pp. 19–33). Oxford and New York, NY: Routledge.

Cunningham, S. (2004) The creative industries after cultural policy: A genealogy and some possible preferred futures. *International Journal of Cultural Studies* 7 (1), 105–115.

Einsiedel Jr, A.A. and Einsiedel, E.F. (2004) Museums as Agora: Diversifying approaches to engaging publics in research. In D. Chittenden, G. Farmelo and B.V. Lewenstein (eds) *Creating Connections: Museums and the Public Understanding of Current Research* (pp. 73–85). Lanham & Oxford: Altamira Press.

Florida, R. (2002) *The Rise of the Creative Class: and How it's Transforming Work, Leisure, Community and Everyday Life*. New York, NY: Basic Books.

Grassby, R. (1999) *The Idea of Capitalism Before the Industrial Revolution*. Lanham and New York, NY: Rowman & Littlefield.

Habermas, J. (1992) *The Structural Transformation of the Public Sphere: An Inquiry into a Category of Bourgeois Society*. Cambridge: Polity Press.

Hartley, J. (2005) *Creative Industries*. Oxford: Wiley-Blackwell.

Hartley, J. and Keane, M. (2006) Creative industries and innovation in China. *International Journal of Cultural Studies* 9 (3), 259–262.

Hénaff, M. and Strong, T.B. (2001) Public space, virtual space, and democracy. In M. Henaff and T.B. Strong (eds) *Public Space and Democracy* (pp. 221–31). Minneapolis, MI: University of Minnesota Press.

Kohn, M. (2004) *Brave New Neighborhoods: the Privatization of Public Space*. New York, NY: Routledge.

Kundera, M. (2006) *The Curtain: an Essay in Seven Parts* (L. Asher, trans.). London: Faber and Faber.

Livy (Titus Livius) 1905 [c27-25BCE] The History of Rome (trans Rev. Canon Roberts), London: J. M. Dent & Sons.

Merrill, S. (1977) *Ancient Jerusalem*. New York, NY: Arno Press (original work published 1908).

Ovid 1931 [c1BCE-1CE] *Fasti* (trans James George Frazer), London, William Heinemann.

Parkhurst, H.B. (1999) Confusion, lack of consensus, and the definition of creativity as a construct. *Journal of Creative Behavior* 33 (1), 1–21.

Polanyi, K. (1957) *The Great Transformation: The Political and Economic Origins of Our Time*. Boston, MA: Beacon Press (original work published 1944).

Prickett, S. (1981) *The Romantics*. New York, NY: Holmes & Meier.

Rheingold, H. (1994) *The Virtual Community: Surfing the Internet*. London: Martin Seeker and Warburg.

Runco, M.A. (2004) Creativity. *Annual Review of Psychology* 55 (1), 657–687.

Russell, B. (2004) *History of Western Philosophy*. London: Routledge (original work published 1946).

Sahlins, M. (2004) *Stone Age Economics* (2nd edn). New York, NY: Routledge.

See, F. (1994) Mapping amazement: John Irwin and the calculus of speculation. *Modern Fiction Studies* 40 (2), 343–353.

Smith, A. (1909) *An Inquiry into the Nature and Causes of the Wealth of Nations*. New York, NY: P.F. Collier and Sons (original work published 1776).

Throsby, D. and Hollister, V. (2003) *Don't Give Up Your Day Job*. Sydney: Australia Council.

Virgil 2005 [c30-19BCE] *Aeneid* (trans Stanley Lombardo), Hackett Publishing; Book VI: lines 37–40.

Williams, R. (1981) *Culture*. Glasgow: Fontana.

Weber, M. (2003) *The Protestant Ethic and the Spirit of Capitalism* (T. Parsons, trans.). New York, NY: Courier Dover Publications.

Webster's Third New International Dictionary of the English language 1981 Philip Babcock Gove (ed), Springfield: G. & C. Merriam Co.

Zolberg, V. (1990) *Constructing a Sociology of the Arts*. Cambridge and New York, NY: Cambridge University Press.

4 The Publishing Paradigm: Commercialism versus Creativity

Jeremy Fisher

Introduction

On 4 May 2009, I was on a panel at the inaugural Alice Springs Writers Festival. The festival was small, but the enthusiasm of the writers there was enormous. The Chair of the panel, Peter Bishop – then of Varuna, The Writer's House – encouraged the audience of would-be writers to retain their creativity, to keep their individual voices, despite what editors, publishers and agents might tell them the market needed.

I was more cautious. While it is, of course, very important creative writers maintain their individual voices, if they are going to develop a sustainable career path through writing, authors need to be aware of the market they are entering and the forces that operate within it.

For instance, authors need to be cognisant of the role of the acquisitions or commissioning editor in the development of publishing lists and their rejection policies. While most editors and publishers I know profess to be, and, on the face of it, are, open-minded and genuinely interested in quality manuscripts, they have their own foibles and idiosyncrasies. These are further compounded by the strictures of their employers. In the main, a great non-fiction book is not going to be taken up by a publisher whose eye is focused only on the fiction market, even when an editor champions it. Likewise, a literary novel with potential sales of 3000 is not going to be considered in the acquisitions meeting of a publisher that has decided it will only publish books capable of selling 20,000 copies or more.

These days, much more so than in the past, an editor also has to convince the sales force that a book will sell, why and to whom. In this context, a chick-lit title is an easier option than a beautifully crafted novel aimed at teenage boys. Why? Teenage boys are not reading and rarely buy books (Australia Council for the Arts, 2009). Young women, however, are still avid readers and book-buyers.

There are other factors at play as well. Australian publishing flourished from 1939 to 1959, thanks to wartime restrictions on the import of printed products from overseas, but particularly from the United States (Johnson-Woods, 2006). This gave some legs to publishing entrepreneurs who were creative, though perhaps only in their accounting practices. Since the invention of the printing press, the publishing industry has not advanced much in terms of the creativity of its product. The success of the industry is still predicated on sales of books bound in set and regular sizes. In Australia, books are currently produced in the following formats: C format (235 x 153mm) trade paperback and B format (200 x 130mm) mass market paperback. The major changes that have affected publishing have been less to do with creativity than packaging. The paperback, for instance, was a major change, and the entrepreneurial Australian publishers of the Fourties and Fifties grabbed the format with gusto. The production of pulp fiction provided a sustainable income for Australian writers, such as G.C. Bleeck and A.G. Yates (better known under his pseudonym Carter Brown). Like Yates, Bleeck was a full-time writer, even while working for the NSW Railways, and produced a vast number of titles over the years (Johnson-Woods, 2002).

But did full-time work as an author bring about any greater creativity for writers? Possibly it did, but not perhaps as a greater licence for artistic expression. Nor was full-time writing necessarily a great advance for an author's income. Yates was contracted to his publisher, Horwitz, for £30 a week against his royalties. For this, he was expected to write a book and rewrite another each month (Johnson-Woods, 2004).

G.C. Bleeck, who wrote for Horwitz's predecessor, Associated General Press, was required to write two westerns, a science fiction work and a 24,000 word space opera each two months (Johnson-Woods, 2002). Working across such wide-ranging genres requires enormous literary creativity. Many writers of the time developed their skills in this environment. Bleeck was once asked to write a screenplay in three weeks, but declined for personal reasons. He claimed he was replaced by the latterly more famous D'Arcy Niland, but Kylie Tennant is credited for the script in the National Library of Australia catalogue (Johnson-Woods, 2002). The acclaimed Australian poet Bruce Beaver also wrote pulp fiction for this market (Fisher, 2005b).

There were other creative opportunities as well. While crime and romance were once first published in hardcover, paperbacks made them more affordable and opened up markets. Writers could extend and develop characters over a series of books, confident of keeping a readership, as A.G Yates did with his Carter Brown books and, as I have shown, Joseph Hansen did in the United States with his detective character Dave Brandstetter (Fisher, 2005b).

Genres and Publishing

The categorisation of fiction into the various genres by which we know it today commenced early in the 20th century and continued with paperback development and other forms of mass marketing. By the end of that century, genres were firmly in place in fiction publishing. Fantasy fiction, replete with boy wizards and vampires, has tended to dominate that market for the first decade of the 21st century. These works were remarkable more for how conventional they were in narrative form and characterisation, than for any creative challenges. Their conventionality allowed for easy crossovers to audio-visual storytelling and harmonious marketing of both the print and audio-visual forms. Such marketing success has tended to discourage publishers from exposing themselves to risk by tampering with either the physical form of the book or the conventions of the genre, even when digital technology has begun to tap them firmly on the shoulder.

One genre where the conventions are blurred is literary fiction, a genre which has developed as a natural evolution of the process of categorisation of books into marketable types. From the time of James Joyce, who challenged the traditional narrative structure of the novel, writers have been playing with the form with varying degrees of success. Numerous writers in this category – William Burroughs, Frank Moorhouse and Haruki Murakami being just three examples – have further experimented with the narrative form of the novel. English novelist B.S. Johnson even challenged the physical form of the book. His *The Unfortunates* (1969) was produced in 26 sections which were contained in a box and permitted the reader to read them in any order (though two sections are labelled 'first' and 'last'). They could be tossed up in the air, then read in whatever order they fell, the story changing with each reading. By and large, this experimentation has not been embraced by the mass market and, as a consequence, literary fiction has tended to be regarded as elitist by readers and book-buyers. Artistic creativity does not easily translate into commercial success, even when the technology and form of narratives change. The market still expects traditional narratives, even with digital delivery of content. In the United States, in 2010, e-book sales in genre fiction, such as romance, mystery and thrillers, was 'especially robust' (Bosman, 2011: C1).

This was of no significance to poor B.S. Johnson, who committed suicide frustrated by his lack of success (Coe, 2004). Ironically, his work has remained in print and his experimentation is now highly regarded (Coe, 2005), proof of the fact that the development of a writer is not an overnight process. And proof, too, if it were needed, that creativity in and of itself is not the essential part of a writer's commercial success.

Commercial success is most likely to be due to writers keeping to the tried and true, working within the established publishing framework and limiting their creative experimentation and boundaries. This is because publishers and readers like to be able to label and categorise books. An evolving author may vary his or her audience focus, but once an author has been accepted by readers and is commercially successful, the established brand name sets up audience expectations and so the author is limited in how much they can vary their creative focus. It is difficult for established writers to shift genres without a different brand name. Their publishers, and their readers, expect them to fit their market niche, be it non-fiction, crime, chick lit, sci-fi, romance or fantasy.

Robert Dessaix once recounted to me how he felt obliged to meet the expectations of his purple-haired female readers 'of a certain age', because they were the ones who bought his books and that this placed certain constraints on him as a writer. There were things he wanted to write about he knew his readers didn't want to know. Some authors invent a pseudonym to overcome this problem, as the Australian Young Adult author Gillian Rubinstein has done with her fantasy-writing alter ego Lian Hearn; and children's writer Sonya Hartnett has done, writing for adults under the name Cameron S. Redfern. American author Joseph Hansen also used the pseudonyms James Colton and Rose Brock for different genres (Fisher, 2005b). Agatha Christie, the great crime novelist, wrote romances under the name Mary Westmacott.

By and large, though, publishing in the 21st century is little changed from the 19th, and this is a problem for both authors and publishers. The economic history of the 20th century is littered with the skeletons of industries that have been conservative in their practices and resistant to change.

The Digital Revolution

Profit, of course, is the motivating driver for commercial publishing, whether that be Elsevier's vast network of scientific journals, Pearson's various learning management systems, Harlequin's myriad romance imprints or Bertelsmann's many names for its publishing businesses. Some publishing, literary journals, for example, exist on tiny budgets and goodwill, but such publishing tends to operate on the fringe of both the trade and education markets. However, while most 'for profit' businesses spend some money on research and development to extend markets and market share, publishers on the whole do not and have not. Partly, this relates to the success of the business model of the industry and its acceptance by consumers. Books are respectable products and regarded warmly.

But this is a generational attitude. People aged 30 years or less, particularly males, have less respect and warmth for books, and they read them less, though this does not mean they are not reading at all, just that they choose to read something other than books (Australia Council for the Arts, 2009). These people tend to be more focused on information and entertainment delivered through digital channels. Publishers, by and large, have ignored such trends, perhaps because these trends were so slow in their emergence that they were not easily discerned. But their businesses have been affected by them, nevertheless (Fisher, 2010).

The digital revolution has had a more gradual impact on the marketing relationships in the publishing industry than in other creative industries such as music. Digital technology began to revolutionise publishing production processes in the 1970s and 1980s. By the 1990s, publishers were transmitting digital files to their printers, but the books that were subsequently sent to bookshops still looked the same and sold the same. However, in music, the downloading of digital files rapidly replaced or reduced sales of physical products, such as compact discs, cassettes and vinyl discs. Up to now, the effect on publishing has been insidious, rather than sudden. The major effect has been on the economic dynamics of the industry.

Even as late as the 1980s, publishing was very often a mixed business. In Australia, for example, Law Book Company and Methuen, a trade publisher, were once part of the same operating company. But legal and professional publishing quickly adapted to digital delivery – loose-leaf services, immensely profitable in print format, were even more so when digitally delivered to a rich niche of lawyers and accountants (Fisher, 2010).

Reference publishing was also affected, but not as fortuitously. Encyclopaedias in print form have largely disappeared, replaced by Wikipedia and other online reference sources. Divisions of companies that once thrived on the door-to-door sales of 12 or more volumes, paid for in monthly instalments stretching over years, vanished overnight. Shareholders panicked and sought to minimise their risks. As a consequence, publishers merged and then broke apart, segmenting themselves into more streamlined companies, delivering to viable market niches.

At first, this appeared advantageous, as profit levels for the specialist publishers rose. In 2004, the profit margin for Reed Elsevier – the world's largest 'specialist' publisher and dominator of the academic journal market – was 19% (Fisher, 2005a: 31). In 2007, profit before income tax (PBIT) for Australian publishers in this segment (which, in Australia, includes higher education) was 13.4%, an increase over 2006 (Australian Publishers Association, 2009: 8). In contrast, the PBIT for trade (general market) publishers was 10.4% in 2007 – still a respectable return and greater than retail, for example, but a worrying discrepancy for shareholders in trade publishing companies.

Profitability still remains high for Australian trade publishers (Australian Publishers Association, 2009: 8), but trends in the United States and United Kingdom are running the other way. Publishers face very significant challenges to their traditional printed product business models from digital alternatives, and they are racing to adapt. For instance, Pearson is a large, global company that operates both as a trade publisher, in the form of Penguin, and an educational publisher, as Pearson Education, in an attempt to balance its print-product options, but the digital economy still creeps, in fact, leaps upon it.

In June 2009, then California Governor Arnold Schwarzenegger announced that his state, which previously spent AUS$437 million a year on textbooks for its school students, would switch to online teaching resources as of August 2009, because the global financial crisis had almost bankrupted California, and it could no longer afford the luxury of state-funded textbooks (ProPrint, 2009). The California textbook market was previously the largest single market for US educational publishers, of whom Pearson is the largest.

The loss of this market is likely to have an enormous impact on Pearson's projected profits and publishing projects. While educational publishers have been working with digital and online technologies for a decade or more, none has yet translated its investment in these new technologies into a revenue source to rival that from printed product. At the same time, digital and online resources for education have emerged from a wide range of other players, including many educational authors, and these have found wide acceptance in the educational community, to the detriment of printed products. Schwarzenegger's decision will hasten this process.

A dilution of the profits of Pearson, resulting from decreased sales in California, puts more pressure on the Penguin division of Pearson to deliver more profits. The United States and United Kingdom sales in the trade market have been lethargic in 2008 and 2009 (Publishers Association, 2011; Association of American Publishers, 2011). Paradoxically, the fastest growing part of the market has been e-books, but this presents all traditional publishers with a problem, as in this market, they no longer control distribution and, thus, their share of the sales revenues has been diluted. As an example, Amazon first paid publishers just 30% of revenues from sales of e-books through its Kindle electronic reader (Miller, 2010: B7), while publishers generally receive from 60% to 40% of revenues from sales of printed products. Self-publishers and authors licensing direct into Kindle, however, may receive as much as 70% of revenues. At the same time, the price of e-books is lower – at around US$9.99 – and decreasing, compounding the revenue problem for publishers (Amazon, 2011).

Part of the problem is that publishers have struggled to adapt to the changed economic circumstances brought about with digital technologies and their implementation. As one example, Thompson (2005: 216) reports how higher education publishers in the United States have pushed up the prices of textbooks and then maintained them 'in what is virtually a state of continuous revision', because of a perceived need to provide instructors with an expensive package of free digital teaching supplements. As another, trade publishers have not led the move to e-books; this has been accomplished by bookseller Amazon (and others) and computer company Apple. Any responses from publishers to digital challenges have been within traditional market paradigms – they have assumed an e-book is just a printed book presented as a digital file. Publishers have assumed they can control the supply of these, much as they do books, but this is proving not to be the case.

This makes it ironic that the one major positive effect of these challenges to publishers is that they have become more efficient in their core business – the provision of printed product. The general trade market has been radically overhauled in the light of new information available to publishers through new digital technologies and delivered as data collected directly at sales points and provided by sources such as Bookdata. Using this information, publishers have been able to make decisions that reduce their investment risk as much as possible.

The essential business model has not changed at all. In publishing, profits come from sales, and one book selling hundreds of thousands of copies makes more profit than several books selling the same number of copies, since there is a greater return on investment for the publisher. This, of course, is also beneficial to the author, whose book sells many thousands of copies.

It leaves few opportunities for new and emerging authors, since, as a consequence of this, editors, marketers and sales representatives have tended to stick with the tried and true, even when keeping a somewhat blinded eye on the digital threat. Repetition of the same becomes inbuilt into the sales process. Most publishers offer their sales representatives some form of bonus for increased sales. Even though it is more difficult for a sales representative to persuade a bookseller to take 50 copies of a new, unknown, Australian author than 50 copies of a well-known, highly publicised Stephenie Meyer, Dan Brown or J.K. Rowling title, most publishers provide no incentive for representatives to make the extra effort for the new book. Not unnaturally, sales representatives pursue the easiest option to earn their bonuses, so new writers, perhaps more creative writers, struggle to find any place in the market.

The advent of data sources, like Bookdata, at the turn of the century encouraged and enhanced this process even further. As a result, readers are starved of choice, at least in terms of authors of whom they have never heard. Since there is little information or feedback on new writers, either from word of mouth or reviews, readers by and large stick with the known – a safer alternative than wasting money on a book they find, upon reading, they dislike.

This is perpetuated in so-called marketing campaigns, such as Books Alive, which is funded by the Australian Government, now as part of its cultural programme, but, initially, as part of a package delivered to the book industry as some compensation for the imposition of a Goods and Services Tax (GST) on books in 2000. Books Alive pays little attention to new authors, except those backed by major publishers. At one point, it was also using Australian taxpayers' money to market mostly overseas authors, but, thanks to protests from Australian authors, this focus has changed. The programme claims benefits in improved reading rates and sales of books in the period in which it runs (Books Alive, 2009), but it is firmly in the hands of large publishers who, it could be argued, do not need such marketing assistance given to them.

Small publishers, such as those in the Small Press Underground Networking Community (SPUNC), lack marketing funds and effective distribution mechanisms and would seem most in need of a marketing campaign such as Books Alive, but at this point they remain shut out of the system. Their books and writers remain relatively unknown, thanks to a chronic lack of marketing and promotion.

Of course, publishers do promote new writers, but the task of publicising and marketing a new, unknown author is daunting when this requires interaction with the elements of the mass media that are more interested in known celebrities, paid endorsement or contra deals – all somewhat at odds with artistic creativity. A 'writer' with an immediately recognisable profile – a sports star, perhaps, or an errant politician or a television star – is a safer option in guaranteeing sales.

As a result, the cost of establishing a media presence for a new 'creative' author and, thus, some mass-market credibility, involves payments for interviews and appearances, gratuities and gifts – an expenditure not viable for a publisher anticipating a moderate return on a new novel or scholarly biography. These sorts of costs are impossible for 'kitchen table' publishers, such as most of those in SPUNC, very few of whom can even afford to join the Australian Publishers Association, the peak body representing Australian publishers.

These small publishers also become the victims of their own success. Should a small press author attain some success, larger publishers will very quickly offer inducements for them to change imprints. An author such as Peter Carey remained loyal to his first Australian publishers, the medium-sized University of Queensland Press, for decades, until the offers of the German-owned giant Random House proved too much to resist.

Authors can't be blamed for this. The median income for authors in Australia is a mere $11,700 (Throsby & Hollister, 2003: 45). Authors are constantly struggling to survive in their chosen profession and will work for years for little financial reward or public recognition before they are 'discovered' – if, indeed, that ever happens. Literary agent Jenny Darling referred to this as 'the amnesia in the industry that most authors are not an overnight success' (Australian Bookseller and Publisher, 2005: 13). The creation of a recognised author is a slow process that does not fit well with publishers' desires for immediate profits. But the process of creating such an author tends also to have an impact on an author's creativity, pushing them towards what is deemed to be commercially successful, rather than creative.

The result, at least as demonstrated in best-seller lists, is a strong homogeneity in both fiction and non-fiction. As for-profit businesses, publishers sensibly attempt to minimise their risk and exposure and guarantee sales, ensuring they tend to be reactive to successful publishing decisions already made. This means when the success of authors such as Dan Brown, J.K. Rowling and Stephenie Meyer comes as a surprise, such extreme success was not envisaged by their publishers (but, nevertheless, wonderful for profit margins).

These authors have not materialised suddenly – their creativity has developed over time, generally un-nurtured by publishers. Rowling, in particular, had her manuscripts rejected time and again before being successfully published. Jenny Darling makes the point, as well, that Dan Brown was not an overnight success (Australian Bookseller & Publisher, 2005). However, rather than look for new creative voices, publishers chase their last successful book. They are not interested in something new to challenge and entertain readers, unless it has guaranteed sales.

Common sense suggests this should be a self-defeating process, but this business practice has not yet translated into lower revenues for publishers. In fact, there is evidence, in Australia, that it is having an opposite effect. The 2007 Industry Study conducted by the Australian Publishers Association (the most recent statistics available) showed that 2007 increased on 2006 in both book sales (3.8%) and profit (6.1%) (Australian Publishers Association, 2009: 4).

However, whether or not such increases are sustainable is a moot point, given the decline of books sales in other markets. Also, a focus on sales is a mere distraction from the real issue – that authors themselves rarely have the opportunity to be truly creative in their artistic output, as they are too dependent on the role of the publisher.

That does not mean that publishers are totally in control, but, at this point in time, there is little room to operate outside the traditional marketplace. However, that marketplace is not as monolithic as has been supposed. New research shows that there is considerable publishing activity occurring that, traditionally, has not been measured.

In Australia, the most significant analysis of the publishing industry was completed by the Australian Bureau of Statistics (ABS) between 2000 and 2004, as yet another part of a Goods and Services Tax (GST) compensation package to the publishing industry. The figures that were collected by the ABS, from around 244 organisations identified as publishers, showed that 8602 books were published in Australia in 2003–04.

However, Andrew Wilkins (2008), using the number of titles recorded in the *Australian Books in Print* database, has shown that over 14,258 titles were published in Australia in 2007. Wilkins (2008) identified 8924 of these titles as coming from the 244 publishers identified by the ABS. The other 5334 titles, published by entities not included in the ABS publisher category, had previously been floating under the radar, but they represent a considerable and diverse output. For example, poetry titles were almost non-existent from the 244 ABS publishers, but poetry represented 2% of Wilkins' (2008) total. At the same time, almost 32% of the books published in 2007 were published by just 0.1% of all publishers – the top 20 publishers – yet, 70% of publishers (2782 of them) published just one book in 2007 (Wilkins, 2008).

The situation is similar in the United States. A report by the US Book Industry Study Group (BISG), *Under the Radar*, indicates that, in the US, approximately 63,000 publishers, with annual revenues of less than $50 million, produce aggregate sales of US$14.2 billion (Book Industry Study Group, 2005: 7). The sales of these publishers had gone unreported previously. About US$11.5 billion of that amount comes from around 3600 of those publishers with annual revenues of US$1 million to US$49.9 million. In contrast, the older, more visible segment of the industry produces annual revenues of around US$25 billion. The BISG reports that the number of small and mid-size publishers has been increasing and, often, prospering, while the largest publishing companies have been consolidating. These smaller publishers have been using routes to readers outside traditional bookshops. They are often selling more books outside trade channels than within them, with more than 50% of their business outside book-trade channels.

Yet, the traditional publishing industry has ignored these other publishers, even though their output competes with, and may evolve into that of, traditional publishers. The sector has been discounted as amateur and inconsequential, even though its sales and revenues approach those of traditional publishing, and the people working within it may display greater creativity than traditional publishers. The *Going Down Swinging* anthology is an example of this, featuring multi-genre works in print and audio form.

Their lack of perception and vision has also meant that traditional publishers have given only scant consideration to the income streams that digital technology and internet distribution may offer. While the sales of e-books has been a growth area, it is still only a small part of the market and is dependent on delivery to specialised readers, such as Amazon's Kindle, Sony's book reader and the Apple iPad, through territorial licensing agreements.

Google has stolen a march on publishers, though, through its controversial library project, where Google began to digitise the print collections of a number of libraries in the United States, Europe and Japan. Google claimed the right to do this under the fair use provisions of the US Copyright Act (the Australian Copyright Act offers no such rights and such a practice could not be legally replicated here). Google was challenged in its claim by the US Authors Guild and US publishers and taken to court. A settlement was proposed in 2009. As I write, this settlement is still awaiting ratification by US courts, but it has already established several benchmarks and debunked some myths.

The essential myth the Google book settlement puts to rest is that digitisation of books is expensive. Publishers claim this over and over again as a means of persuading authors to accept very low royalties for digital rights. Google has stated that the average cost of digitising a book from a library collection is a mere US$30 (Palma, 2009, personal commumication). Also, since most books these days are created as digital files, the cost to publishers of outputting them as print or e-books is minimal.

Many publishers have now entered into partnership agreements with Google Books and have uploaded digital files of their books for searching and display. The object of this is to allow online users of Google Books to gain some perspective on a book and then buy the print edition.

But Google already has plans in place to download digital versions of the books from its Google Library project direct to iPhones and other readers (Palma, 2009). This will have a dramatic effect on the publishing industry, since many of the works digitised in the Google Library projects are controlled directly by their authors, rather than publishers. Google is also proposing that 63% of the revenues from these digital uses flow to rights-holders (United States District Court for the Southern District of New York, 2009), which is a much better return than that offered to authors by traditional publishers and it has now been matched by Kindle.

More than anything else, the Google initiative breaks the hold that publishers have over the distribution of books, and it enables authors to effectively self-publish. Authors themselves have been less constrained than publishers in reacting to the digital economy. Technological innovations have been quickly adopted by writers. Blogging and multimedia are examples of new forms of works from the digital world. The problem is how this creativity can be chained into a source of income that can sustain the writer.

Combined with digital communications and technologies, this opens up channels for authors to directly interface with their readers and either forgo, or enhance, traditional publishing methods. Cory Doctorow, a US science fiction author, has worked with his publisher Tor (a division of Macmillan) to show that, by releasing online versions of his books, he was able to increase sales of the print version (Doctorow, 2009). His successes in this are detailed in his blog at craphound.com.

This is where creativity exists within the publishing industry at present, right at the cusp and led by authors.

References

Australia Council for the Arts (2009) *General Book Reading and Buying Research Report.* Sydney: Australia Council for the Arts.

Australian Bookseller and Publisher (2005) July 2005 issue.
Australian Bureau of Statistics (2005) *Book Publishers Australia 2003–04* (1363.0) Canberra: ABS. (http://www.ausstats.abs.gov.au/ausstats/subscriber.nsf/0/5D65642E28A86ADC CA25705F0075012E/$File/13630_2003-04.pdf) accessed 12 December 2011. P. 5.
Australian Publishers Association (2009) *2007 Industry Study.* Sydney: Australian Publishers Association.
Amazon Kindle Pricing Page. https://kdp.amazon.com/self-publishing/help?topicId=A2 9FL26OKE7R7B (accessed 12 December 2011).
Association of American Publishers (2011) Bookstats Overall Highlights. http://publishers.org/bookstats/highlights/
Book Industry Study Group (2005) *Under the Radar: A Breakthrough, In-Depth Study of the Book Industry's Under-Reported Segments and Channels.* New York, NY: Book Industry Study Group.
Books Alive (2009) *Presentation to Stakeholders.* Sydney: Books Alive.
Bosman, J. (2011) Publishing Gives Hints of Revival, Data Show. *The New York Times,* 9 August 2001, C1. Online at http://www.nytimes.com/2011/08/09/books/survey-shows-publishing-expanded-since-2008.html
Coe, J. (2004) *Like a Fiery Elephant: The Story of B.S. Johnson.* London: Picador.
Coe, J. (2005) Nothing But the Truth. *The Guardian,* 17 June. Online at http://www.guardian.co.uk/books/2005/jun/17/biography.samueljohnsonprize2005
Doctorow, C. (2009) *Craphound,* website, accessed 27 July 2009. http://www.craphound.com
Fisher, J. (2005a) *Current Publishing Practice.* Sydney: Australian Society of Authors.
Fisher, J. (2005b) In Praise of (Gay) Pulp. *Journal of Publishing,* 1 (1), 78–96.
Fisher, J. (2010) E-Books and the Australian Publishing Industry. *Meanjin,* 69 (3), 117–124. Online at http://meanjin.com.au/editions/volume-69-number-3-2010/article/e-books-and-the-australian-publishing-industry/
Johnson, B.S. (1969) *The Unfortunates.* London: Panther Books.
Johnson-Woods, T. (2002) Bleeck house: Australian pulp fiction. *National Library of Australia News,* November, 3–7.
Johnson-Woods, T. (2004) The mysterious case of Carter Brown: or, who really killed the Australian author. *Australian Literary Studies,* 21 (4), 74–88.
Johnson-Woods, T. (2006) Pulp friction: Government control of cheap fiction, 1939–1959. *Script & Print,* 30 (2), 103–119.
Miller, Claire Cann (2010) Amazon increases Kindle Royalties to Publishers. *New York Times,* 9 November, B7, http://www.nytimes.com/2010/11/09/technology/09kindle.html
Palma, C. (2009) Google Executive in Conversation with Jeremy Fisher. [personal commumication]. Sydney, Australia, 19 March.
Publishers Association (2011). The UK Book Publishing Industry in Statistics 2010. Market Research and Statistics.
ProPrint (2009) *Printed Textbooks Won't Be Back: Schwarzenegger,* Online article, accessed 29 July 2009. www.proprint.com.au/News/147276,printed-textbooks-wont-be-back-says-schwarzenegger.aspx
Thomson, J.B. (2005) *Books in the Digital Age.* Cambridge: Polity Press.
Throsby, D. and Hollister, V. (2003) *Don't Give Up Your Day Job: An Economic Study of Professional Artists in Australia.* Sydney: Australia Council for the Arts.
United States District Court for the Southern District of New York (2009). Final Notice of Class Action Settlement. http://static.googleusercontent.com/external_content/untrusted_dlcp/www.googlebooksettlement.com/en//intl/en/Final-Notice-of-Class-Action-Settlement.pdf accessed 12 December 2011
Wilkins, A. (2008) Australian publishing: The stats. *Bookseller and Publisher Magazine,* 88 (3), 16–17.

5 As Good As It Gets? National Research Evaluations

Gerry Turcotte and Robyn Morris

Introduction

Despite the origins of universities, the interface of creativity and academic industry has long been problematic. Separating the creative and academic in this way produces a spurious dichotomy, but one that has nevertheless dominated the academic environment, where employment, government funding, promotion, enrolments and a great many other factors have all danced around the notions of research value and quality and, particularly, how this is evaluated in a metrics-dominated system. The question of how to measure and rank academic and creative output has immediate consequences for the arts, creative arts and humanities, and Australia is not alone in undertaking government-initiated, research-measurement exercises. Australia trialled the Excellence in Research Australia (ERA) scheme in 2009, with a full roll-out across all university clusters/disciplines occurring in 2010[1] (Australian Research Council, 2011). Comparable nation-based measurement exercises include New Zealand's Performance-Based Research Fund (PBRF), which assesses individuals, and the United Kingdom's Research Assessment Exercise (RAE), which assesses departments. The RAE has recently been replaced by the Research Excellence Framework (REF). Whatever the assessment acronym (or nation), these national research evaluations are not going to go away. Moreover, it is unrealistic to think that such major government-initiated policy changes will not dictate the way national and international institutions think about research, recruitment and promotion.

The focus of the Australian ERA exercises purports to be the measurement of research quality. As soon as measurements are invoked, debates about the instruments and mechanisms used to produce and interpret the data inevitably dominate and, indeed, questions about both, and about the viability of a national research measurement system, abound in the media. These debates are also pursed in academic journals, conferences and seminars. For example, ERA's accuracy, impact, strengths and weaknesses, long-term and short-term effects upon the publishing and research behaviour of Australian researchers and publishers were examined by the National Academics Forum (NAF) during a two-day seminar in September 2009. Two key issues of debate, arising from this seminar, circulated around the reliability of using bibliometrics as a measurement system for academic output and the contentious 'eligible' journal list compiled by the Australian Research Council (ARC). This list assigns each journal a discipline code (although some are coded 'Multidisciplinary') and a ranking (although some are listed as 'not ranked'). The controversy arises not only from the level of the ranking – from A* through to A, B and C – but also from the ARC-assigned discipline coding that might see a multidisciplinary journal ranked only for its contributions to historical studies. A literature scholar with a publication in such a journal would effectively find their work devalued so that it did not attract research dollars, while their history colleague in the same publication would receive top marks. To add to this, many journals were left off the list entirely, including key humanities journals (ie. *Ariel*).[2] Whilst rankings apply across the disciplinary sector, it has had a particular impact on the humanities, especially those with a regional emphasis. As Guy Redden has argued:

> It is apparent that journal ranking creates particular problems for the humanities. One of the critical issues is the ranking of 'local journals' – that is, journals with a local, regional or national focus and readership – in a system which is designed to establish international benchmarks for 'impact' or 'quality'. (Redden, 2008: 7)

It is this issue of quality that is perhaps most contentious, and one which impacts upon both the humanities and creative arts. Redden further notes that ERA:

> ...will put more weight on ranking of publication outlets by 'quality'. The results of these processes of review in Australia may define the nature of the academic enterprise for many years to come. It remains to be seen whether they will overturn the legacy of the Dawkins reforms of the 1980s and early 1990s, which created a competitive level playing field as higher education colleges became universities able to compete with the established research-intensive institutions for research funding (through a new set of grant schemes of which the IGS is one component). What is at stake is not just the nature of the academic vocation and the conditions under which academics work, but also the rationale of the modern university, or differing rationales of different universities. (Redden, 2008: 7)

The development of ERA, as the latest government research quality framework, has coincided with the inclusion of the creative industries on the Federal Government's development of a proposed national high school curriculum and attendant workshops by the Australian Curriculum, Assessment and Reporting Authority (ACARA). ACARA is 'the independent authority responsible for the development of a national curriculum, a national assessment programme and a national data collection and reporting programme that supports 21st century learning for all Australian students' (ACARA, 2009).

For creative writers, increasingly embedded in whole or in part within universities, it has long been the case that they have struggled – like their fellow artists – to have their outputs acknowledged by a 'measurement' system designed to cater to the sciences, imperfectly modified and applied to the arts and humanities and, arguably, antagonistic to the creative industries. Lobbying from the sector has recently resulted in a reformed process of evaluation, and universities and funding bodies – not to mention the sector itself – are now working to develop a mechanism that will incorporate the creative industries into a system of measurement upon which university careers are evaluated and rewarded. Creative arts submissions to ERA, such as a painting or work of fiction, needed to be accompanied by a 250-word background statement, which had to identify how the output being submitted met the ERA definition of 'research'[3] (ARC, 2009: 50).

Difficulties in defining the terms 'quality' and 'research' can perhaps be linked to the stated aim of ERA, which is 'to establish an evaluation framework that gives government, business and the wider community assurance of the excellence of research conducted in Australia's higher education institutions' (ARC, 2009: 12). The linking of business with government is worrying indeed and begs the question of who is being measured by whom? Interestingly, in 2002, the United Kingdom House of Commons Science and Technology Select Committee published a report on RAE, in response to widespread criticism, defining 'research' as:

> …a public good with substantial economic and social benefits. In the UK, as in all advanced countries, the Government funds a key segment of the nation's research effort. Although industry and commerce have a large research commitment, their research investment is, quite rightly, mostly near-market. Business does not tend to engage in speculative basic research, where the returns are often uncertain, long-term, and difficult for one company to capture. Government investment is required to provide the basic new knowledge on which further research can build. A strong publicly funded knowledge base also has benefits in ensuring a supply of highly skilled people with the capability to carry

out research in the public and private sectors, to innovate and to make use of new knowledge not just from the UK but from across the world. (The Science and Technology Committee, 2002: 4)

In this sense, the notion of research has shifted from being curiosity driven to an element of national government policy; funding spent on research needs to be seen to be producing results. Despite this, and as Redden (2008: 8) notes: 'In a world where such frameworks are inevitable the current Australian system [ERA] is about as good as it gets'. Terry Cutler's August 2008 Report, 'Venturous Australia: Building Strength in Innovation', has made it clear that the funding of research activities and even the right to enrol honours and postgraduate students, will be contingent on ERA outcomes. As noted in the Report's section titled 'Incentives For Achieving Research Excellence':

To the extent that funding is increased and the allocative criteria for the block grants and funding for research training are aligned to the ERA rankings of research quality, we can expect more high quality research to emerge. Competition amongst universities for quality based research funding can be expected, following the UK example, to encourage academic entrepreneurship which will improve the quality of research through specialisation and concentration of resources. (Cutler Report, 2008: 70)

This report aligns future institutional research funding with results from ERA, which recommends that the government should:

Base the distribution of research block funding to universities on success in winning national competitive grants and on evidence of excellence in research, such as the research quality rankings to be produced by the Excellence in Research for Australia initiative. (Cutler Report, 2008: 70)

The 2009 ERA results were released on the ARC website on 31 January 2010 (ARC, 2010b). How this impacts upon research in all clusters, not just the humanities and creative arts, remains to be seen.

We Regret That We Are Unable to Fund Your Project, Mr Shakespeare: Living with Research Measurement Exercises

So, if measurements of research quality are here to stay, what impact does this have on the creative arts? To address this in part, the government has attempted to develop standards and outcomes for teaching the creative arts. The Australian Learning and Teaching Council's (ALTC) appointment of a Discipline Scholar to develop standards for the creative industries, as they relate to the higher education environment, was a direct response to the Australian Government's Higher Education Regulatory Framework. This section will examine the issue of quality research measurement from the position of a creative practitioner, who has also been a long-standing administrator and supervisor. My career[4] as an academic coincides almost exactly with my experience as a published writer. While the creative side of my portfolio has always been valued by colleagues and students, it is also true to say that it has counted for little in terms of what has come to be known as ERA 'outputs' – the product, as noted earlier, that is measured and rewarded by institutions such as academe and government. Because I tended to alternate between an academic and a creative output, I used to refer to the 'creative' year, sardonically, as the fallow period. Those who evaluated my output were happy, because I still met my targets for journal articles, book chapters and the like, but I recall once having a senior mentor note to an appointments committee that I would be further ahead if I had not spent so much of my time 'busying myself writing poetry'. After a series of poetry books appeared in quick succession, another colleague noted wryly that I was going overboard to get promoted. The irony was that I had just been dressed down by my academic adviser for spending time in the creativity zone. I was told, 'we need your *academic* outputs! I hope the creative isn't slowing you down.'

Both views, relating to such 'outputs', are valid. It is pointless to beat oneself on the breast and bemoan the fact that within academic regimes certain types of academic product are more valued than others (consider the significant effort assessment bodies are investing to establish Esteem Measures). One would have to be superhuman, however, not to feel a twinge of annoyance or regret that the landscape in Australia, for the creative practitioner, has been so skewed and for so long. While it is true that the 'market' is changing, with new instruments and categories of research being promoted and new panels for the creative industries being developed, all this is very new indeed, and the terms of reference for measuring such activity is ambiguous, at best. Although the ALTC appointed a Discipline Scholar to oversee the development of indicators and guidelines for the visual and performing arts, and while ERA has come along prepared to capture creative materials, it is still worth remembering that the baselines for such measurements are vested in a review process that does not radically alter the field. Colleagues, or assessors, are still being asked to measure the *research* component of the creative work that is produced, tacitly suggesting that, in academe, the creative has no value in and of itself. The search for the 'critical' or research component of the work now drives the process, hence the 250-word statement that has to support and explain the research value of each creative arts output submitted for appraisal under the ERA exercise.

The very model of measurement, putatively designed to capture what has hitherto been excluded from such categorisations, in fact, interprets the creative through a filter that effectively denies its legitimacy. It is the equivalent of designing a research model that is drawn from the sciences to assess the humanities, or to pay lip service to collaborative and inter-disciplinary targets on the one hand, whilst designing capture mechanisms that invariably penalise truly interdisciplinary endeavours on the other. Ask any Dean about her, or his, experience interpreting the ERA data and conveying the results of the four-unit and two-unit digit Fields of Research codes to their staff, as identified in the Australian and New Zealand Standard Research Classifications (ANZSRC) (ABS & Statistics NZ, 2008).

All this is akin to reading the Australian writer Peter Carey's extraordinary *The True History of the Kelly Gang* (Carey, 2000) and awarding it kudos for the substantial research done into the Kelly legend, as though the novel were somehow reducible to this; as though you could extract and measure the research component that informs the fictional content, without assessing how the two are, in fact, the true achievement of the work. Indeed, one could go so far as to argue that the magnificence of the accomplishment is precisely in the way that the research dynamic is erased, except in the closing notes at the back of the book that provide a bibliography of sorts.

In other cases, it may well be the case that the research is transformed, travestied or refuted by the creative work in question. One could approach Shakespeare's *Richard the Third*[5] and bemoan the historical inaccuracies – the way Shakespeare, sloppy academic that he was, telescoped 13 years of history into one at the beginning of the play. Alternatively, one could more correctly understand that the mechanism of the historic functions differently within the creative agency of the work. What would our assessment protocols do with Shakespeare if he were operating within modern grant and assessment regimes today?

We regret that we are unable to measure or fund your project. In the eyes of the committee, significant historical inaccuracies and poor and impartial analysis of data betray the weakness of the foundational research. We recommend that the project be reviewed, reworked and resubmitted in a later round. Similarly, the clear plagiarism that appears between an Italian novella and your own Romeo and Juliet *has been referred to the Ethics Committee for investigation. We do not rule out further disciplinary action in the latter matter. We should note that the committee was impressed by the fine copperplate handwriting that was displayed throughout the forms. We hope you will not be discouraged in your future endeavours. As an Early Career Researcher (hereafter ECR), we feel that you have much to contribute (though the clock is ticking!).*

Please note: the committee would like to use a quote from one of your texts to provide a pithy saying for a promising scientific project. This would be an effective embellishment to a real research endeavour.

Uncanny Shotgun Weddings

The job of administrators within research centres and groups, schools, colleges and faculties is specifically to encourage, measure and, at times, police the paradox of compliance and regulation within the fiction of diversity. The Uncanny is invoked here as a possible model for understanding this fraught space, particularly as it has been used in the last two decades to explain how generic forms – and, especially, the Gothic mode – have been modified in new world contexts (see Turcotte, 2009). A key pillar of this analysis has been Sigmund Freud's wonderful and, arguably, atypical essay on 'The Uncanny', one of his few ventures into literary analysis (Freud, 1956: 368–407). In this essay, which has now filtered into many interpretative fields, Freud outlines a number of useful constructions that seek to explain how feelings of dread, unfamiliarity and the uncanny are generated in literary products. This insight has since been applied to national models, to understanding colonial encounters, to national imaginaries, to pedagogical understandings and more (see, for example, Gelder & Jacobs, 1998; Kertzer, 1998; Sugars & Turcotte, 2009; Turcotte, 1998a, 1998b, 2004, 2009).

For Freud, the sense of uncanny develops in literature through a number of factors, not least of which when the familiar is made somewhat unfamiliar or when the homely (*heimlich*) is made unhomely (*unheimlich*) through a change in perspective, orientation or understanding. For the Gothic heroine, to use one example, the uncanny moment traditionally manifests when she is involuntarily transported – usually by a monstrous force – into an alien space, where all of her values are rendered meaningless or are disrupted by the inappropriate or antagonistic environment. Her 'homely', secure space is, through this rupture, made unhomely or insecure. One might speculate that the kidnapping of creative knowledge by governmental processes risks replicating this scenario.

In many respects, the process of analysing the creative industries through a science-based research filter is profoundly uncanny. Many would agree that creative practitioners – from dancers, to actors, to writers and animators – research extensively to produce their art. As many have shown, even spontaneous production is informed by significant analysis and reflection. But such processes may also have the effect, at times, of stilting the imaginative product or denaturing it, because it assumes that the one is not profoundly constitutive of the other. In other words, the process renders the creative uncanny, but not in an entirely productive capacity. This last sentence, therefore, suggests two effects of the process – one positive and one negative. The positive emerges in the way such measurements can come to legitimate both the art and the artist. For those who can find a way to 'quantify' their creative output through the prism of ERA-style metrics, there can be the validation that comes with a successful acquittal of a work that might otherwise be dismissed as 'merely' spontaneous or unscholarly. Encouraging creative artists to think differently about their art can also generate positive energies as they look 'askance' at their work and discover new possibilities. In this sense, the creative is rendered uncanny to many, but the uncanny register has a positive effect all round. It refocuses the academic stance, perhaps textures the administrative view of the creative industries and allows the creative to speak in particular, perhaps unexpected, ways.

It is true to say, however, that this 'denaturing' can also have a negative effect. Asking the creative industries to 'gloss' their submissions with a contextualising frame implies a deficit and asks practitioners to jump through an additional reporting hoop, in order to address that unspoken deficit: show us *how* the work you do has a particular value within *our* system of measurement, beyond the mere fact of its existence (see ARC, 2010a: 50 for the format of the *Research Statement for Peer Review of Creative Works for the HCA Cluster*). While it is also not uncommon for artists to say that their creative energies have been diminished by the academic enterprise, the significant number of creative artists in academe, the large number of creative writing theses, productions and studios embedded in universities, and the close collaboration of the creative industries with the higher education providers, suggests that the marriage works, by and large, even if it is a shotgun wedding.

Issues arising from this 'marriage' and, more particularly, of how to measure the research quality of a creative arts output, were the focus of a two-day Innovative Research Universities (IRU) Workshop on ERA and the Creative Arts, run from the 16th and 17th November 2009 at Griffith University. Questions that were addressed included: can or should creative arts research quality be assessed in the same way as other kinds of research? Does the ERA definition of research work for creative arts? Does it exclude any important categories of creative arts research endeavour? How easy was it to 'fit' creative research outputs into the four ERA categories? How effective is peer review in isolation as a measure of research quality in the creative arts? Could any of the traditional bibliometrics act as a proxy for overall research quality? Should performing or visual arts outlets or venues be ranked? Might ranking have unwanted side effects? Can the outputs of creative arts groups or institutions be credibly benchmarked against one another? How much value will be added by the support statement suggested for inclusion with each individual creative output?

The questions raised during this two day workshop are ongoing, and one can only feel that the valuing of the creative industries within governmental and university settings is long overdue. The need to account for key indicators is simply part of that necessary enabling and empowering process. The key, though, must be to develop mechanisms that measure the work on its own terms and according to its own field and then to reward them accordingly. There is nothing wrong with learning how to measure and assess the different dimensions of a project, especially if they don't denature the work at hand or if they contribute to an uncanny reconceptualising of the work, the field or the industry. For the latter to happen, it means that the measuring instrumentalities must learn to see differently and must learn to measure more creatively, so that it is not always the same partner being asked to compromise.

Lost in Translation

In light of recent changes in academe, arts practitioners have complained about scientific models being used as the baseline for measurements, and, typically, the response has been to characterise the humanities, arts and social sciences (HASS) sector as perpetually disgruntled. Nor has the sector had much luck in lobbying for changes to the pressure for collaborative endeavours. Arguments suggesting that many art forms and humanities projects are individual projects or that the assessment tools favour a scientific approach are rarely given much credence. On the issue of measurement models and structures, scientists have attacked the HASS criticisms, arguing that the ground rules are all about accountability, that collaborative structures are the most productive and transparent and that grants and research papers are structured as they are to ensure transparency and accountability. The myth of scientific objectivity and transparency, however, especially in regards to research write-ups and funding applications, raises just as many questions. Brian Martin, for example, has argued that a:

> ...common misrepresentation of research work is exaggeration of its quality, progress and social importance. This is almost essential for a successful scientific career. A modest and honest grant application stands

little chance of success: the applicant, to obtain money, must puff up the quality and importance of previous work and give a highly unrealistic assessment of the likely results of funding future work – or, as is common, request money to carry out research which actually has been completed. Most grant applications are convenient fictions. (Martin, 1992: 85)

Clearly, the sector's greatest need is for a more textured mechanism to assess productivity, but such requests are always put into the too-hard basket. Certainly, the challenge would be difficult. As Stephen P. King has suggested:

A differentiated system of funding and fees would require the government to decide which areas of study provide the greatest social spillovers. Such a decision would be difficult and controversial. Every area would claim its importance. Business faculties would proclaim their benefits to Australia's international competitiveness. Science faculties would cite the links between research and development and economic growth. Engineering would mutter darkly about lives lost when a bridge or building collapses. While deciding appropriate levels of support for different areas of study will be difficult, this is not a reason to avoid the task and simply treat all areas of study as essentially identical. (King, 2001: 192)

This is an important point: just because a process is difficult, is not a reason to ignore reform, especially where equity is concerned. After all, if humanities' style indicators were imposed on scientific methodologies, there would be outrage. For example, were the humanities to determine the laws of authorship as a principle of funding success, insisting that supervisors could not add their names to a postgraduate student's paper just because the project originated in their lab or because someone advised on the statistical model used, there would be an outcry. Or, conversely, if a humanities supervisor were to insist on co-authorship on the basis that they had spent extensive hours, months, years advising in-depth on what, eventually, became a sequence of papers emanating from a thesis, theatrical production or script, there would be few, if any, single author ECR studies in the field. But it would be perverse to expect one field to operate according to the logic of the other.

In the metrics market, it is crucial, therefore, that we allow the measures to fit the industry. If this means that the metrics used have to be thrown out or that existing mechanisms have to be rewritten, then that is certainly what needs to be done. Similarly, although it is important that the creative industries continue also to address this changed environment, it is, arguably, exactly what creative practitioners within academe *have* been doing for decades in their assessment of undergraduate and postgraduate work.

The dynamic way that the creative practitioners in dance, visual media, creative writing, drama and many other areas collaborated with discipline scholars to identify industry-wide standards, similarly demonstrates the availability of the creative arts to measurement systems. The case, surely, is in developing approaches that respect the specificity of the modes of production *and* the resultant production itself. At times, then, it is about translating the metrics into language that applies to the task at hand, whilst ensuring that this translation does not have the effect of denaturing the project; rather, it must texture the environment in which the work is received. To do otherwise is to guarantee that we are always lost in translation.

Notes

(1) ERA's abandoned predecessor was the Liberal Government's Research Quality Framework (RQF).
(2) In the most recent issue of *The Australian* newspaper's Higher Education supplement, Jill Rowbotham reports that in order to avoid the controversy that attended the first ranking exercise, the Australian Research Council (ARC) would put the journal and conference rankings advice 'out to tender' to ensure both greater transparency in the process, but also to assure the academic community that this transparency was central to the exercise (see Rowbotham, 2011).
(3) In Section 5.1 of the ERA 2010 Evaluation Guidelines research is defined as follows: 'For the purposes of ERA, research is defined as the creation of new knowledge and/or the use of existing knowledge in a new and creative way so as to generate new concepts, methodologies and understandings. This could include synthesis and analysis of previous research to the extent that it is new and creative'. See http://www.arc.gov.au/pdf/ERA2010_eval_guide.pdf for the complete ERA Guidelines (accessed 15 April 2010).
(4) See biographical details.
(5) The liberties Shakespeare took with his retelling of the *Tragedy of King Richard the Third* are widely understood and significant scholarship on this topic is available, though clearly not the topic of this paper.

References

Australian Bureau of Statistics (ABS) & Statistics New Zealand (Statistics NZ) (2008) *The Australian and New Zealand Standard Research Classification (ANZSRC)*. Canberra: ABS. Online at http://www.arc.gov.au/pdf/ANZSRC_FOR_codes.pdf
Australian Curriculum, Assessment and Reporting Authority (ACARA) (2009), website, accessed 25 January 2011. http://www.acara.edu.au/default.asp
Australian Research Council (ARC) (2009) *ERA 2010 Submission Guidelines*. Canberra: Australian Government. Online at http://www.arc.gov.au/pdf/ERA2010_sub_guide.pdf

Australian Research Council (ARC) (2010a) *ERA 2010 Evaluation Guidelines*. Canberra: Australian Government. Online at http://www.arc.gov.au/pdf/ERA2010_eval_guide. pdf

Australian Research Council (ARC) (2010b) *ERA 2010*. Canberra: Australian Government. Online at http://www.arc.gov.au/era/era_2010.htm

Australian Research Council (ARC) (2011) *Excellence in Research for Australia 2010 National Report*. Canberra: Australian Government. Online at http://www.arc.gov.au/pdf/ ERA_report.pdf

Carey, P. (2000) *The True History of the Kelly Gang*. St. Lucia: University of Queensland Press.

Cutler & Company Pty Ltd (2008) *Venturous Australia - Building Strength in Innovation (The Cutler Report)*. Canberra: Australian Government Department of Innovation, Industry, Science and Research. Online at http://www.innovation.gov.au/Innovation/ Policy/Documents/NISReport.pdf

Freud, S. (1956) *Collected Papers: Papers on Metapsychology, Papers on Applied Psycho-Analysis* (Vol. 4) (trans. Joan Rivière). London: Hogarth.

Gelder, K. and Jacobs, J.M. (1998) *Uncanny Australia: Sacredness and Identity in a Postcolonial Nation*. Melbourne: Melbourne University Press.

Kertzer, J. (1998) *Worrying the Nation: Imagining a National Literature in English Canada*. Toronto: University of Toronto Press.

King, S.P. (2001) The funding of higher education in Australia: Overview and alternatives. *The Australian Economic Review* 34 (2), 190–94.

Martin, B. (1992) Scientific fraud and the power structure of Science. *Prometheus* 10 (1), 83–98.

Redden, G. (2008) From RAE to ERA: Research evaluation at work in the corporate university. *Australian Humanities Review* 45, 7–26. Online at http://epress.anu.edu. au/ahr/045/pdf/essay01.pdf

Rowbotham, J. (2011) Journal rankings out to tender. *The Australian Higher Education Supplement* (p. 18), 23 February 2011. Online at http://www.theaustralian.com.au/ higher-education/journal-rankings-out-to-tender/story-e6frgcjx-1226010304425

Shakespeare, W. (1968) *King Richard the Third*. E.A.J. Honigmann (ed.). London: Penguin.

Sugars, C. and Turcotte, G. (eds) (2009) *Unsettled Remains: The Postcolonial Gothic in Canada*. Toronto: Wilfrid Laurier Press.

The Science and Technology Committee (2002) *The Research Assessment Exercise: Government Response to the Committee's Second Report*, online document, accessed 8 August 2009. http://www.publications.parliament.uk/pa/cm200102/cmselect/cmsctech/995/ 995.pdf

Turcotte, G. (1998a) Australian gothic. In M. Mulvey-Roberts (ed.) *The Handbook of Gothic Literature* (pp. 10–19). London: Macmillan.

Turcotte, G. (1998b) English–Canadian gothic. In M. Mulvey-Roberts (ed.) *The Handbook of Gothic Literature* (pp. 49–53). London: Macmillan.

Turcotte, G. (2004) Compr(om)ising post-colonialisms: Post-Colonial pedagogy and the uncanny space of possibility. In S. Sugars (ed.) *Home-Work: Postcolonialism, Pedagogy and Canadian Literature* (pp. 151–166). Ottawa: University of Ottawa Press.

Turcotte, G. (2009) *Peripheral Fear: Transformations of the Gothic in Canadian and Australian Fiction*. Bruxelles: P.I.E. Peter Lang.

6 Creative Writing, Neo-Liberalism and the Literary Paradigm

Jeff Sparrow

1.

Creative writing as a discipline has – in the last four years (indeed, in the last decade) – virtually exploded onto the university sector in a sudden and ungainly manner. Like a rude girl she sits in the senate, her bright red lipstick out of place amongst all that beige and grey. (Krauth & Brady, 1999)

The editorial extract above, from the journal *Text*, offers an arresting visualisation of creative writing at the time of its consolidation as an academic discipline in Australia. It is a scholastic riot girl: hip, sexy and fundamentally transgressive.

As the long-running debate about the value and function of academic creative writing programmes takes new forms internationally (Batuman, 2010; Genoways, 2010), an investigation of that self-depiction provides a useful reframing of arguments about the past and future of the discipline. What were the sources of this striking image? Why was creative writing imagined in 1999 as an academic rabble-rouser, blowing raspberries at the haughty legislators of the university?

In Australia, Paul Dawson has argued that, in many places, creative writing entered the tertiary sector alongside critical theory, as part of the same challenge to the traditional hegemony of the discipline of English (Dawson, 2005: 126). That challenge was mounted in a particular political context, or, to be more exact, emerged out of a particular political project. The social movements of the Seventies – New Left developed critiques of power, gender, race and sexuality in the course of the campaign against the war in Vietnam and for women's liberation, gay liberation and Aboriginal rights. That period of critical theory – and academic creative writing – represented, amongst other things, a generation, radicalised in the early Seventies, turning its focus onto the transformation of the university. The push for creative writing stemmed, in part, from a renewed interest in Australian culture, attributable, at least to some degree, to the anti-imperialist sensibility of anti-Vietnam activists, influenced by Left nationalism most forcibly articulated by Maoism.

As Paul Dawson documents, creative writing established its first toe-holds in TAFE professional writing courses, where the staff self-consciously sought a radical pedagogy. For example, the pioneering programme at the New South Wales Institute of Technology explicitly focused both on feminism and Marxism:

The emphasis, as always, was on craft as a means of breaking down the myth of the writer as inspired and isolated genius. [. . .] There was less concern with producing published writers, however, than with the political ideas emerging from other parts of the department. The textual studies major, commonly taken by writing students, was not concerned with traditional English studies but with new Theory. Although there was an incredible diversity of ideas and motivations among the teaching staff, the central concern, Graham Williams relates, was a vision of the writer as 'a worker with a particular kind of position in society'. [. . .] The dominant ideology of authorship was Marxist, in the form popularised by Terry Eagleton's *Marxism and Literary Criticism*. (Dawson, 2005: 148)

Another description of the rise of the discipline illustrates how easily tropes from that radical past can be deployed to express an apparent dis-junction between creative writing and the contemporary university. Nigel Krauth writes:

[T]here has been a power-shift. English Departments, prior to the nineties, were all about readership, reception and reaction. By enrolling, students defined themselves in 'Other' terms, in disempowered terms. 'Here is the canon,' English Departments said, 'cop it!' 'The hierarchy states this,' they said, 'respond to it!' Unsurprisingly, in the developing cultural context, albeit prompted by English Departments themselves in several cases, students have oriented towards pro-active, innovative behaviours – discarding re-active, history-bound activity. Writing looks like 'doing it'; reading looks like 'suffering it'. Students react to all sorts of cultural and social imperatives, but the 'practical' has gained an advance against the 'academic' in attracting students to university courses.

Creative Writing Departments, in this context, have offered not only readership, but also writership. They have replaced re-action with pro-action. They have empowered students to tell, and not just to read and reply (to re-tell the telling); they have encouraged production and not just reception. They have put expression, not just impression, into the hands of students. (Krauth, 2000)

On the one side, the edgy innovators of creative writing; on the other, the stuffy, resentful traditionalists. Again, the images overtly evoke Seventies campus radicalism: faced with a hierarchy telling them to 'cop it', students 'empower themselves' through self-expression.

Creative writing's history provides a reservoir of oppositional tropes suitable for deployment in response to subsequent institutional challenges. Indeed, despite tremendous growth within higher education – undergraduate and postgraduate degrees, professorships, specialist journals and research programmes, etc. – those tropes continue to reoccur, since creative writing in Australia still seems, both to many of its opponents and to some of its practitioners, an uneasy fit within the university. One of the anonymous interviewees, in Rjurik Davidson's survey of creative writing academics, explains that she feels her field is considered less valuable than other disciplines, with creative writing teachers seen as 'some naive blind primitives ... just working on instincts' (Davidson, 2010). The sentiment is widespread. Why is it, asks Sue North, in a common lament, 'that creative writers in universities struggle to have their work recognised as being on an equal footing with other disciplines, especially when it comes to research?' (North, 2006). Creative writing academics often perceive themselves as misunderstood, underappreciated and marginalised by university administrations, uncertain as to how to measure and assess their outputs.

The actuarial mentality of a corporate university seems incompatible with creativity, not simply in terms of research, but also pedagogy. Creative writing rests, for the most part, on the workshop – a peculiarly intimate and expressive process, especially when contrasted to the established traditions of the humanities. Students are as likely to workshop a self-consciously autobiographical story of a failed love affair, as they are to produce a sober work of conventionally scholarly gravitas. Hence, the rude girl's hostility towards the university's beige men – the stuffed shirts who hem and haw at creative writing's innovations. Hence, her ungainliness and, perhaps, the brightness of her lipstick.

Yet it is also important to understand the rise of creative writing in the context of the massive changes in higher education over the period in which creative writing has entered the university. As David Harvey notes, the industrialised world has made an:

...emphatic turn towards neoliberalism in political-economic practices and thinking since the 1970s. [. . .]Neoliberalism has, in short, become hegemonic as a mode of discourse. It has pervasive effects on ways of thought to the point where it has become incorporated into the common-sense way many of us interpret, live in and understand the world. (Harvey, 2005: 2–3)

Within the tertiary sector, the neoliberal turn has reshaped the traditional institution into what Simon Marginson calls the 'Enterprise University' (Marginson, 2002). Crucially, Marginson suggests that the 'Enterprise University' should be understood in part as a:

...neoliberal political response to the 'red bases' strategies of the late 1960s and early 1970s, in which the new left student movement sought to reorder the university on the basis of participatory democracy and turn it into a factory of social intervention and political revolution. (Marginson, 2002: 110)

In other words, the neoliberal university has appropriated the form of the New Left critique to express a very different content. That is, the generation that entered academia as a transformative project, denounced the elitism and exclusivity of traditional universities and advocated for popular accountability and social relevancy. Today, that rhetoric still echoes throughout the Enterprise University, but it is now utilised to facilitate the marketisation of the institution. Where the New Left project was explicitly anti-capitalist (or, at least, anti-market), neoliberalism posits market forces as the source of all legitimacy. The Enterprise University thus emphasises relevance and accountability, but relevance and accountability measured by supply and demand, rather than social engagement. The Enterprise University seeks, like the New Left, an expansion of higher education, but does so not to open education to the disadvantaged, but on the basis of a universalised user-pays philosophy. Most of all, the neoliberal opposition to any authority other than the market forces means that the university can embrace the New Left's hostility to stiff-necked traditionalists and hide-bound canons, albeit in the name of the market rather than popular democracy.

In this light, the radical tropes used to explain creative writing's struggle against reactionary professors, fussy bureaucrats and literary Tories take on a different colouration. For instance, Graeme Harper and Jeri Kroll write:

The growth of the subject in universities over the past 10 to 15 years, and the slower but still considerable growth for the 40 years or so before this, has meant that Creative Writing practice is now undertaken by individuals with a range of backgrounds and expectations. Universities were once far more elitist places; mass higher education has introduced notions of 'access for all', which naturally has opened up the number of possible individual 'life plans' that might exist in any one university. (Harper & Kroll, 2008: 5)

Now, nothing in that formulation is untrue, but the frame of discussion needs only shift for the passage to appear much more ambiguous. It seems strangely naive to discuss 'access for all' and the 'opening up of the university' without any reference to the political and economic context in which those individual 'life plans' are now mapped. It is true that universities now embrace innovations such as PhDs in creative writing, but it is equally true that these degrees can cost the student something like $20,000. What is more, this fairly obvious point has elicited very little discussion in the scholarly literature on creative writing, an absence all the more remarkable given that the limited data available suggests that the cost of creative writing is a major factor in the 'life plans' of the students wishing to enrol in it. A survey conducted in 1997, for instance, concluded:

> Financial considerations were very significant to the postgraduates at the University of Adelaide. This was heightened by the announcement during their Diploma year that up-front fees for 1998, the first Masters year, would be roughly double the 1997 charges. The fees change may be severe enough to place continuing enrolments in jeopardy, according to student comments. (Evans & Deller-Evans, 1998)

One wonders if the Adelaide postgraduates, as they prepared to enter further into debt, saw much distinction between the rude girl of creative writing and any of the other beige bureaucrats.

In other words, the naïve populist account of creative writing's development tends to uncritically accept a key argument of the Enterprise University and neoliberalism in general – the market as a democratic facilitator of choice. As Kathleen Lynch writes:

> Choice is the carrot with which people are duped into believing that they will have freedom to buy what higher education they like in some brave new market. This drive to increase 'choice' and shift control from the school or the university to the sovereign consumer is indicative of a broader political shift to the Right. A distinctive neo-liberal interpretation of fairness and efficiency based on the moral right and supremacy of the market has taken root across the public sector. (Lynch, 2006: 3)

Thus, at the very least, the populist narrative needs to be problematised by a more detailed exploration of creative writing's relationship with neoliberalism.

2.

In the 19th and early 20th century, those who proposed integrating writing into the university generally suggested that its acceptance as an academic discipline would bolster the status of literature. Of Walter Besant, for instance, Paul Dawson notes:

> His point was that if the novelist's craft was taught in the university, by writers, then, as with other arts, fiction would have greater credibility in the public sphere. The presence of a university in the realm of literature would influence public perception of authors and hence increase their professional and social standing. (Dawson, 2005: 9)

Today, the university is sufficiently present in the realm of literature for the 'academic novel' (that is, the novel written as part of a higher degree) to be declared 'a significant evolutionary leap for the novel species' (Krauth, 2008). But compare the assessment by novelist and literary editor Malcolm Knox, as to what the production of literary fiction does for his professional and social standing:

> I am placing strain on my marriage, I am depriving my children of time with their father, I am not providing as well as I could be for their future, I am jeopardising the friendships I have by modelling my characters on people I know, and I am risking my parents' shame with my explicit and confronting images, not to mention my children's embarrassment when they are old enough to read my diseased outpourings. And I am doing all of this for a dying form, with ever fewer readers, pouring my energies into an anachronistic black hole. And it's not even fun anymore, because I know that when I'm published, all I will face is momentary anxiety over reviews and the slowly-ebbing expectation of selling enough books so that my next novel might be published as well. Why the hell would anyone bother? (Knox, 2006)

There are plenty of such novelistic laments, perhaps, as David Carter suggests, there always have been (Carter, 2007: 231). Nonetheless, Knox's essay scarcely suggests that the encroachment of writing upon the university has bolstered the status of literary novelists.

In fact, though data is hard to come by, the rise of academic creative writing seems to correlate with a quantitative decline in the publication of literary fiction in Australia. Nicola Boyd's invaluable database of creative writing PhDs in Australia and New Zealand shows in 1996, only one creative writing PhD; in 2004, there were 25; and in 2006, 35 (Boyd, 2009). Her figures can be read against Mark Davis' compilation of the combined number of literary novels published by Australia's multinational publishers, Allen & Unwin. In 1996, he counts 60 novels; in 2004, the figure is 32; and in 2006, 28 (Davis, 2007: 120). In other words, the fewer novels published, the more creative writing PhDs.

The different directions in which these two sets of numbers trend suggests that the rise of academic creative writing can be usefully understood in relation to what Davis calls the 'decline of the literary paradigm' (Davis, 2007). He contends that in the 1960s, 1970s and 1980s, the Australian publishing industry defined itself by the literary fiction it published. This was, he says, a period of cultural nationalism, in which progressive governments made, through funding programmes and other incentives, the promulgation of a national literary canon a priority. Publishers paid relatively large advances to the Australian novelists, the books these writers produced featured on the front lists of catalogues and literary fiction ranked high in the 'best-seller' lists that independent retailers compiled (Davis, 2007).

By the early 2000s, the situation was very different:

> [A]lmost no major Australian publisher was aggressively seeking or promoting new literary fiction at the forefront of their lists, and literary fiction was no longer the cornerstone of the industry's self-perception. In the late 1990s Penguin Books, which had been at the forefront of the 'cultural renaissance' of the 1960s–1980s period, first dropped its poetry list and then culled its mid-list (that is, books with moderate print runs, often middlebrow fiction). Instead, Penguin decided to 'pick winners' by shifting emphasis to publishing mass-market titles by high-profile popular authors such as Bryce Courtney, who was reportedly signed up for a multi-book deal worth more than a million dollars. Since 2003, HarperCollins, too, has gradually been divesting itself of its mid-list, and in 2004 published 40 per cent fewer books, citing weak sales of literary fiction. In 2004, Simon & Shuster announced it would no longer take on first-time authors. In the past decade, entries in the Miles Franklin Award, Australia's premier literary award have dropped by a third. In the same period, entries in an annual award for new novelists run by the *Sydney Morning Herald* have sunk from between fifteen and twenty-five titles per year, of which more than half were literary, to a total of eleven entries in 2005, of which four were literary. (Davis, 2007: 120)

Now, 'death of literature' theses have been formulated throughout Australian literary history (Carter, 2007: 231). Such arguments regularly air in 'Culture War' skirmishes, and the image of academic novelists sucking the vitality from contemporary literature remains a favourite of conservatives, polemicising against tenured radicals. But Davis makes a different case: not an argument about cultural decline so much as economic periodisation.

His thesis suggests that the neoliberal imperatives driving reforms in the university sector (and elsewhere) have also restructured the publishing industry, and this restructuring has impacted not only on how publishing works, but also on the kinds of books it supports. Throughout the 1990s, the industry embraced globalisation, with many of the major houses consolidating into transnational corporations in which the production of books became merely one part of global information businesses. Modern marketing encroached upon book promotion, with publishers aggressively pursuing new retail outlets, embracing discount stores and even supermarkets alongside traditional bookshops. If, traditionally, literary publishing saw itself as a gentlemanly occupation in which commercial titles allowed the cross subsidisation of underperforming but culturally important books, today each text competes financially on its own merits. BookScan (the accurate, real-time system that replaced the idiosyncratic sales charts produced by independent book sellers) was merely the most obvious manifestation of a more thoroughly marketised management system. Publishers needed exact sales figures, in part, because accurate data enabled them to shift their investments to maximise profits. Literary fiction generates the same returns as sports memoirs and cookbooks. What is more, books as a whole must prove themselves as profitable as other forms of entertainment. Knox writes:

> Most of our main book publishers are owned by Pearson, Bertelsmann, Viacom, Holtzbrink, News Corp. [...]The governing management principles of such organisations include segmentation and internal competition. If you are the shareholder of such a company, you don't say, ah, our movie and new media sections are doing well this year, they can cross-subsidise our book or newspaper division, where the return on investment is on par with cash. What you do is, you pit these divisions against each other. You reward your more successful divisions with more resources, and punish the less successful by taking resources away. (Knox, 2006: 6)

The absorption of book publishing into media corporations encourages cross-platform licensing of product. Davis suggests that, in this environment, non-fiction – even literary non-fiction – proves more profitable than fiction, providing content that can be broken down into component parts for magazine articles, web pages, newspaper features, television segments and so on. The reliance on the sale of extracts to other media, both for publicity and as a source of revenue, creates a pressure for topicality and instant returns, in which literary titles that sell slowly over a long period suffer against mass-market titles with an instant readership (Lee, 2007: 25). Not surprisingly, backlist sales are declining and the shelf life for new titles has shrunk (Carter, 2007: 245).

The consequences for literary fiction can be seen at different, albeit intersecting, levels. In production, for instance, literary writers – especially debut authors – could once rely upon publishers for extensive structural editing, a process justified on aesthetic, rather than economic, grounds; the production of fine literature took as long as it took, with the costs absorbed by more profitable projects. Today, many publishing companies have embraced the management buzzwords of the Nineties, duly 'delayering' (that is, shedding various levels of staff), 'disaggregating' (ridding themselves of extraneous functions) and 'reengineering' (finding less labour-intensive ways to operate). Even if publishers wanted to devote more editorial time to a dense and complex novel than to the latest cricketer's diary, in all probability, they will not have the staff available. Accordingly, in a much, much tougher market for literary novels, structural editing has become a rarity (Poland, 2007: 102).

Perhaps more importantly, the same pressures impinge on the social infrastructure on which literary fiction depends. Throughout the 20th century, most quality newspapers maintained a stand-alone book review section, with a strong focus upon literary fiction. The book pages directly advertised literature, as well as signalling the cultural importance of contemporary literary fiction. Newspapers retained a reviews section, because knowledge of new books was assumed to be important to the idealised reader. In the United States, however, these dedicated book sections have disappeared from all major papers, other than the *San Francisco Chronicle* and the *New York Times* (Meyer, 2009). Only the bravest of pundits would bet against a similar trend asserting itself in Australia.

The decline of newspaper book reviewing itself represents the application of neoliberal management principles. In the past, the book section might have been subsidised because of its cultural status; today, companies simply cut back on non-performing sectors. More generally, the fate of the review reflects a broader crisis in the newspaper industry, a crisis that stems, in part, from issues also affecting literary publishing. One of the more well-established sociological trends of recent decades is the ongoing withdrawal from public life in industrialised nations, expressed most famously in Robert Putnam's study of social capital in the United States:

For the first two-thirds of the twentieth century a powerful tide bore Americans into ever deeper engagement in the life of their communities, but a few decades ago – silently, without warning – that tide reversed, and we were overtaken by a treacherous rip current. Without at first noticing, we have been pulled apart from one another and from our communities over the last third of a century. (Putnam, 2000: 27)

That decline of community can be plausibly correlated to the hyperindividualism and atomisation associated with neoliberal globalisation (Steger, 2002). Newspapers depend for their cultural authority (and, hence, their advertising revenue) upon engagement with a public sphere and, so, an inability to identify, let alone reach, a unified readership renders their whole project problematic. The internet is, thus, a symptom, rather than a cause, of newspapers' woes: in Australia, circulation has been steadily falling since 1980 (Simons, 2007a: 29).

That decline in collective identity creates similar problems for the 20th century literary project – the creation of a national identity around a national literary canon. Davis argues:

[The] changes in literary publishing are part of a wider trend towards the commodification of all cultural forms; this trend is typical of the drive within neoliberal societies to transform social relationships of the sort that once underpinned literary production, with its reliance on government support, coterie culture and education systems, into market relationships wherein all potentially profitable forms of cultural productions become media properties... (Davis, 2007: 128).

Hence, his conclusion that 'the activities of reading, studying, writing and publishing literary fiction will increasingly become the preserve of a rump of "true believers"' (Davis, 2007: 129).

The trends Davis identifies makes the rise of academic creative writing over precisely the same period seem anomalous, even perverse. Paul Dawson argues, reasonably enough, that 'the crucial factor for the wide-scale attraction of Creative Writing ... is not only a desire for individual self-expression which was cultivated in schools, but a cultural environment in which it seems possible and attractive to become a published author' (Dawson, 2001). Why, then, does the success of the discipline correlate so closely with Davis' periodisation of literary decline?

The neoliberal project was always as much about shaping a new kind of citizen, rather than merely reforming the economy. As Margaret Thatcher explained, 'Economics are the method but the object is to change the soul' (cited in Harvey, 2005: 23).

But engineering the soul is a complex business, with contradictory effects. If neo-liberalism fosters social atomisation, it also creates a corresponding yearning for community, authenticity and transcendence. These contradictory pressures can be seen in studies of contemporary religiosity. On the one hand, traditional church attendance has been (like trade unionism, membership of political parties and local sporting teams) in steady decline in the industrialised world (Boucher & Sharpe, 2008: 105). Yet the drop in identification with mainstream denominations has corresponded with a sharp up-tick in Pentecostal and Charismatic Christianity (Simons, 2007b: 15). Marion Maddox notes the incompatibility between the traditional, community-based church and the frantic individualism of, what she calls, the 'Market God' and concludes that 'the Market God cannot rule alone. It has proved too dynamic and unsettling. It sabotages family and community life and tears away safety nets. It has had to make Olympian room for another deity, one who brings "Us" a renewed sense of the security that the Market God took away' (Maddox, 2005: 292). In other words, the Evangelicals – with their mega-church convenience, their un-self-conscious 'Gospel of Prosperity' and their emphasis on individual salvation – offer a marketised consolation for the soullessness of a marketised society.

Phil Edmonds makes a similar argument about creative writing classes. 'They have become,' he suggests, 'in a sense, a site of the post-modern confessional, a search for community in an instantaneous, yet disconnected world' (Edmonds, 2005). The contours of Edmonds' claim can be fleshed out with survey data from Donna Lee Brien and Philip Neilsen. Concerned that 'the proportion of our students who are "readers" is disconcertingly low', they polled students about their attitudes to reading and to writing. Most respondents (78%) said they enrolled because they wished to become writers. But only 40% of undergraduate students read 'for pleasure' more than once a week, and 20% read 'for pleasure' once a fortnight or less (Brien & Neilsen, 2001).

How to explain this puzzling enthusiasm for a profession that produces books, in which students take little pleasure? Hans Abbing suggests that the desire to become an artist (or writer) reflects 'a social need to have a sacred place'; that artists 'offer a romantic alternative to a society of more or less anonymous and replaceable employees – from managers to street sweepers' (Abbing, 2002: 290). That alternative – 'authorship' – seems to exist as an abstraction, unrelated to writing as a communicative practice or a social phenomenon. As Jyotsna Kapur argues:

> An old narrative about the arts still persists in the academy: it is that artists are genius outsiders, voices of dissent, rugged lonesome individuals who live on the margins, victims of economic marginalisation and

social misunderstanding, with a special, even sacred, relationship to their art which must be protected from the intrusions of the world. (Kapur, 2007: 2)

It seems plausible, then, that the popularity of creative writing rests, at least in part, on the desire of students for authorship, as a representation of the imagination, passion, inspiration and other values directly counterposed to the antiseptic exchange of buyer and seller.

The correlation between the rise of creative writing and Davis' thesis of a literary paradigm in decline becomes clearer. The Australia Council's 2010 report – *Do you really expect to get paid?* – records that in 2007–2008, the median income from creative writing for professional writers in Australia was $3,600 per annum (the mean figure is less influenced than the average by the anomalously high incomes of the few very successful authors) (Throsby & Zednik, 2010: 44; *cf.* Throsby & Hollister, 2003). But what do such dire statistics mean for authorship, in the sense discussed here? Abbing argues that, in fact, the extreme difficulty of artistic life makes art more attractive, rather than less, since it is assumed that 'if so many take the plunge and fail, those who succeed must be special indeed' (Abbing, 2002: 289). Similarly, Malcolm Knox's description of novelistic life might have been intended as a warning, a text that a conscientious creative writing teacher might show students to disabuse them of unrealistic expectations. Yet Knox reproduces all the main elements of Kapur's 'old narrative': the author as lonely, marginal outsider, misunderstood and victimised, but still pursuing a sacred calling.

The novel might be, as Davis suggests, less central to culture, but its actual standing does not necessarily impact on a reified notion of authorship that, if anything, bears an inverse relationship to the social status of actual writers. The argument might seem a confirmation of the populist assumption of a fundamental incompatibility between creativity and the neo-liberal university and, in some respects, it is. Many students, it seems, enrol in creative writing because the university – indeed, the world – seems depressingly beige, and they, by contrast, identify with the ungainly rude girl and her red lipstick. Yet, almost by definition, academic creative writing succeeds because it offers an escape from commodification *in the form of a commodity*. As Thomas Frank points out, there have always been 'new products. . . to facilitate our rebellion against the soul-deadening world of products, to put us in touch with our authentic selves, to distinguish us from the mass-produced herd, to express our outrage at the stifling world of economic necessity' (Frank, 1997: 229). As Hillsong repackages Jesus for the market, so the university bundles the outsider experience of authorship into units purchasable by the term.

Creative writing might, then, be anomalous in the modern university, but it is, also, to some degree, exemplary. Despite its outsider image, academic creative writing actually integrates far more easily with industry than comparable traditional liberal arts programmes, such as English Literature or History. Insofar as publishers still do seek literary novels (and a declining interest by major publishers provides commercial opportunities for small and very small publishing houses), a writing course, particularly at postgraduate level, offers direct access (that is, without the intercession of literary agents) to a concentration of high quality manuscripts that have already been extensively edited. The university, in other words, substitutes for the work that many publishers can no longer perform (sorting through slush piles, reworking flawed manuscripts, structurally editing promising books, etc.). It makes commercial sense for commissioning editors to establish relationships with institutions and, in effect, provide a de facto subsidy (Davidson, 2010). Equally, universities recognise the importance of introducing publishers to their students. As Tony Birch, a writer and academic at the University of Melbourne, says, 'There's a pressure on university staff to produce writers who become published and then we can advertise our writing classes … that, you know, this great author came out of this program' (Birch, 2005). Writing programmes that cannot offer access to publishers will suffer in comparison to those that do and, so, it seems likely that the relationship between industry and creative writing will only grow.

Of course, the great majority of graduates do not become professional authors, a fact that reinforces a perceived incompatibility between creative writing and the commercial imperatives of the modern university. Again, however, this is more apparent than real. Graduates of creative writing, like graduates from other humanities, will drift into a variety of industries. Indeed, the growth of academic creative writing opens an internal career path, with many graduates finding work in higher education, either as career academics or as part of that army of sessional employees on which the universities now depend. In that context, consider the following description of word practices by a creative writing academic.

I supervise Creative Writing PhDs, those new-breed, non-traditional doctorates that worry university administrations, attract scorn from some older writers and academics, and bring in more candidates than we can handle. I supervise three times more PhDs (18) than my university's recommended load (only 6) because: (1) I like watching new work come to fruition; (2) I crave discussion with other writers over bottles of wine; and (3) I am, like most academics I know, a workaholic. (Krauth, 2008: 10)

Imagine such a statement in a different industrial context. Would, for instance, a builder's labourer boast about how she performed three times as many concrete pours as contractually required because: (1) she liked watching buildings completed; (2) she enjoyed the companionship of her workmates; and (3) she loved hard work? If the question seems incongruous, it is not because construction workers find no satisfaction in labour (in fact, they often do), but because they, as workers with a strong union tradition, possess sufficient political sophistication to recognise that exceeding accepted norms undermines industry conditions.

The comparison, trivial in itself, illustrates another of Kapur's arguments. She suggests that idealised employee of the neo-liberal economy is not the blue-collar labourer of the construction site, but, instead, looks very much like. . . an artist: 'Workers, like artists, are expected to function perpetually as freelancers who constantly update their skills and knowledge: ie they retrain themselves at their own expense and also own their tools' (Kapur, 2007: 10). If a building worker would find the notion of cheerfully labouring without pay both absurd and reactionary, a writer would not – indeed, it is something that most writers take for granted. So what does the student of creative writing learn about working life? She is taught that she must work long hours (on her manuscript) without any guarantee of payment; she learns that, with opportunities (for publication) so scarce, she must do everything possible to attract an employer; she learns to accept an individual, short-term contract (for a book) as an almost utopian outcome. When, as is likely, she finds work in another industry, she is thus, as Kapur suggests, an ideal employee.

In this context, the populist rhetoric in which creative writing is steeped takes a particular significance. Krauth's claim to worry the starchy administrators and scornful professors faintly echoes the militant past of a discipline too radical for squares and traditionalists. Yet if, in some senses, creative writing does trouble the university management, in another sense, the administration doubtless yearns for more of these employees so enthusiastic about donating their labour. A comparison might be drawn with Frank's description of the young employees of the dot com boom: contract workers who self-identified as anti-authoritarian creatives and sported wild haircuts, brought their pet birds to work and generally stuck it to the Man. As Frank notes, these free-spirited hipsters did, in fact, shock traditionalists, but a new breed of managers found their antics entirely admirable, since their rebelliousness was explicitly individualist (and implicitly anti-union) and, so, at the first sign of economic turmoil, they (and their birds) could be summarily dismissed (Frank, 2002).

3.

In the wake of Elif Batuman's (2010) much discussed *London Review of Books* essay on Mark McGurl's *The Programme Era: Postwar Fiction and the Rise of Creative Writing*, Emmett Stinson (2010) noted 'the burgeoning semi-genre' of what he called 'the Creative Writing exposé'. In response to the essay, he contended that:

> ...there *is no* crisis within contemporary literature as such, but *there is* a crisis in how literature is produced, disseminated and advertised within the marketplace. The failures are *systemic failures* that cannot be separated from larger economic structures.

Accordingly, he argued:

> What Creative Writing programs provide is precisely a space in which such writers can feel that their writing (and literature more generally) *matters*, which is pretty useful if you're going to devote an enormous amount of time to writing your first 60,000 to 100,000 word manuscript. I suspect that the rise of Creative Writing programs is as much a response to the increasingly monolithic, corporate, 'superstar' model of publishing as anything else.

Stinson's approach seems broadly correct.

Certainly, academic creative writing offers aspiring authors discipline and structure, mentors and peers, all of which may prove difficult to find elsewhere. While many students go into debt for their studies, the study of writing may, through scholarships and bursaries, provide an income for some. Most of all, because of its links with industry, academic enrolment enables would-be authors to overcome the awful catch-22 facing emerging writers, who cannot attract a publisher without an agent and cannot attract an agent without prior publication. For that reason, formal study will, in all likelihood, become (if it has not already) the most common path to publication for new writers.

Furthermore, a recognition that the phenomenal growth of the discipline rests upon a reified notion of creativity is not a claim that creative writing has somehow been co-opted. Writing has always been a commercial activity and, in any case, contrasts between 'authentic' and 'inauthentic' discourses make increasingly little sense in contemporary capitalism. As Mark Fisher argues:

> What we are dealing with now is not the incorporation of materials that had previously seemed to possess subversive potentials, but instead,

their precorporation: the pre-emptive formatting and shaping of desires, aspirations and hopes by capitalist culture. Witness, for instance, the establishment of settled 'alternative' or 'independent' cultural zones, which endlessly repeat older gestures of rebellion and contestation as if for the first time. 'Alternative' and 'independent' don't designate something outside mainstream culture; rather, they are styles, in fact, the dominant styles, within the mainstream. (Fisher, 2009: 9)

The task is, thus, not to stand 'for' or 'against' academic creative writing (whatever that would mean) so much as to recognise the implications of creative writing's location in a particular social and economic context. The relationship between the growth of creative writing as a discipline and the rise of neoliberalism both inside and outside the university necessarily entwines the economic and the aesthetic. To use the most obvious example, the concern of Adelaide postgraduates about the cost of their studies has implications reaching beyond equity within the university itself. If creative writing courses are, as has been suggested, providing the next generation of literary novelists, then Australian literary culture will be disproportionately shaped by those who can either afford fees or secure a scholarship. Obviously, there have always been economic barriers to authorship. It is striking, however, that, today, they are both so overt and, yet, so rarely noted.

Understanding academic creative writing in this way is particularly important, not only because higher education faces continuing uncertainty, but also because the publishing industry seems set to enter a period of renewed turmoil as it grapples with electronic formats, challenges to traditional copyright and changes to the laws governing parallel importation. Arguments about the future of creative writing will necessarily involve arguments about these and other broader issues.

In some respects, then, remembering the radical past of creative writing seems more important than ever, since, today, efforts to shape the future of literature must, of necessity, once more involve attempts to shape the world.

References

Abbing, H. (2002) Why are artists poor? *The Exceptional Economy of the Arts*. Amsterdam: Amsterdam University Press.

Batuman, E. (2010) Get a real degree [Review]. *London Review of Books* 32 (18), 3–8. Online at http://www.lrb.co.uk/v32/n18/elif-batuman/get-a-real-degree

Birch, T. (2005) The World of Creative Writing courses. [Interview]. *ABC Radio National Interview with Ramona Koval*, 7 August. Online at http://www.abc.net.au/rn/arts/bwriting/stories/s1430412.htm

Boucher, G. and Sharpe, M. (2008) The Times Will Suit Them: *Postmodern Conservatism in Australia*. Crows Nest: Allen & Unwin.

Boyd, N. (2009) Describing the Creative Writing thesis: A Census of Creative Writing doctorates, 1993–2008. *Text* 13 (1). Online at http://www.textjournal.com.au/april09/boyd.htm

Brien, D. and Neilsen, P. (2001) Why don't our students read? *Text* 5 (1). Online at http://www.textjournal.com.au/april01/neilsen_brien.htm

Carter, D. (2007) Boom, bust or business as usual? literary fiction publishing. In D. Carter and A. Galligan (eds) *Making Books: Contemporary Australian Publishing* (pp. 231–246). St Lucia: University of Queensland Press.

Davidson, R. (2010) Liberated zone or pure commodification? *Overland* 200 (Spring), 103–109. Online at http://web.overland.org.au/previous-issues/issue-200/feature-rjurik-davidson/

Davis, M. (2007) The decline of the literary paradigm in Australian publishing. In D. Carter and A. Galligan (eds) *Making Books: Contemporary Australian Publishing* (pp. 116–131). St Lucia: University of Queensland Press.

Dawson, P. (2001) Creative writing in Australia: The development of a discipline. *Text* 5 (1). Online at http://www.textjournal.com.au/april01/dawson.htm

Dawson, P. (2005) *Creative Writing and the New Humanities*. London: Routledge.

Edmonds, P. (2005) The romantic ego in the Creative Writing workshop. *Text* 9 (2). Online at http://www.textjournal.com.au/oct05/edmonds.htm

Evans, S. and Deller-Evans, K. (1998) True lies? 1997 survey of Creative Writing students. *Text* 2 (2). Online at http://www.textjournal.com.au/oct98/evans.htm

Fisher, M. (2009) *Capitalist Realism: Is There No Alternative?* Winchester: Zero Books.

Frank, T. (1997) *The Conquest of Cool: Business Culture, Counterculture, and the Rise of Hip Consumerism*. Chicago, MA: University of Chicago Press.

Frank, T. (2002) *One Market Under God: Extreme Capitalism, Market Populism and the End of Economic Democracy*. London: Vintage.

Genoways, T. (2010) The death of fiction. *Mother Jones*, Jan-Feb 2010, online article, accessed 16 January 2011. http://motherjones.com/media/2010/01/death-of-literary-fiction-magazines-journals

Harvey, D. (2005) *A Brief History of Neoliberalism*. Oxford: Oxford University Press.

Harper, G. and Kroll, J. (2008) Creative Writing and the university. In G. Harper and J. Kroll (eds) *Creative Writing Studies: Practice, Research and Pedagogy*. Clevedon: Multilingual Matters.

Kapur, J. (2007) The Ideology of the Aesthetic in the Neo-Liberal Turn. [Presentation]. *Paper presented at the Annual meeting of the American Sociological Association*, August 11. New York, NY. Online at http://www.allacademic.com/meta/p181957_index.html

Knox, M. (2006) Pushing against the real world: The case for 'original' Australian Fiction. *Overland* 182 (Autumn), 4.

Krauth, N. (2000) Where is writing now? Australian university Creative Writing programs at the end of the millennium. *Text* 4 (1). Online at http://www.textjournal.com.au/april00/krauth.htm

Krauth, N. (2008) The novel and the academic novel. In G. Harper and J. Kroll (eds) *Creative Writing Studies: Practice, Research and Pedagogy* (pp. 10–20). Clevedon: Multilingual Matters.

Krauth, N. and Brady, T. (1999) Editorial. *Text* 3 (2). Online at http://www.textjournal.com.au/oct99/editorial.htm.

Lee, J. (2007) Exploiting the imprint. In D. Carter and A. Galligan (eds) *Making Books: Contemporary Australian Publishing* (pp. 17–33). St Lucia: University of Queensland Press.

Lynch, K. (2006) Neo-liberalism and marketisation: The implications for higher education. *European Educational Research Journal* 5 (1), 1–17.

Maddox, M. (2005) *God Under Howard: The Rise of the Religious Right in Australian Politics*. Crows Nest: Allen & Unwin.

Marginson, S. (2002) Towards a politics of the enterprise university. In S. Cooper, J. Hinkson and G. Sharp (eds) *Scholars and Entrepreneurs* (pp. 109–136). North Carlton: Arena.

Meyer, D. (2009) *Literary Death Spiral? The Fading Book Section*, February 19th 2009, online article, accessed 25 July 2009. http://www.npr.org/templates/story/story.php?storyId=100828803

North, S. (2006) Creativity: The fire in the fennel stalk. *Text* 10 (2). Online at http://www.textjournal.com.au/oct06/north.htm

Poland, L. (2007) The business, craft and profession of the book editor. In D. Carter and A. Galligan (eds) *Making Books: Contemporary Australian Publishing* (pp. 96–115). St Lucia: University of Queensland.

Putnam, R. (2000) *Bowling Alone: The Collapse and Revival of American Community*. New York, NY: Simon & Schuster.

Simons, M. (2007a) *The Contentmakers: Understanding the Media in Australia*. Camberwell: Penguin.

Simons, M. (2007b) *Faith, Money & Power: What the Religious Revival Means for Politics*. North Melbourne: Pluto Press.

Steger, M. (2002) Robert Putnam, social capital and a suspect named globalisation. In S. McLean, D. Schultz and M. Steger (eds) *Social Capital: Critical Perspectives on Community and Bowling Alone*. New York, NY: New York University Press.

Stinson, E. (2010) *Literary Links: (What's So Funny) 'Bout Peace, Love and Creative Writing Programs*, blog, accessed 16 January 2011. http://emmettstinson.blogspot.com/2010/09/literary-links-whats-so-funny-bout.html

Throsby D. and Hollister V. (2003) *Don't Give Up Your Day Job: An Economic Study of Professional Artists in Australia*. Sydney: Australia Council for the Arts. Online at http://www.australiacouncil.gov.au/__data/assets/pdf_file/0007/32497/entire_document.pdf

Throsby, D. and Zednik, A. (2010) *Do You Really Expect to Get Paid? An Economic Study of Professional Artists in Australia*. Sydney: Australia Council for the Arts. Online at http://www.australiacouncil.gov.au/__data/assets/pdf_file/0007/79108/Do_you_really_expect_to_get_paid.pdf

7 Nothing is Free in this Life

Antonia Pont

Years ago, while suffering from extreme seasonal allergies, I came across something on the internet which clarified for me a crucial aspect of the business of marketing. I had tried everything for my tears, runny nose and grating, itchy throat, but nothing had worked, and I wasn't willing to exacerbate my dependence on antihistamines.

Willing to read anything that might have a connection to my condition, I happened upon an area of alternative therapy, hitherto unknown to me, going under the euphemistic name of 'uropathy'. Now, stated bluntly, uropathy consists of drinking your own wee – fresh, sometimes allowed to 'breathe' – and my source referenced all manner of very interesting research on the matter.

I recommend a web search, if only out of curiosity. The thing that struck me, however, in relation to uropathy, which claims for itself amazing curative powers (and there were numerous miraculous testimonials), was a statement by one of its advocates, explaining why uropathy was not likely to be promoted by pedestrian, allopathic healing modalities. The writer explained that due to the fact that uropathy primarily works when the patient consumes their own urine (due to the specific hormonal profile of the filtrate), it was never going to be of any use to the medicine business. Uropathy, in other words, offers absolutely nothing that can be sold. Urine is available enough and since one needs to use one's own, it subverts any kind of exchange economy. Abundant *and* specific – an odd combination in itself – urine consumption would then be analogous to an unusual kind of self-sufficiency and self-healing potential contained in every human body and placing that body – to some degree – out of the reach of 'pharmaceutical tithe'.

It is beyond the scope of this chapter to inquire into the current state of my hay fever. However, the example of uropathy, as a playful analogy, raises certain important questions in relation to the central concern of this book: *What is it that the creativity market purports to sell?* Or, *what is creativity and how do we situate it theoretically?* And, finally, *is it scarce?*

To this end, I would firstly like to take up some writings of the French thinker Jacques Derrida and his contributions to our understanding of the possible readings of 'creativity' and, more specifically, how creation may be distinguished from the category of invention.

Creation and Invention

In his work, *Psyché – Inventions of the Other,* Derrida (1987) brings attention to the distinction between 'creating' and 'inventing'. To create, he explains, relates more to notions of genesis. God *created* the world, for example. One does not normally say that he 'invented' it. Creation would imply that out of nothingness, came some*thing*. Noting that the category of invention can imply both 'invention' that pertains to the things invented (invention as noun) or to the activity of inventing itself (invention as the name of an activity), Derrida writes:

> But in the two cases, according to the two points of view (object or act), invention doesn't create an existence or a world as an assembly of entities, it doesn't have the theological meaning of a creation of existence, as such, *ex nihilo*. (1987: 35)

Creation, therefore, implies an almost magical process or, at least, a theologically inflected one. It would have to do with generating (out of nothing) something. It would not relate to a new approach or an innovative utilisation of what was already there. Its definition, in other words, would not be satisfied by a mere rearrangement, or alteration of form, based on existing categories or elements.

If we borrow Derrida's instructive question in this regard: 'Does one invent a child?' (1987: 14) or does one create one? the answer – conventionally and, somehow, intuitively – is that one *creates* a child. The angle on this matter points us towards the *biological* aspect of creation. All living creatures are 'creative', in that they create themselves down the genealogical line. It would be a natural happening and not an exclusively *human* one. Out of nothing (or, at least, two *very* small things), comes a new being. This is a kind of creation. God gave birth to, that is, *created* the world, and we – beasts and creatures – give birth to the next generation. Creation, paradoxically, would be both more, and less, surprising than invention, with the *theological* kind of creation lying completely beyond the reach of the mere human and the *biological* kind being typical of the human qua animal.

Derrida's *approach* here is useful for our wider inquiry, even if his choice of terms might appear to derail our discussion. Yes, we are talking about the so-called *creativity* market, but if this is a self-given title, the term 'creativity' might well be the result of advertising rhetoric, rather than definitional accuracy. Aggrandising its promise and desirability, as well as its importance within a marketplace, have those agents who make up the 'creativity market' auto-assigned a name for it that rings the most impressive and works the most strategically?

On the other hand, it is worth noting that the term 'creativity' can also function as a slight. The 'creative' within tertiary education has been viewed at times disparagingly by other faculties and disciplines of the academy, as if it were somehow less serious, more immature and less related to the adult preoccupations of *épistémè* (knowledge) and *istoria* (history). 'Creativity', in this sense, can be another term for the unrigorous, unscientific and flippant.

If we allow ourselves to split hairs, we find that the so-called creativity market does not at all pertain to the realm of mating frogs, budding wizards or gods who might be imagined as being capable of Derrida's idea of creation *ex nihilo*. Rather, the creativity market more commonly claims to be able to sell *inventiveness* (following the Derridean definition), to nurture it and teach its whimsical ways. Perhaps the name 'creativity market' prevails since it flatters a human consumer to believe that she, or he, might have this power of the gods to make something (other than offspring) appear where there was nothing before. However, to summarise Derrida again, God did not *invent* the world, and parents do not *invent* their children. A novelist, however, might invent a new technique in fiction, or a dancer might invent a new choreographic syntax.

Restricted to the so-called biologically natural or to the supernatural, creativity may therefore be theoretically distinguished from inventiveness, which – according to Derrida (1987: 36) – is restricted on the whole to the realm of the *human* and relates to the human's capacity for *techné*.

The creativity market, then, might be a misnomer for the market which offers to sell to the public the skills, luck and practices that relate to being inventive. Simultaneously, it is also that market which facilitates the production of the outcomes of inventiveness. In other words, this market would produce both invent*iveness* (as act or experience) and invent*ions* (as objects: films, novels, images, happenings). To explain this in another way, the creativity market has both a *process* aspect and a *product* aspect, purporting to generate the double-edged outcome of experiences and objects – that which can be 'lived' and that which can be 'had'. This reminds us of the old Aristotelian distinction of *praxis* and *poiesis*, where the former relates to activity in-and-of itself and the latter emphasises the products of activity.

Individuals and groups who approach the 'creativity market' with various wishes, agendas or hopes may be framed in relation to this double-edge. Let us just make a loose division and say that some may seek the *experience* of being (what is called) 'creative', while others might seek the know-how, mostly in order to produce the saleable objects or entities that fall somehow into the category of 'creative' or, even, 'artistic'. These might include quirky clothing, re-imagined homewares, industrially designed children's furniture, or noise music for advertising and so on.

We might also speculate that some consumers in 'creativity markets' are, in fact, unconsciously seeking something theological or 'metaphysical'. Beyond the scope of this discussion, it would be interesting to interrogate whether there is a relation between secularisation and an increase in the number of people seeking 'creative avenues' as a means of facilitating a particular kind of existential encounter.

The invention for Derrida, despite appearing less magical or miraculous than his 'creation', is, upon closer inspection, at least as complex a notion.

The Six Criteria of the Invention

There are six important criteria relevant to our discussion that help frame the notion of the invention. These are:

(a) the invention's illegality;
(b) the invention as a category pertaining to form and composition;
(c) the paradox of the invention;
(d) the iterability of the invention;
(e) the invention as both a first and last time; and
(f) invention as 'finding there for the first time'.

These criteria assist in the identification of inventions already in the world. Let us examine them more closely.

(a) Illegality

The first interesting thing that Derrida notes about this category is that 'an invention always supposes some illegality, the rupture of an implicit contract, it introduces disorder into the peaceful order of things' (1987: 11).

An invention would somehow always be illegal, radical and a break with tradition, existing codes or the status quo. An invention goes against the grain of the order as humans have established it, forcing something new into its grid, making something that was previously not possible, possible and via a contravention. I read this to imply that unless the order is ruptured in some way, there will have been no invention as such. Or, without such disturbance to the way things are, the so-called invention will have been a mere reshuffling a predictable link in an existing chain of everyday goings-on.

(b) Form and Composition

The next aspect of the invention, Derrida goes on to explain, referencing the development of patent law between the 17th and 19th centuries, is that, curiously, it has legally been defined in relation to form and arrangement, rather than to actual content (1987: 14). This would support the aforementioned creation/invention distinction, wherein it is implied that, in creation, something materially new is called into being, whereas invention would involve a different kind of 'newness' and one intricately bound up with the human sphere and measurable against it. Inventions emerge from a context at a particular moment and both that 'moment' and the particularities of the context are *human*.

(c) Paradox of the Invention

An invention, according to Derrida's definition, operates paradoxically. Insofar as it (see a.) always involves a rupture with the existing order and legality, it also, in order to be classed as an invention, must be taken up and recognised by laws and society (Derrida, 1987: 16). The invention breaks traditions so as, ultimately, to be called into being via their acknowledgement, thereby adding to them. Derrida will say this amounts to the impossibility of a 'private' invention and that inventions are therefore creatures of the public and, by implication, the social or political realm (1987: 15). It is, in this sense, also, presumably, that they are not 'natural', but rather, produced by, and producing of, human worlds.

(d) The Invention's Iterability

Iterability here refers to a capacity to be repeated. Closely related to the previous aspect, it suffices here to quote, a little lengthily, from *Psyché,* in order to make clear the consequences of both the necessity of invention breaking with tradition and also its being called into being by it:

> [The invention] will receive its status of invention, moreover, only to the extent that this socialisation of the thing invented is guaranteed by a system of *conventions* that will assure at once inscription in a shared history, belonging to a culture: heritage, patrimony, pedagogical tradition, discipline and chain of generations. The invention *begins* by being able *to be repeated, exploited, reinscribed* [my emphasis]. (1987: 16)

For the invention not just to be a one-off, abhorrent breaking with tradition or a queer anomaly, it must demonstrate the capacity to be repeated, used and/or exploited. Derrida will even call it a *machine* (1987: 21), thereby hinting towards the invention's close, but unexpected, link with human technology.

(e) Invention as First-and-Last Time

Stemming from the previous point, the invention is the coincidence of both an *inaugurating* time (a 'first' time), but also of a *last* time, insofar as it must be unique. As the only 'first time', other 'times' will not be classed as inventive moments, but will be merely examples of its inscription in the tradition, or the system, that will take up the invention's machinic possibilities (Derrida, 1987: 16).

(f) Finding-There For the First Time

In this final aspect, Derrida recalls the reader to the fact that – according to pure definition – invention can be understood as meaning 'finding there for the first time' (1987: 16). Within this definition, we find the antithesis of 'creation'. Invention *finds* and finds what was already *there*. It is inventive because it finds for the *first time*. The *finding* is unique, but *what* is found was already at hand with potential, but in an as yet unacknowledged form.

To risk a simplifying summary, then, invention would be a new relationship to the raw substance/content already available in the existing context. Rather than pertaining to the creation of fresh *matter*, it involves a discovery of an approach, perspective or structuring that would render the same old 'stuff' uniquely new, enabling this relationship/configuration to be repeated and taken up by the system of relationships in which the matter previously existed.

If, then, the criteria outlined above are the means to recognising an invention when one comes along, we are still no closer to understanding how inventions arise. Since this is the primary concern of the industries or markets that would declare themselves 'creative', let us examine what Derrida says about this.

What Has Happened When an Invention Happens?

At this point, we are able to identify an invention after the fact, but, obviously, the 'creativity market' would wish to make some claim about its ability to shepherd, coerce or facilitate inventive capacity. Derrida distils the mechanism of invention down to a very straightforward, but also *impossible*,[1] coincidence.

To use Derrida's example, we need to clarify several concepts stemming from *Speech Act Theory* in linguistics. An important area of debate within linguistics relates to the classification of certain statements into those that are descriptive (called 'constative') and those that are themselves *acts* (called 'performative'). To make it simple, examples of the latter are usually statements that, in fact, effectuate some change (in legal status, for example) or action through their being uttered. The obvious example is always 'I do' in marriage. On the other hand, an example of the former would be something typical, like 'the sky is blue today', a statement that doesn't make anything happen (superficially, at least).

We will leave aside Derrida's other work that has challenged this simplistic division in Speech Act Theory, however, what is useful here is the way a discipline (linguistics), or indeed any system, can set up categories and rules that are deemed complete and self-evident, almost 'naturally true'. This is where the idea of the 'impossible' becomes central. Invention arrives in a system or a context where it had seemed that nothing new or radical were possible, and this arrival happens via 'impossibility'. In other words, the impossible can happen and its happening relates to what we understand invention to be.

Taking a work by Francis Ponge, Derrida gives the reader an example of when the constative and the performative categories of linguistics collide illegally in a happening that can be deemed 'inventive' and related to the so-called 'impossible'. As a rupture, whose outcome is iterable, but also unique, it will be both reliant upon convention *and* totally subverting of its typical use. 'By the word by begins therefore this text' (Derrida, 1987: 19). This simple sentence of Ponge, grammatically sound, at once *performs* itself and *describes* itself *at the same time*. Since most (actually, all, except those that are inventively rupturing) statements tend to manage to fall into only one of the categories of Speech Act Theory, it is a kind of *event* when a statement simply and quietly inhabits the two at once.[2] Such an 'event' – of co-inhabiting – is astounding and 'unpre-emptable', but (after the fact) *not* impossible at all. Once uttered, any prior, apparent impossibility of the statement's invention drops away and is nowhere to be found.

Put simply, once the invented is found, it is difficult to unthink its *found*ness.

Round things existed, for example, before the invention of the wheel, but the application of round-cylindrical-ness to movement may be classed as an 'event' for human animals. It is difficult for us (now, at this historical moment) to imagine a time prior to the obviousness of the wheel's existence. It has already, in other words, been found for *that* first time. Once employed and used as a machinic pattern, it can never be *found*, in that initial way, again.

Inventive Instability

To describe the movement out of which inventiveness emerges as a 'collision' between two apparently mutually exclusive states (the 'performative' and 'constative', for example, in linguistics) is perhaps to simplify what will prove, upon closer observation, even more interesting. Referencing the Belgian theorist Paul de Man's comments about the relationship between fiction and autobiography, Derrida writes:

The infinitely fast oscillation between performative and constative, language and metalanguage, fiction and non-fiction, auto- and hetero-reference etc. does not only produce an essential instability. This instability constitutes the event itself, let's say the oeuvre, the norms, statutes and rules of which the invention normally perturbs. (1987: 25)

By satisfying the definition of the performative and the constative in one gesture, Ponge's line ('by the word by begins therefore this text') constitutes a rupturing of an established convention of linguistic logic. To think it geometrically: *that which was parallel has become circular*. The rupture only, however, puts to use that which our existing grammar and 'sense' had already provided. The inventive structure is found, for the first time, there, *where it always was*.

So the event, for Derrida, is characterised by an essential instability, a rapid change of state and a failure – so to speak – of imperatives to obey the established categories provided by a system. In this sense, to invent would amount to the subversion of binary categories through the *taking up of both sides* of them in an infinitely accelerated fashion.

Derrida's Invention and Badiou's Event

I have used the term 'event' above, to designate Derrida's notion of invention, but – given the theoretical players contributing to thought today – this sphere of inquiry must also, I believe, give us to think the Badiouian *event*. I would claim, here, that the 'event', as framed by Badiou and then Derrida's notion of invention, each speaks to the other and that this definitional conversation can persuade us to take notice of what these thinkers offer to our understanding of how events come about and what agency humans have in relation to them.

A 'creativity market', whether it chooses to share such a theoretically rigorous understanding with its consuming public or not, could still do well to have the capacity to think invention-events. On the other hand, one can argue that consumers should be informed about the kinds of things money can realistically buy, and whether inventiveness is one of them.

Despite relying on vastly different methodological approaches, Derrida and Badiou, I believe, inform us about potentially foundational veracities concerning 'events'. Let us take up this idea and see if it can contribute to clarifying our inquiry about 'creativity markets'.[3]

An event, for Derrida and Badiou, would be something that ruptures. For the former, in relation to invention, the rupture – always somewhat illegal – would arise via a kind of manoeuvre within a context that is both perfectly *possible* retrospectively, but pragmatically impossible to *stage* prior to itself. The unique constellation that opens the event's possibilities pertains to an odd coincidence of naming-as-doing or an oscillation between these mutually exclusive categories. As simple as it sounds to describe, this coincidence *cannot be made to happen*.

For Badiou, comparatively, the event is undisputedly random and beyond human coercion. In his use of set theory, Badiou is able to depict very clearly using mathematical 'syntax' what is at play in the rupture that his event constitutes. He offers the following definition:

> The event (at a given evental 'site') is 'the multiple composed of: on the one hand, elements of the site; and on the other hand, itself (the event)'. (2007: 506)

The matheme, or formula, of the event is able to be identified as an extraordinary kind of set, since it *contains itself*: $e_x = \{x \in X, e_x\}$ (Badiou, 2007: 179). Such scenarios within mathematics have often been outlawed or, at least, designated as destabilising and undesirable. See, for example, Douglas Hofstadter's book *I am a Strange Loop* (2007) for a very accessible description of these issues for the field of mathematics. Or, the other option has been for mathematicians to employ different systems of classification so as to prevent certain inconsistencies from arising (Goldblatt, 2006: 9–12).

Badiou's matheme of the event is not unrelated to the arising of the event that Derrida outlines in *Psyché*. Ponge's 'By the word by . . .' is also a kind of set that contains itself. By self-referencing, that which would be both *itself and the invention of itself at the same time*, it initiates a feedback loop, and this looping or whirligig 'acceleration' (to use Paul de Man's vocabulary [1979: 921]) is essential for whatever it is that constitutes the moment of the invention-event.

We can conclude that, with its possibility contained within the elements of the context or situation itself, the invention is both an exception to the rule and also reliant on *nothing* that is (not) already there. What does this mean?

Abundant Voids

For Badiou, an event happens when somehow our day-to-day reality – its rules, statutes, practices, technologies, language systems – fails to secure itself, and the *void* of which it is the structured organisation (and only that) reveals itself as the ontological foundation. To quote Roffe on this point: 'Its border status, its exposure to uncounted, inconsistent being, is what opens it up to the aleatory' (2006). The rupturing that the event is – completely outside of any kind of inscription system that could document or record it – disappears as soon as it has occurred. Or, to quote Roffe again, 'it also has no temporal reality other than the moment of its (dis)-appearance' (2006). The event leaves *nothing* in its wake and sometimes this 'nothing' is noticed by humans and a process begins.[4]

Whether events are common or scarce is, to me, not completely clear from the sum of Badiou's work I have read, and perhaps the point is that *we cannot really know*. In relation to our ongoing inquiry, what remains central is that whether scarce or not, the stuff of inventiveness – that is, Nothingness, the Void or accelerated instability – is not something that the market can annex, privatise or patent. This Void (of Badiou's) cannot be made to disappear entirely, no matter how tightly the reigns of the State or the status quo might pull and appear to cover it over. Always there, this 'nothingness', however, must be *secured* – that is, locked down in the 'count' of structuring, organising and disciplining – and we must understand that for *there to be* anything, this, too, is crucial.[5] It is also interesting to note that the void, for humans, is pure horror, since we do not exist there and are irrelevant. Or, to anthropomorphise a little, the void is not *dis*-interested in the human, simply *non*-interested.

Due to both the importance of the securing of the void, in order that 'there is' anything at all, and the necessity that this order be ruptured from time to time, added to, destabilised, re-invigorated and toppled, even, humans seem to have a justifiably ambivalent relationship to liminal experiences, such as inventiveness.[6] This ambivalence can give us a hint about the role of the 'creativity market' and also its limits.

So, What Can Money Buy Me?

Given the theoretical, even ontological, discussion above, we return to our question of what it is that can be sold under the rubric of 'creativity'. Let us quote Derrida again:

> If the word 'invention' knows a new liveliness, upon a foundation of anguished exhaustion, but also since the very desire to re-invent the invention itself, and to the point of re-inventing its statute, it is without doubt in relation to a scale that is unmeasurable against that of the past, that which one calls the 'invention' to be patented finds itself programmed, that it is to say, submitted to powerful movements of prescription and authoritarian anticipation, of which the modes are most numerous. And this as much in the domains called art or fine arts, as in the techno-scientific realms. Everywhere the projects of knowledge and research are firstly programmatics of invention. [. . .] One could evoke also all the institutions, private or public, capitalist or not, who declare themselves the machines for the production and orientation of the invention. (1987: 39)

Derrida notes an urge to want to re-invent what inventiveness is and notes that, at the same time, powerful forces are at work hoping to corral the stuff of inventiveness. Seminars, self-help books, tertiary institutions, privately-run weekend retreats, think-tanks, research institutes (to name a few) the market that sells creativity and the bodies that would claim to have its key seem to have something to offer, but, as we've read above, they can't have *nothing* to sell.

If the Badiouian Void, or the inherent instability or oscillation of which Derrida speaks, is somehow always already there *and* un-quashable, what factors influence or enhance a person's or organisation's ability to mobilise or to promise the delivery of that from which inventiveness springs?

Let us acknowledge a disconcerting coincidence. As a Caucasian, female, Australian-born, human animal, I can say that at this historical moment I am regularly subjected to forces demanding an obedience to statutes, laws, etiquettes, career and life trajectories, financial behaviours, etc. *and*, at the same time, am constantly targeted as a unit who might wish to consume products or services that declare themselves the means for the escaping of such confining (yet securing) structures. Allowing for specific geographical and societal differences, one could speculate that this bind is something shared by many people across the globe who are subjected to considerable amounts of media and advertising, at the same time as knowing acutely the demands of the conventions and lore of their specific context.[7]

Beyond the narrow definition of the 'creativity' market, perhaps markets *in general* do, and have always, to a certain degree, promised the kind of existential escape routes that the creativity market, of late, explicitly claims to offer.

This may be exactly what Derrida is pointing to when he says that we dream of re-inventing the invention:

> Today, it is perhaps because we know too well the existence at least, if not the functioning of invention-programming-machines, that we dream of reinventing the invention beyond the matrices of the programme. For, is a programmed invention still an invention? Is it an event through which the future comes to us? (1987: 40)

In relation to this question, I would emphasise here a strategic necessity. It is the importance of paying very close attention to vocabulary, with a view to paying close attention to ontology, so to speak. We need to clarify the ontology of inventions in the face of markets that are seeking to do what markets do, that is, generate velocities of exchange. We need to think, with curiosity and fierceness, into the possibilities of what money can buy, since it buys very many lovely things.

Nothingness, I would like to propose, finally, is not for sale, but instruction regarding, and environments conducive to, particular 'nothingness' practices might be.

The Lucrative Wisdom of Inventiveness?

Let us call again on the distinction noted above between the experience of inventing and the products of invention – *experiences and things*. It is quite obvious that 'newness' is a very saleable quality. Much of what passes for newness, however, is of the stale, programmed type noted by Derrida in the passage above. As a mere rearrangement of existing elements, it would not constitute a rupture.

Bombarded with the advertising speak of 'all new!', consumers may, and will, allow themselves to believe that some trace of the void (or a rupture of their unbearable daily normality) will grace them if they acquire a new style, a new piece of technology, etc. This is a furphy, and anyone who has shopped knows the let-down of this mistaken hope. A particular intellectual rigour or simple street-smartness might be enough, at least, to *decelerate* the incidents of unnecessary consumption elicited by claims of pseudo invention-events. Or, in the absence of this, shopping (and this includes for education) might simply emerge as *what it is*: the acquiring of more things/skills, some necessary, some not. A justifiable and pragmatic human activity among many, but by no means expected to be revolutionary or revelatory.

On the other hand – as is often the case with the fine arts and its products, so-called 'design', the literary business, etc. – something else is at stake in the wanting to attain proximity to someone else's invention event. In the absence of being inventive oneself, the possession of the trace of inventiveness (so-called creative products) may still seem appealing. This more vicarious aspect comes, perhaps, closer to what might be a driving factor in those markets termed specifically 'creative'.

So if most 'newness' isn't really new and being close to the traces of inventiveness is not the same as inventiveness itself, what, then, *is* saleable, given all our previous discussions about the nature of invention-events?

Let us propose that, despite humans not being able to influence the arising of events, specific human animals may have more or less aptitude, or practice, in noticing events *when they do happen* and being there to 'follow through' when events/invention arrive. Were there to be anything in which a 'creativity market' could trade, it might be in the teaching of what I propose to term an 'evental sensitivity' – a kind of preparedness. This may be what is purportedly on offer during creativity seminars, in the university classroom and within the covers of self-help books. If creativity markets are able to offer anything realistic, it is via this aspect. Providing employment for many people (many of whom are artists, researchers and creative practitioners themselves), these markets are clearly 'selling' something, and their product is neither toxic, unethical, nor even – if they pay attention to invention's ontology – deceitful.

Conclusion: Nothing *is* for Free

The old traces of inventiveness make up the majority of what we would call our cultural and technological canons, indeed, our civilisations. To read, 100 years after the fact, the literary works of an originally inventive writer is surely to be graced by beauty and to be groomed in sensitivity to *something*. This something might be human psychology, certain aesthetic qualities or grammatical elegance, among other things. In other words: light, colour, form, imagination or rhythm. To read will not necessarily constitute inventiveness, but it will not necessarily impede it, and it may even contribute to the possibility of the reader's noticing, and being able to respond,[8] to an event when it does arise.

The void of Badiou is *mostly* quite securely 'locked up' in structure . . . but not entirely. As Badiou will explain, it can be seen to 'haunt' the situation, but in non-presentation (see 2007: 94). This void is beyond the reach of any market – a fact which renders it both frustratingly evasive to those wishing to herd it into an exclusive and lucrative form by promising to sell the paradox of inventiveness, but also reassuringly resistant.

To conclude, then, let's say that an artist (in the broadest sense) may be that kind of creature who practices both a fluency in the rules, codes and techniques of the situation or current historical context, but who does not confuse this programmatic competency with the stuff of true invention, which is, in fact, nothingness or the void – that which is always there to be found and which is always already *for free*.

Notes

(1) This use of the term 'impossible' in Derrida's thought is not casual. 'Impossibility' for Derrida may be the very condition of that which renders any inventiveness, change, or justice-to-come possible at all. In other words, he proposes that something able to shift dominant patterns or old hierarchies is likely to involve a passage through 'impossibility'.

(2) I say this, well aware that Derrida's work of deconstruction challenges such bifurcations. The mutual exclusiveness, however, of these categories traditionally persists within systems that declare them – linguistics, for example, but it could be art, history or literature at given historical moments – and the system supports itself upon the very structure of that categorisation.

(3) This chapter is clearly not the forum for a detailed and rigorous interrogation of this claim concerning the resonance between a Derridean and Badiouian thinking of the event. However, for the purposes of opening the debate and stimulating discussion pertinent to this book, the claim, I believe, is useful or at least fruitfully provocative.

(4) This is a colloquial summary of the central argument of *Being and Event* (Badiou, 2007). Please refer to this work for closer elaboration.

(5) This difference between 'is' and 'there is' is central to 'Meditation One' of *Being and Event* (Badiou, 2007: 23ff) and nods in the direction of the old question 'why is there something rather than chaos?'

(6) Just as they might be ambivalent about the four categories of truth procedures outlined in both volumes of *Being and Event*: the amorous, the political, the scientific and the artistic (see, for example, Badiou, 2009: 77).

(7) The discomfort of this kind of irresolvable bind is, in any case, surely good for encouraging spending, the mantra of marketing pedagogy being to create a glaring problem and then to offer the solution at a price.

(8) This touches on an important similarity, but apparent distinction, between Derrida and Badiou. Derrida collapses two aspects of the invention – namely the event of its rupture and then the taking up of its possibility within the human context through statute, patent, etc. Badiou, on the other hand, but really in a comparable gesture, separates the event (as rupture) from the 'truth procedure' of the subject, who works to force into encyclopaedic knowledge the new truth revealed by the event. Derrida will name both phases the 'invention'; Badiou will use two different terms. Nevertheless, the theoretical manoeuvre is arguably comparable.

References

Badiou, A. (2007) *Being and Event* (O. Feltham, trans.). New York & London: Continuum.

Badiou, A. (2009) *Logics of Worlds* (A. Toscano, trans.). New York & London: Continuum.

Derrida, J. (1987) *Psyché – Inventions de l'autre*. Paris: Editions Galilée.

Goldblatt, R. (2006) *Topoi – The Categorial Analysis of Logic*. New York, NY: Dover.

Hofstadter, D. (2007) *I am a Strange Loop*. New York, NY: Basic Books.

Man, P. de. (1979) Autobiography as de-facement. *Modern Languages Notes* 94 (5), 919–930.

Roffe, J. (2006) Alain Badiou's being and event. *Cosmos and History: The Journal of Natural and Social Philosophy* 2 (1–2). Online at http://www.cosmosandhistory.org/index.php/journal/article/view/42/84.

8 The Ghost in the Machine: Creative Writing and its Malcontents

Phillip Edmonds

In this chapter, I discuss links between the current economic situation and the changing nature of cultural formation, specifically, where the 'industry' of creative writing in Australia is located within a crisis of 'theory' and 'practice', in literary studies and the broader society and the extent to which it is sustainable in broad terms. I will discuss what I believe is the developing bureaucratisation of 'literary' structures, including creative writing courses (CW), writers' centres, literary agents and writers' festivals in Australia. My observations have international parallels.

In 1996, D.G. Myers wrote of his experience in the US of college creative writing courses, where, rather than carrying the baton for the liberal arts, such initiatives, he claimed, had lost their way in a sea of bureaucracy and business (Myers, 1996). I suggest that we are currently seeing similar tendencies, yet individuals can make a difference, even though many of us were wilfully ahistorical in the lead up to the global financial 'crisis'. The 'crisis' of theory and practice I allude to above is, and was, implicated in the lead-up to the so-called 'global financial crisis' of 2008, where the contradictions of late capitalism spun out of control, firstly, in the financial markets.

Implicit in such a discussion is a belief that we can use a language which privileges the complex nature of cultural formation and determination. I also need to follow up on a challenge Robert Dixon made in 1998 when he suggested a link between developments in literary theory, the privatisation of the Australian economy and the growing corporatisation of the education system during the 1980s and 1990s. He suggested that:

> We would need to ask, what relation might there be between the importing of theory, with its cult of expertise, and the Dawkins reforms, which, among other things, helped to produce a new humanities

reshaped in the image of corporate culture and technocratic expertise. (Dixon, 1998: 201)

My invocation of 'commodification' and 'financial' is a contention that cultural analysis can no longer inhabit the anorexic, aseptic space it has defined for itself over two decades in Australia and overseas, even though I take up John Frow's (1995) point that:

> The theoretical analysis of social class has become deeply unfashionable and for good and persuasive reasons ... that class analysis reduces political and cultural struggles and determinations, and the specific institutions through which they work, to the singular underlying logic of the economy and of places generated in economic production [...] (Frow, 1995: 97)

For all that, Frow added that there were dangers:

> In throwing out reductionist concepts of class – and they have virtually all been reductionist – we have lost an indispensible analytical tool. We can understand neither the most delicate and subtle nor the crudest and basic movements of social power [...] (Frow, 1995: 98)

In other words, in our 'literary' conversations, we talk of the political economy of publishing when we recount stories of student successes, or otherwise, in terms of commercial publishing. That is, we talk about the economy, even when we don't talk about it. In broad terms, bankers and CEOs of major companies know intimately the link between economics and culture and the revolving nature of base and superstructure. In contrast, it is the 'knowledge class' that has tried to forget the surplus value expended in pursuit of its own compromised independence.

As I have suggested elsewhere, the upsurge in creative writing courses and the postmodern moment of celebrity (in Australia and elsewhere) is, in a sense, a type of 'unrequited desire', in that too much work is searching for too few publication opportunities, and we have been witnessing a repressed quasi-spiritual moment (Edmonds, 2005: 3). Such an obvious point is central to capitalist economics, which, of course, creates surplus value (through desire), both use and exchange. But we need to venture further, because our moment (post- the global financial crisis) is one of high drama, even if it is inside a fading economic rationalist rhetoric.

For example, what we are now seeing, despite the free floating signifiers and evangelical language of the past two decades, is the painful realisation that late capitalism, in universities and colleges at least, is currently corporatising 'creativity' and, by stealth, the possibility of a 'free' floating post-modernity. This is despite the commitment of people working in the creative arts setting in place resources for new writers and artists through postgraduate scholarships and helping to create good books and new writing through undergraduate and postgraduate courses. As Drusilla Modjeska noted nearly 10 years ago in an article that asked why publishers and readers then preferred non-fiction or memoir to fiction and still do:

> Writing that began as a challenge slowly became an orthodoxy. During the 1980s creative writing was established as a subject in our universities; students were learning the theories of post-structuralism and post-modernism ... there was a lopsided relationship between theory and feeling, with feeling often confused with sentimentality [...] (Modjeska, 2002: 204–205)

Walter Benjamin had prefigured as much in earlier times, in terms of the perceived contradictions of 'theory' and 'practice', when he discussed the cultural formations of Europe in 1934:

> Contrasts, which in happier epochs, used to fertilize one another have become insoluble antinomies. Thus, science and belle letters, criticism and original production, culture and politics now stand apart from one another without connection or order of any kind. (Benjamin, 1977: 89)

Such contradictions, in contemporary Australia (and also in the United Kingdom and the United States), have occurred against a backdrop of countervailing social moods and the onset of the 'war on terror'. Frank Moorhouse has called it 'a form of neurotic social hyperesthesia'. He cites examples of self-censorship and charts how such a social mood is institutionalised, in that, 'hundreds of Australians are employed to decide what we should watch and then to decide what is offensive in what we do watch' (Moorhouse, 2009: 3), observing that there are review boards, authorities of various types, and ethics officers and ethics committees in university humanities departments.

At this point, it is necessary to define, in some way, why such accommodations, other than mere practicality, have occurred. Frow contends that (we), 'the knowledge class', work in a:

> ... universe of discourse at once rule-governed and open-ended. The second determination is their membership of a social class with real, though ambivalent, class interests in the implementation of modernity. (Frow, 1995: 165)

The exercise of its power, then, can 'take the form of an apparent self-negation or self-abasement' (Frow, 1995: 165). Quoting Bourdieu, he suggested that, 'culture is our specific capital, and even in the most radical probing we tend to forget the true foundation of our specific power' (Bourdieu, 1990: 107).

My point is that such an involuntary bureaucracy is implicated in our institutional need to expand (as was the way with the credit economy), and by our contradictory role as intellectuals in advanced capitalism, in that we are involved in promoting our institutional 'products', while being at times internally critical of the direction of such initiatives. We are then 'structured by our indirectness of insertion in the relations of production, and by the fuzziness of its boundaries with other classes' (Urry, 1990: 88).

Furthermore, we are 'a class which is necessarily-not-for itself, and a class which is coherent only in its lack of structural cohesion' (Frow, 1995: 127).

To paraphrase, a class faction that cannot organise, and which prides itself on its partial independence from the production of cultural capital, is almost the perfect target for corporate ideology and an ideal representative for an inefficient bureaucracy that has facilitated some of the current cultural ground. A contrary view has recently been expressed in the United States by Steve Healey, who argues that contemporary capitalism needs a creative class of multidimensional thinkers working in, what Richard Florida has termed, 'the creative industries' (Healey, 2009: 35) to revitalise the cultural means of production in a globalised world notable for intense competitiveness. Conversely, such developments, in Australia, at least, have been satirised in the so-called campus novel by authors such as Michael Wilding, who has picked over the bones and satirised the very contradictions (Wilding, 2002) of what he believes is the partial strangulation of 'creativity' in the new corporate universities.

I am, therefore, in the spirit of contradiction, being kind and unkind to formalised creative writing in the academy. There is the potential that some graduates can become public intellectuals, even if only to promote their own egos, or indeed, their repressed desires. There is also potential to develop a relationship between the estranged twins of 'theory' and 'practice', if only because as intellectuals in the humanities, they are consciously, or unconsciously, going about issues of production *and* reception, in contrast to the relatively inward state of much of postgraduate literary and cultural studies in Australia, at least.

Creative writing in the academy can, then, if teachers get students to read more in different ways, interrogate the multiplicities of the breakdown between high and popular culture and engage, as Collins suggests of broader trajectories, in struggles between discourses that 'destabilize the very category of "the dominant" by asserting multiple, competing hierarchies' (Collins, 1989: 25). In other words, the popularity of creative writing is partly a statement about a crisis in the humanities itself, which is a crisis of volunteerism.

Let me be more specific, because on the 'literary' ground, there is a lot to look at. The most obvious link between the economy and 'culture' in the literary area in Australia is that book publishing is still dominated by a handful of large multinational firms who operate in the world of venture capital and whose interests aren't solely devoted to local considerations. This is despite the percentage of locally published books increasing markedly over the past two decades and the stable existence of a number of Australian-owned middle-sized firms, including Text Publishing and Allen & Unwin. The question for the immediate future is whether they will cut back on local publishing programmes.

There are, of course, other causal links that have determined what is published and why. Over the past 20 years, determinants, such as the abolition of the book bounty (which subsidised the local printing of books), the abandonment of the standard trade discount of 33% and the introduction of sale and return in the book trade has meant that it has become harder for publishers to take risks on new authors, because stock has a shorter shelf life, which aids bestsellers.

As Anne Galligan has noted:

> Publishing today is front-list driven, with advertising potential directed to the latest publications; the emphasis is fast production and quick sales ... this is the opposite of publishing for cultural value. (Galligan, 1998: 151–152)

The relatively recent rise of the role of the literary agent in Australia, between the primary producer and publishers, also needs examination, as it represents both a larger and more diversified market for books and a perceptible increase in literary production, partly as a result of creative writing courses. Most large publishers don't look at new manuscripts, unless they come through a respectable agent so that they are largely abrogating their role as innovators (in the 'literary' field) in a time of repressed desire and inflationary production. It needs to be said, though, that those publishers have rarely been innovators; they have, rather, published worthy books to gain broad cultural cache for their lists. In this way, prestigious, slow-selling titles have marginal exchange value, but enlarge the corporate image of the publisher as a destination of power and influence.

In a sense, most agents are acting as handmaidens akin to the literary equivalent of *Australian Idol* – a televised local musical talent quest where only a few people can ever be promoted in a relatively small marketplace at any one time. Because of the economic imperatives they work with, it is hardly surprising that, in most cases, agents are only of use to best-selling authors and established names. But, unfortunately, many new authors seem to regard acquiring an agent as an act of quasi-publication and status and, for most, such an arrangement comes to nothing. In such an environment, the editors of under-resourced, small magazines and 'literary' journals are the people committed to encouraging new writers.

Presumably, away from the grinding gears of political economy, a major trauma for those working in the creative arts in universities in Australia has been the lack of peer review points and validation for 'creative research'; that is, the publication by academics of novels, volumes of poetry, short stories and creative non-fiction, in contrast to writing for peer review academic journals, which is evidence that large parts of the educational system in Australia are inefficient, relatively bureaucratic and symptomatic of a society that wedges the 'theory' and 'practice' of its constituents. Currently, there are moves to validate 'creative research' within the Australian Research Council, but the administration of potential changes is breaking down at local levels and intense dispute characterises the ranking of journals, whether they be 'academic' or 'creative'.

Consequently, some of us still write endless articles on teaching 'pedagogy' and/or the nexus between the PhD creative work and the exegetical essay. Are we trying to legitimise our practice to the pure theorists? In so doing, is not the crisis over 'theory' and 'practice' exposed and left unresolved as universities revert back into the harbour of 'theoretical' criticism?

As Modjeska has noted:

There is a divide I find painful to witness between students doing research degrees which give little attention to ways of writing, and those doing writing degrees which attend to the writerly content without sufficient challenge to the quality of content. (Modjeska, 2002: 210–211)

How should we think? How can we retain even a modest sense of agency if academics and their pupils behave anti-socially?

But there is a problem, similar to that behind the initial onset of the global financial crisis, in that too much cultural capital has been lent out in performative ways that have refused definition and determination. For all the talk of 'difference', plurality and democracy in Western capitalism, much of it was predicated on the assumption that resources were relatively infinite, when, in fact, they were based on notions of on-going 'credit', which was an attempt, as we discovered, to wish away the politics of the economy. As Glucksmann has suggested, the cultural ground was prepared by 'postmodernism, which placed itself "beyond good and evil", beyond true and false, and inhabited a cosmic bubble' (Glucksmann, 2009: 4).

Furthermore, a perceived lack of agency has gone hand-in-hand with a sense of increasing powerlessness in the universities and the broader society in Australia and elsewhere. Concentrating on the Australian experience, Robert Dixon has suggested that the trajectory for part of the problem can be traced back to the 1980s, when 'the cult of theoretical expertise continued to fracture the public sphere for Aust. Lit. Crit,' (Dixon, 1998: 198) so much so, that any notion of a 'national' literary project was weakened by the positioning of structuralism and post-structuralism as oppositional discourses. He extrapolated further, into links between the economic rationalism of the Eighties and Nineties and the onset of 'theory' and cultural studies in humanities departments of Australian universities. Referring to the 'internationalist' discourse of the Hawke-Keating years, he suggested, 'these descriptors of economic rationalism have an alarming resemblance to theory's impact ...' (Dixon, 1998: 201). My point here, is that despite the advances of the economy and its intimate relationship with 'cultural' change, agency, as a political gesture, has become so decentred, that delineation, as ethical problem solving, in this instance, has become almost indistinct.

There has been one utilitarian, patronising ruling idea in the Australian literary world: that we Australians should be thankful for what we get as readers and cultural producers. After all, these multinationals are doing us a favour, it is hard to get published, we are a small country, and writing is a kind of voluntary activity staffed by a lumpen-proletariat of semi- amateurs who have little or no bargaining position.

I suggest that this has led us into some equally inefficient and visionless moments that have been hidden underneath the veneer of cultural modernisation and compromised any further advances, even though nationalistic, in the first instance. Such a position also articulates what Benjamin suggested was a central question for intellectuals. Rather than the purely descriptive 'what is a work's position vis- a- vis the production relations of its time', a more thorough question is 'what is its position within them?' (Benjamin, 1977: 87). Speaking specifically of the mainstream theatre of the 1930s, his insights are acute for *our* times. Referring to the perceived consciousness of the writers, musicians and critics:

Believing themselves to be in possession of an apparatus which in reality possesses them, they defend an apparatus over which they no longer have control, which is no longer, as they still believe, a means for the producers but has become a means to be used against the producers. (Benjamin, 1977: 98)

In Australia, writers' centres were established during the 1980s, funded by the Australia Council for the Arts, to cater for an upsurge in literary production after a period of cultural nationalism in the 1970s, as a broad gesture in a time of reduced funding. They have, therefore, become an example of theory and practice spinning out of orbit. Created over 20 years ago as a type of inclusive community arts agenda, they are now in a position where few young people are members and, structurally, much of their income and time goes into keeping themselves afloat, even if they have helped some new writers as a first port of call. Most of them (particularly the metropolitan centres) run a myriad of 'how to' courses, in an effort to increase their cash flow. Writers basically need publication and money and time to write, which writers' centres rarely provide them with. In remote regional areas, they can be useful as meeting places, but overwhelmingly, their model is to promote *their* cultural capital to would-be writers, rather than to readers.

A well-known literary critic and retired academic recently resigned from the board of one centre on being told that the place wasn't interested in readers. This is an extraordinarily 'small' moment, but something strikingly symptomatic of excess 'theory' out of control. Will writers' centres have to change the way they operate without their existing level of state support? A broader question could be, how can any non-for-profit structure survive in the new 'crisis' environment, whether small publishers or writers' centres?

The contemporary success of writers' festivals in Australia is also instructive if one wants to look at links between the economy and cultural formation and commodification. They are a relatively recent contradictory phenomenon in Australia – on the one hand, a celebration that Australian literature has ventured into popularity from obscurity and marginalisation and incorporated a desire for 'community' that is often unrealised in the broader society; on the other hand, they are evidence of increasingly restrictive commodification in Australia and of the intensification of our current moment of celebrity and spectacle.

By this, I mean that it is difficult for new writers and small publishers to gain access to the programmes of the larger metropolitan festivals, because sponsorship and resources are still largely in the hands of large multinational publishers, whose authors dominate. The smaller festivals can still fulfil a 'community' focus, as they don't have the pressure to become 'the biggest and the best'. Even so, there are now festivals in every state capital, coupled with generous state and federal government support, and suggestions that the promotion and publicity at these events is distorting the free market possibilities of the book trade (Galligan, 1998).

There are parallels between writers' centres and festivals in that both structures are showing similar symptoms to the corporatisation in the universities. My point is that the gathering crisis showed (and shows) itself in cultural formations, in these instances, in bureaucratic procedures and the fetishisation of existing structures to the point (as with the global money markets) where efficiency was a minor consideration because vested interests were entrenched.

But are they the only culprits? Aren't we, those involved in creative writing courses (although, I acknowledge that we aren't only trying to create new writers), continuing to ride a late wave of unrequited desire if we don't support publishing initiatives and community engagement as more valuable than writing for peer review journals? Are we in danger of creating insular clubs of creative writing PhDs who feel safe from the world and only validated internally? Few of our students will ever win the Vogel Prize (the major prize for new novelists in Australia), so skills in publishing and editing and the economics of the book trade have to be part of our responsibility. To give credit to where it is due, there are people and departments who are always proactive, my point, though, is that in a climate where we have often felt defensive, more active institutional encouragement within specific departments is essential.

Another challenge is to find new readers and spaces in which to communicate, by supporting existing publications and encouraging new ones, (whether hard copy or digital) particularly outside institutional frameworks so that the insular 'student anthology' model isn't further encouraged. Universities have to behave cooperatively, rather than competitively, in this new environment, because efficiencies can be created through sharing infrastructure and resources, rather than in the kind of inefficient 'competition' that characterised the lead-up to the first wave of the global financial crisis. We may mean well, but if we ignore much of the above, are we not becoming bureaucrats of desire? I have been pushing to also teach Australian literature as well – that is my confession.

References

Bourdieu, P. (1990) *Other Words, Essays Towards a Reflexive Sociology* (M. Adamson, trans.). Stanford, CA: Stanford University Press.

Benjamin, W. (1977) The author as producer. In A. Bostock (trans.) *Understanding Brecht* (pp. 85–103). London: Verso, New Left Books.

Collins, J. (1989) *Uncommon Cultures: Popular Culture and Post-Modernism*. New York and London: Routledge.

Dixon, R. (1998) De-regulating the critical economy: Theory and Australian literary criticism in the 1980s. In A. Bartlett, R. Dixon and C. Lee (eds) *Australian Literature and the Public Sphere* (pp. 194–201). Toowoomba: ASAL.

Edmonds, P. (2005) The romantic ego in the Creative Writing workshop. *TEXT* 9 (2), 3. Online at http://www.textjournal.com.au/oct05/edmonds.htm

Frow, J. (1995) *Cultural Studies & Cultural Power*. Oxford: Clarendon Press.

Galligan, A. (1998) Build the author, sell the book: Marketing the Australian author in the 1990s. In A. Bartlett, R. Dixon and C. Lee (eds) *Australian Literature and the Public Sphere* (pp. 151–158). Toowoomba: ASAL.

Glucksmann, A. (2009) The postmodern financial crisis 'It is true because we say it is' has run its course. *City Journal* 19 (1), 4. Online at http://www.city-journal.org/2009/19_1_snd-postmodern-financial-crisis.html

Healey, S. (2009) The rise of Creative Writing & the new value of creativity. *The Writer's Chronicle* 41 (4), 30–39.

Modjeska, D. (2002) The present in fiction. In *Timepieces* (pp. 201–212). Sydney: Picador.

Moorhouse, F. (2009) Warning: Life can be fatal. *The Australian Literary Review,* 4 February, p. 3. Online at http://www.theaustralian.com.au/news/arts/warning-life-can-be-fatal/story-e6frg8px-1111118683669

Myers, D.G. (1996) *The Elephants Teach: Creative Writing Since 1880*. Englewood Cliffs, NJ: Prentice Hall.

Urry, J. (1990) *The Tourist Gaze: Leisure and Travel in Contemporary Societies*. London: Sage.

Wilding, M. (2002) *Academia Nuts*. Sydney: Wild & Woolley.

9 Creativity, Compromise and Waking Up with the Funding Devil

Mike Harris

In a paper given to the annual conference of the Australian Association of Writing Programs, the editor of this volume, Dominique Hecq, suggested that: 'in the current socio-political climate, creativity is trivialised, commodified and commercialised ...' so that '... the talk is about producing marketable artefacts rather than about the worth of creative writing courses or benefits gained from the ethical and ontological journeys that writing a PhD entails ...' (2008: 1–2), but was there ever a 'socio-political climate' in which the processes we loosely term 'creativity' weren't in some way trivialised, commodified or commercialised? Was there ever a time when that subset of what we call 'creativity' – the thing that universities now call 'Creative Writing', whether undertaken as a PhD or not – went on an exclusively 'ethical and ontological' journey?

Some of the writers most associated with self-sufficient, 'ontologically' individual creativity and with notions of poetry as inherently 'ethical' are probably the early English Romantics. But here is Wordsworth on his motives for writing his ground-breaking *Lyrical Ballads*: 'I published those poems for money and for money alone ... money was of importance to me ... I care little for the praise of any other professional critic, but as it may help me to pudding' (2005: 337). The biographer Richard Holmes (1987: 513, 695) assures us that Shelley wrote his verse play *The Cenci*, because he desperately wanted commercial success; and Tom Mole (2007), in *Byron's Romantic Celebrity*, describes the poet commodifying his own image as mad-bad-sexy Byron almost as effectively as Colonel Parker commodified the image of Elvis Presley, with much the same effect on female fans and personal bank balance. One final example, for now, Joan Hedrick (1994: 136) tells us how Harriet Beecher Stowe (later, and in another medium) only turned to writing because her husband's salary could not support her hitherto total commitment to motherhood and, yet, still, according to

Stowe's son Charles, *Uncle Tom's Cabin* did more to 'pry open' a dominant power than any novel before or since if Abraham Lincoln really *did* declare at their first meeting: 'So you are the little woman who wrote the book that started this great war!' (Stowe, 1911: 203).

In this context, it is probably worth noting that, according to Kathryn Holeywell (2009: 23), the first official writer-in-residence at a British University was the novelist and playwright Angus Wilson, whose term of office eventually led to the setting up of the first creative writing degree in the United Kingdom at the University of East Anglia in 1971. A former graduate student of Wilson's at UEA recalled that 'he (Wilson) was looking for a good post that could bring him a certain amount of money in per year, rather than the difficult job of balancing the books as a novelist'(Sage, cited in Holeywell, 2009: 23). Wilson's somewhat less than idealistic motives are corroborated by Margaret Drabble, in her biography of Wilson, citing the man who interviewed him for the job, the literary academic, Ian Watt: 'Watt described what he had in mind, and Angus listened patiently. Then he asked his own questions, the first of which was "would the position be pensionable?"' (Drabble, 1995: 314).

The intimate relationship between writers, commerce and power has a longer timeline than triumphant postmodern capitalism. When Medieval and Renaissance artists wrote for, and about, the landed aristocracy in exchange for payment in cash or kind, we find that very few of their works fail to praise the truly remarkable human qualities of the paymaster. In this context, the sadly neglected verse of Ewen McTeagle springs unavoidably to mind:

'Upon Reading Chapman's Homer in Selfridges'

Owe gie to me a shillin for some fags
And I'll pay yer back on Thursday.
But if you can wait till Saturday
I'm expecting a divvy from the
Harpenden Building Society.

(Idle, 1971)

If writing for money and truckling to power has been constant in poetry and the novel, what must have been the state of affairs in my own field, *drama,* as it marshalled material forces far more costly than ink, paper, pen and printing press?

The theatre of Arles, in Roman-occupied Gaul, had a capacity of 10,000 and a triple function of distracting, impressing and culturally assimilating the conquered. The importance of theatre to the Roman Imperium is best appreciated on-site. The Theatre, near Nimes in the Gard department of southern France, was built even before the city's Coliseum. Both dwarfed all the other buildings in the Roman city and, even ruined, are still by far the biggest in the old city centre. The classicist David Wiles notes how the enormously expensive theatrical presentations were funded by wealthy Roman citizens, and we can be certain that they allowed writers scant freedom to question too hard the blessings of empire, attack the ethics of their sponsors or go on ontological journeys of subjective creative discovery (1997: 49–65).

Moving on 1200 years or so, it seems unlikely that the anonymous writers and improvisers of medieval 'Mystery Plays' would have kept their jobs if they had tried to add the tale of 'Mack the Manichean' or 'Christ the Cathar' to the cycle. 'Mystery Plays' were part theological propaganda and part sanctioned safety-valve, through which dangerous plebeian energies were released into slapstick, irreverence, carnival and riot. Once a more effective means of psychic policing had been devised – Protestantism – the 'Mysteries' and other such public celebrations were slowly suppressed, as Wiles (1997), Chambers (1963) and Ehrenreich (2007) recount.

And just to make perfectly clear that it isn't just writers in this craven creative relationship with *pouvoir,* we only have to look at some of the greatest works of Renaissance painters. In these, we not infrequently find the corpulent figure of a Medici banker prominent amongst the crowds waiting to adore the baby Jesus. A good example of such 'sponsor placement' is Benozzo Gonzelli's fresco, *Procession of the Magi,* in the Medici Palace in Florence. Gonzelli's paymasters, Piero and Cosimo Medici, are clearly visible, queuing to see the son of God, 1459 years before they were born. This teleportation of two early modern bankers into the birth scene of Christ surely puts into the shade the paid-for 21st century appearance, by the millionaire businessman and self-publicist Richard Branson, in the James Bond film *Casino Royale?*

Sadly, it seems that writers have always been more McTeagle than Mandelstam (1975) (whose courageous – or foolhardy – satirical poem about Stalin is thought to have provoked his arrest, imprisonment and ultimate death).

The tainted dollar paid to scribblers in the globalised 'knowledge economy' is not the perversion of a norm, but rather the norm itself. It follows from this that the many different processes we call 'creativity' arise within, and from, this unequal relationship with power, cannot easily be detached from it and probably never could. Therefore, pending some revolution in which all inequalities of power are successfully abolished, the individual writer will have to go on her 'ontological creative journey' within that relationship and try to smuggle her oppositional ethics into creative work *despite* it. Either that, or resolve never to publish, perform or broadcast.

It is certainly possible to argue that the obstacles and limits imposed by power and commerce (and their attendant ideologies) can provide the friction that sparks creativity. For example, in the 1940s and 1950s, the British playwright Terence Rattigan embedded his illegal homosexuality into apparently heterosexual dramas of respectable middle class angst. In his best work, for example, *The Deep Blue Sea*, there is an atmosphere of suppressed tension, behind a facade of terribly British respectability. This tension is felt, by contemporary critic Reballato (1995), to arise from his attempt to enact the legally un-actable and not be caught in the act.

This is not to suggest that all 'creativity' is *ipso facto* sourced in, or facilitated by, repression, nor that it always sets out to provoke power. 'Creativity', more often than not, has no problems with commerce and power and profits from the relationship. Most British playwrights complied easily with the theatrical censorship that only ended in 1968. The 18th century society portraits of Sir Joshua Reynolds and the self-commodified 20th century works of Andy Warhol sit well on, respectively, the walls of aristocratic mansions and corporate boardrooms. And John Sutherland (1978, 2006) has amply evidenced the many ways in which the intimate relationship between novelist and capitalist publisher in 19th century Britain was instrumental in shaping the form's most creative products.

Rather than claim for all 'creativity' the power to 'pry open the strategies set up by the dominant power' (Certeau, cited in Hecq, 2008: 4), it might be more accurate to say that the relationship between writers, commerce and power is perpetually shifting between assent, dissent, compromise, resistance and happy commercial compliance at different times and for different reasons.

By way of illustration, I now want to describe something of the process involved in a play I wrote and directed in response to the suicide bombing of the London Tube system on July 7th 2005 by violent Islamic extremists in which 56 people died and 700 were seriously injured. This play was eventually funded by a government I regarded as deeply culpable in provoking those bombings.

Shortly after the bombings, I was sitting in a pub with Qaz Hamid, a Muslim actor and friend, working with GW – the Theatre in Education [TIE] Company I set up 25 years ago and for which I still regularly write and direct. Like everyone else in the country, we were depressed and angry, though not for exactly identical reasons.

We felt the same about the death and suffering, of course. We agreed that decades of rubbing-along and putting-up-with, by ordinary people from all United Kingdom cultures, had just gone up in smoke (*wrong*). We agreed there was going to be a serious white backlash (*mostly wrong*) and that our government would use the threat of terror to introduce repressive legislation that would target Muslims, reduce the freedoms of everybody and ratchet up its drive for a globalism-compliant, ID-carded and consumer-surveillance society (*dead right*). After that, we diverged. Qaz thought the suicide-bombers weren't 'real' Muslims (*I disagreed: they weren't representative, but they were Muslims, just like George Bush is a Christian, but probably not quite what Christ had in mind*); that Islam was peace (*mostly right*); and Jihad was spiritual struggle, not violent struggle (*I discovered later that it can be either or both, depending on circumstances*).

For my part, I was angry because I'd regarded the bombers as my people: working-class lads from the North of England with older relatives who'd worked in textile factories just like mine; they'd played outside in terraced streets in the 1970s and 1980s, just as I had in the early 1960s; and, on their behalf, I had spent 40-odd years arguing fiercely against the bog standard working-class racism of my old dad (amongst others).[1] I felt betrayed. Not rational and not fair, but there you go. Bombs have that effect on people.

Anyway, it was a pile of shit that I wanted to help shovel away, and the only thing I know about is writing and directing plays. So, a little later, I met in another pub with Dave Jones – one of GW's two actor-managers – and we hammered out a proposal for a TIE project, more or less on the back of a cigarette packet. At this stage, it had no story and no characters, no 'creative' content at all, in fact. Just the notion that we wanted to make a play that would get young people talking about the difficult issues that arise when a small number of people from a minority culture try to systematically murder people of all cultures in the name of their religion.

Dave hawked it around funders and, roughly a year later, we had enough money to research, write and rehearse a script and tour a dozen pilot shows.

At this point, some back story is necessary: GW has been doing issue-based theatre for young people since the mid-1980s. Never flush with funding, they have a lean-mean house style: short fast-moving scenes, tiny casts (maximum four, doubling and trebling characters), minimal props and maximum acting virtuosity with no off-stage and no blackouts – everything happens in full view of the audience, like cooking food at a good restaurant. Most importantly, after each performance, the actors come back in character so young audiences can interrogate them. The theatrical style is modelled on 1970s political theatre, the techniques of which I'd loved, but whose frequent predictability – always some variant of 'it's the class struggle comrade' or 'it's patriarchy, sister' – I'd hated. This was partly because predictability is dull, but also because it ensured that the work mainly played to shrink-wrapped audiences of the pre-converted, like political ready-meals.

GW is mostly funded by social agencies and charities, for example, health services, social housing associations, The Brook Pregnancy Advise Service and so on – worthy organisations looking for a novel way of getting their more or less commendable messages across. Occasionally, they mistakenly seem to want a walking-talking leaflet in which young people are piously invited to become social progressives overnight. Then we explain that they already have leaflets, and if the leaflets had been working, they needn't have employed us at great expense (or words more tactfully to the same effect). Our plan is not to lecture, but to give young people real plays about complex situations that don't have easy (or any) answers – to grip them with the plot, make 'em laugh, cry, think and discuss – and then make up their own minds.

Sometimes, though, the worrying social-worker types were right. We'd got something factually wrong, or out of kilter or their suggestion suddenly made a character more complex or offered a more interesting story. Then we were glad to incorporate their ideas in the script. Eventually, we formalised this uneasy, but fruitful, collaborative tango. Now we always set up an advisory group (AG) at the very start of a project. It generally has representatives from funders, social agencies, local people, youths etc. depending on the project, but they have to have some investment (not just monetary) in making the thing work. Since 1985, GW Theatre has toured 24 new plays to half a million young people, mostly in schools, colleges, community centres and youth clubs across the country.

Back to the plot: Dave Jones now has pilot funding for an untitled, unwritten 'extremist show'. A big chunk comes from 'The Pears Foundation' – a charity endowed by a multi-millionaire business family. Another substantial sum comes from Oldham Metropolitan Borough Council. Oldham used to be a thriving mill town, but it's now seriously post-industrial. Its politicians are using government 'social inclusion' funds to address the causes of the race riots that occurred there in 2001. During the riots, police, fascists, young people, poor whites and Asians (that is to say, in British parlance, people of Pakistani and Bangladeshi heritage) clashed violently. The council's plan is worthy, if a bit late. So we meet the head of their 'Social Inclusion Unit'. He gives me an initial list of possible sources for information, and I get on with interviewing, while he puts an advisory group together to our agreed specification.

I find it pays not to have too many fixed ideas at the start of a project, but I'm not a blank sheet, especially not on this most controversial of issues, upon which I have views:

(1) I don't want the show just to be about British Muslin extremists. I want it to be about white British extremists, too. One of the multiple causes of the 2001 Oldham riots had been the crypto fascist British National Party stoking race-hate fires in the borough's ghettoised Punjabi, Bangladeshi and poor-white communities (BBC News, 2001). The far right goose-stepped itself into the play.

(2) I know it has to have teenage relationships at its heart, because young audiences – Muslim or otherwise – are rather more interested in sex and love than they are in Islamic extremism and crypto-fascism, at least, until they're hooked.

(3) I am going to get something in about the British Government's own responsibility for the 7/7 tube bombings. In a word: Iraq. At the time, Prime Minister Tony Blair was denying any connection, like a psychopathic child caught red-handed with blood from the neighbour's cat all over its face – not a good role model for impressionable youth.

(4) I'm not going to censor the illiberal views of poor whites or poor Muslims, however unacceptable. You don't challenge opinions by ignoring them or by patronising people who are struggling to do the right thing, albeit in ways of which you disapprove.
1.

I now start research, e.g. reading *The Koran*, Islamic history, getting up to speed on the recent past of the British far Right and interviewing groups of young people – white and Asian, plus youth workers, politicians etc. I ask them all the same question: what should I put in the play? I then digest their suggestions, add a page about how they might get into the script and take the results to the first AG meeting. This group includes several young people: a young white youth worker and three well-informed 'social inclusion' workers – two Asian (male and female) and a white woman who is a single mother living with a mixed-race child in one of the poorer white areas of town which has active BNP members (one of whom she knows and whom I eventually meet for a drink and a most interesting discussion).

The most important thing about this advisory group is that nobody wants us to avoid the difficult issues. The local riots and the London tube bombings have convinced everyone – local politicians included – that you have to say it how it is if you want to have a chance of stopping it being like it was. So nobody balks at dramatising white resentment of Asian drug dealers on their estates or the widespread white perception that 'the Asians are getting all the council's money' (not true, but understandable when you see new schools and houses going up, and your social housing estate has had a fiver spent on it over 10 years). Nobody tries to stop me dramatising Asian resentment at the unlikelihood of getting a job when an equally qualified white is up for it or the widespread conviction that the government's foreign policy is deliberately anti-Islamic. Nobody tries to stop me putting on stage 'Neville Parkin', the Jew-Asian-and-black-hating local leader of the 'National Democratic Party', or the pro-terror 'Sheik Google' – the 'Ayatollah of Cyber-Space'. And nobody blinks an eye when we let these two say what they *really* believe. Now, remember: this play is not going on at the Royal Court Theatre in London (where you can have Osama Bin Laden and George Bush simulating anilingus and nobody complains). It's going into secondary schools and tertiary colleges. So this advisory group has *cajones*.

The only major objection at the first meeting is to my suggested story, which is: Tony and Jessica were good friends with Ali and his sister Sara at college, but fell out when Ali put Steve in hospital for going out with Sara. Ali went down for 'grievous bodily harm' after Jessica (formerly Steve's and now Ali's girlfriend) shopped him to the police. Steve is now helping Neville Parkin to organise an all-white march through an Asian area, and Ali – mentored by Sheik Google – is organising the brothers to stop it. Jessica, now a journalist for a Right-wing British tabloid, is looking up her old flames so she can get a scoop on the race riot her editor hopes will happen if the march goes ahead. Meanwhile, Ali's younger brother Mo is being manipulated by the Sheik to burn down a mosque so he can blame it on the whites, whilst Steve's younger brother, Karl, is going to torch the old church hall Steve has done up for senior citizens so that Parkin can blame it on the Asians.

Some AG members think this is all too 'soapy' and melodramatic and thus diverts attention away from the real issues. I feel it provides the necessary human focus for *dramatising* the real issues. My audiences watch soap. Good soap is good drama, and, in any case, you start where people are and take them somewhere else. This was too often the problem with 1970s political theatre. It assumed the audience was already there, and then took it on a journey back to the same place.

But we're getting nowhere, so Dave diplomatically suggests that they let me try it in a first draft, and if it doesn't work for them, then we'll re-think. I go away to write that first draft.

I do more research. I web-surf and read more than I interview, because time is short, and websites and books are the compressed time of people who know more than I ever can. Some of the texts consulted are listed in 'works cited' at the end of this chapter. Interviewing people is essential, of course. You get a feel you don't get from books. Anecdotes give scenes and dialogue and characters and themes, and people always snowball you onto someone else interesting to interview.

So, all the time, you're accumulating material. It's crucial to have too much, I find. That way, I don't run out of ideas when the deadline presses. My subconscious is a fat greedy builder who requires a lot of pies or he down-tools (this is an analysis not given by Freud or Lacan). I turn the rough one-page outline into a long scene-by-scene breakdown for myself. This means I don't have to write scenes in order. I can move onto an easy one when I get stuck on a hard one. Then, with luck, when I go back to the hard one, the builder's done the job in the back of my head whilst I was away. Manipulating the unconscious is a practical writing skill which has serious commercial implications: you can't afford to get writer's block if, as a result, neither you nor the actors get paid.

I melt the issues into a plot along standard neo-Aristotelian lines: action, twists, reversals, more action, recognitions, unexpected pay-off and catharsis, but with an open-ending. None of the four central characters are completely reconciled in the end. None of them tries to suggest that the profound differences between them are easy to bridge. Nobody suggests there's any decent alternative but to try.

I then speed-write a draft – it stinks. I've learnt not to commit suicide at this stage as it usually ends up more-or-less competent, so I hold my nose and re-write. I hack away the smelliest bits with a conceptual cleaver. Great rotting pixelated chunks are thrown away to the ravening dogs of cyber space.

At the next AG meeting, we read it aloud. Mostly, they think it's good. This is partly because they do (probably) and, partly, because they're now out of their comfort zone and in my script. I go to a 'final' draft. I show it to the AG – thumbs up. We go into three weeks of rehearsals, followed by a dress rehearsal for the AG and an invited audience of local school kids. We also practice the post-show 'hot-seating' with the audience. As a result, things change. In this localised space, the audience has considerable power to criticise and make suggestions. We do a dozen or so pilot shows to schools, workers and potential funders. More changes. Things can always change. Change is good (when it's not appalling).

Dave gets more funding on the back of the pilots. Over the next year, it tours every town in the Greater Manchester conurbation and goes into every single secondary school and college in Oldham itself. There is blanket coverage of the target market in these areas, better than 'Big Brother'.

Kids interrogate the characters hard during the hot-seating:

S1: 'Why are you on opposite sides?'
S2: 'Why don't you work together?'
S3: 'Why don't you shake hands and make-up?'

S4: 'Ali – why did you beat Tony up for going out with your sister when you were going out with Jessica?

S5: 'Steve – why did you get mixed up with the National democrats? Aren't they a bit racist?'

Sometimes the characters function as stand-ins for their school-mates, parents or whoever, and they ask questions they'd otherwise be scared to, for fear of being called racist or 'Paki lover' or 'Coconut'.

That's the ideal, and it happens a lot. But then again, sometimes nobody asks anything. Perhaps they are cathartically stunned by the drama or, more likely, just eager to get out at break.

Once, just once, in what is now several hundred performances, a member of the audience objected strongly; he stood up and shouted as soon as the show ended:

How dare you come here! Where is this play from? Who do you think you are, who wrote this play, who do you think you are saying these things, what are you doing? You don't know anything. You cannot say these things, it is an insult to me and an insult to Islam, people do not call each other 'paki' in this country it is illegal,[2] people do not say these things, you cannot talk about the Quran in this way, it is wrong and if people knew you were doing this they would bomb you!

The actors then tried to engage with him, but the man walked out. Afterwards, members of the mainly Muslim audience came up to express support for the play and disapproval of our angry guest. The point being: you can't win 'em all.

Meanwhile, Dave is applying for money from Her Majesty's Government, which is distributing millions in PVE (Preventing Violent Extremism) money to try and make good the very situation Her Majesty's Government helped to provoke with its imperialist foreign policy. GW gets £245,000 (AUS$489,000, at the time of writing) to tour the show nationally for three years.

Dave's overjoyed. I'm under-joyed.

In my head, the PVE money's tainted. In Dave's head, it's lots of money for an honest project that manifestly works. And 'nobody made me change a line I didn't want to, did they?' And, 'you're not going to, even if they ask, are you?' (*Am I not? Do I know?*) What I do know is that I want to seriously engage with some British Asian citizens who think their government is a cross between Satan and Richard-the-Lion-Heart and being seen as the user-friendly front end for that government's dubious anti-terrorist policy isn't going to help that. Also, frankly, it's personally embarrassing for my long-term fantasy of permanent oppositionalism.

Then it gets worse.

We're booked to do a show in the Houses of Parliament (not in the Chamber, over the road, in a brand-new sky scraper). We don't know it, but it's the week that the Home Secretary and Hazel Blears, then the Minister for Communities and Local Government, are launching 'Contest 2' – the government's second attempt at an anti-terrorist programme that doesn't alienate the entire Muslim population of the 'United' Kingdom. As Hundal (2009) reports: Contest 2 includes a plan to get 30,000 shop workers to inform on their fellow citizens (*Rule Snitchtania!*). Hazel Blears' spin-doctors tell Dave that she's going to do a national press conference immediately after the show, with Dave fielding questions alongside her. Dave is pleased about the prospect of national publicity, there's been precious little of that for the last 25 years, but I'm beyond embarrassment. I'm looking for a hole to crawl into while I eat my own face. Then, for her own reasons, Blears calls off the press conference, and I'm both relieved, but also disappointed. I don't enquire too much into the source of this disappointment (which is probably more or less craven). Then, just before the show, I peek in the performance space, and Dave is setting up a photo call: the actors, some delightful white and Asian school kids down from Oldham, Hazel Blears and me. There's no way I'm being photographed next to the former 'Minister for Surveillance' with a shit-eating grin on my face. So what do I do? Well . . .

I hide in a broom cupboard.

(OK, it was a room, but it was small and had brooms).

I hide in a broom cupboard to avoid being in the same photo as a politician of whose politics I disapprove. I was 57 at the time. To this, I had come. Like the drunken local hack in my script who drivels on 'I used to be a socialist', before falling on his face.

La lutta continua!

This farcical anecdote is not included in this paper purely for light relief. It is also there to make a serious point. This being that the space available, most of the time, for most writers to 'pry open the strategies of the dominant power' is about the size of a broom cupboard. However, cramped though that space is, it's crucially important, and it certainly doesn't come as a free gift with creativity itself. It has to be made, or negotiated or fought for.

Take the relationship described above with our 'advisory group'. They've got the money, the experience or the inside knowledge, we've got a particular sort of expertise. I incorporated their perfectly good suggestions into the script partly so I could schmooze them into accepting a plot they weren't keen on – *quid pro quo*. This is one of the ways the power gets equalised in negotiation. Contrary to a currently fashionable emphasis in literary theory[3], collaboration isn't the opposite of, or a benign alternative to, bourgeois individualism or the naked exercise of power: it *is* the naked exercise of power and, in collaboration, *all* individualism comes to the fore. You have to argue your case, fight your corner, define who you are in opposition to, and as part of, a group. Effective collaborations come out of groups of *individuals* contesting power and then trying to hold it in balance. The AG let me try my idea: I incorporated theirs. Because of this, we were collectively responsible if some man or woman in a suit decides that someone else with power, money or influence might get offended. Thus, my back was covered.

Collaboration is political creativity.

And then again, the most powerful player in this game – the government of Great Britain and Northern Ireland – *didn't* ask me to change a word of the script or withdraw funds, despite characters in that script voicing clear criticisms of both its foreign and domestic policies. One possible explanation of this is that the project was already, and obviously, working before they got in on the act and Her Majesty's Government was keen to put a human face on its anti-terrorist policy. Another, perhaps, is that individuals in government aren't an anonymous 'hegemonic' mass. Before she went over to the dark side, the minister, Hazel Blears, was a young Left-wing councillor in Salford, where poverty levels were, and still are, high. And so during the discussion after the Parliament show, an audience member asked me why I'd given equal prominence to the white 'extremist', when it was Muslim 'extremists' who posed the immediate threat to life and limb. By this time, the latest capitalist downturn was just kicking in and a quote from Bertolt Brecht sprung into my head and out of my mouth: 'though the world stood up and stopped the bastard, the bitch that bore him is in heat again' (Brecht, 2002).

The quote above is the final line from Brecht's (2002) *The Resistible Rise of Auro Uri* and refers, of course, to the constant danger of fascist revival in times of economic depression. As I said this (wondering if I might get my wrist slapped for publicly using the word 'bitch' in such a derogatory context), I look over and see Hazel Blears nodding in apparently intense agreement. This is a Minister of State in a government that has not only created the biggest gap between rich and poor in my country since the Second World War, but, with its hands-off attitude to City of London bankers, helped cause the latest capitalist downturn to which I referred (and which had, just recently, provided me with a card-carrying fascist as my duly elected representative in Europe) – this Minister is now giving the assenting nod to the wit and wisdom of Bertolt Brecht, communist. The levels of operative unreality all round here are considerable, but the serious point is that 'hegemony', like all other power, is ultimately exercised by individuals, not concepts, and individuals have weak spots, sore spots, politically sentimental spots and sometimes, on the margin, when they have a broom-cupboard of their own to wiggle around in, just sometimes, they act against their collectively hegemonic interests, but not often.

It is, perhaps, only in the (still) relatively protected zone of Western academia that creativity can be imagined as, in any way, 'ontologically' or ethically separable from a deeply compromised process that has always been as ignoble as principled. But because it is often ignoble, that does not mean that it sometimes can't be principled, and sometimes, it can be both at the same time.

Notes

(1)   The 'ordinariness' of the bombers has been much commented on. Begin with: http://news.bbc.co.uk/2/shared/spl/hi/uk/05/london_blasts/investigation/html/bombers.stm

(2)   It isn't, in fact, illegal to call Asians 'Paki' in the United Kingdom and, unfortunately, some people still do, including some of the characters in my play.

(3)   See, for example, Pope (2005) *Creativity: Theory, History, Practice* (pp. 3–33). London: Routledge.

References

Abbas, T. (ed.) (2007) *Islamic Political Radicalism*. Edinburgh: Edinburgh University Press.

Ahmed, N.M. (2005) *The London Bombings: an Independent Enquiry*. London: Duckworth.

BBC News (2001) Race 'Segregation' Caused Riots, *BBC News*, 11 December, online article, accessed 21 August 2009. http://news.bbc.co.uk/2/hi/uk_news/england/1702799.stm.

BBC News (2005) Warning of 'Iraq Extremism Link', *BBC News*, 28 August, online article, accessed 21 August 2009. http://news.bbc.co.uk/2/hi/uk_news/politics/4192188.stm.

Brecht, B. (2002) *The Resistible Rise of Arturo Uri*. London: Methuen.

Certeau, M. de (1984) *The Practice of Everyday Life* (S. Rendall, trans.). Berkeley, CA: University of California Press.

Chambers, E.K. (1963) *The Medieval Stage*. Oxford: Oxford University Press.

Donohue, J.J. and Esposito, J.L. (2007) *Islam in Transition: Muslim Perspectives* (2nd edn). Oxford: Oxford University Press.

Drabble, M. (1995) *Angus Wilson, a Biography*. London: Minerva.

Ehrenreich, B. (2007) *Dancing in the Streets: a History of Collective Joy*. London: Granta.

Gove, M. (2006) *Celsius 7/7*. London: Weidenfeld and Nicholson.

GW Theatre Company, website, accessed 21 June 2009. http://www.gwtheatre.com/.

Hecq, D. (2008) Banking on Creativity? [Presentation]. *Paper presented at the 13th conference of the Australian Association of Writing Programs (AAWP) Conference*. Sydney. Online at http://aawp.org.au/files/Hecq_2008.pdf.

Hedrick, J.D. (1994) *Harriet Beecher Stowe: A Life*. Oxford: Oxford University Press.

Holeywell, K. (2009) The origins of a Creative Writing programme at the University of East Anglia, 1963–1966. *New Writing: The International Journal for the Practice and Theory of Creative Writing* 6 (1), 15–25.

Holmes, R. (1987) *Shelley: the Pursuit*. London: Penguin.

Hundal. S. (2009) Is Contest 2 Talking to the Right People? *Guardian Online*, 24 March, accessed 21 August 2009. http://www.guardian.co.uk/commentisfree/belief/2009/mar/23/counterterrorism-contest-2-muslim

Hussain, E. (2007) *The Islamist*. London: Penguin.

Idle, E. (ed.) (1971) *Monty Python's Big Red Book*. London: Methuen.

Mandelstam, N. (1975) *Hope Against Hope*. London: Penguin.

Mole, T. (2007) *Byron's Romantic Celebrity*. London: Palgrave Macmillan.

O'Neill, S. and McGrory, D. (2006) *The Suicide Factory: Abu Hamza and the Finsbury Park Mosque*. London: Harper Perennial.

Oldham Council, government website, accessed 18 August 2008. http://www.oldham.gov.uk/

Omaar, R. (2007) *Only Half of Me: British and Muslim, the Conflict Within*. London: Viking.

Percival, J. (and agencies) (2009) New Strategy Will Train Shop and Hotel Managers to Tackle Terorist Threats. *Guardian Online*, 24 March, accessed 24 September 2009. http://www.guardian.co.uk/uk/2009/mar/24/anti-terror-al-qaida-weapons.

Phillips, M. (2006) *Londonistan: How Britain is Creating a Terror State Within*. London: Gibson Square.

Pope, R. (2005) *Creativity: Theory, History, Practice*. Oxford: Routledge.

Rattigan, T. (1995) *The Deep Blue Sea*. London: Nick Hern Books.

Rebellato, D. (ed.) (1995) Introduction. In T. Rattigan, *The Deep Blue Sea* (pp. xi–xix). London: Nick Hern Books.

Stowe, C.E. (1911) *Harriet Beecher Stowe: The Story of Her Life*. Boston: Kessinger Publishing.

Sutherland, J. (1978) *Victorian Novelists and Publishers*. Chicago, MI: University of Chicago Press.

Sutherland, J. (2006) *Victorian Fiction: Writers, Publishers, Readers*. Basingstoke: Palgrave Macmillan.

Wiles, D. (1997) Theatre in Roman and Christian Europe. In J.R. Brown (ed.) *The Oxford Illustrated History of Theatre* (pp. 49–92). Oxford: Oxford University Press.

Wordsworth, W. and Coleridge, S.T. (eds) (2005) *Lyrical Ballads*. London: Routledge.

10 Entering the Fictitious: A Play in Two Acts

Christopher Lappas

Characters:

WRITER: published author and academic in his late forties

NURSE / WIFE (played by one actor): hospital nurse / academic and spouse of Writer

STUDENT 1 / STAGE TECHNICIAN (played by one actor): university student and stencil artist / stage technician

STUDENT 2 / WRITER AS A YOUNG MAN (played by one actor): university student and stencil artist / main character in his younger years

Act One

The protagonist, known throughout the play as WRITER, is a published novelist and academic, aged, in his late forties. He is convalescing in bed at home after a surgical procedure. Otherwise healthy, recent medical concerns have caused him to re-evaluate his outlook on life and to question his writing. Significantly, this comes at a time when he is thinking about a paper which needs to be written for a conference he has been invited to attend. The bed, resembling the type found in a hospital, is situated just left of centre stage, the head end closer to stage left. A suspended window frame is visible towards the rear centre stage. An old desk is positioned stage right: it has one leg missing, books stacked under one side keep it standing. It is piled high with papers and books, a computer and other objects (mentioned within the play). The desk is in darkness. WRITER, flat on his back in bed with a book in his hands, stops reading to listen to a couple of STUDENTS carrying shoulder bags. They pause just outside his window.

STUDENT 1: Why bother?

STUDENT 2: Because of the bits in between.

STUDENT 1: Exactly, so why not forget about all the ceremonial and superficial stuff and go straight for the good bits? Go for what's pleasurable and chuck the rest, I say.

STUDENT 2: Because it's all part of the experience. It's like a layer of smooth ice-cream between two biscuits: you persevere with the boring cardboard-like biscuit, because you know it holds the creamy stuff inside.

STUDENT 1: As I said, why bother?

STUDENT 2: *[frustrated]* The reward; the satisfaction; the challenge.

STUDENT 1: *[mockingly]* Pfff, all a waste of time. I can have ten pleasures while you're still trying to experience one.

STUDENT 2: But your pleasure is only a pleasure because of the things around it. The bland cardboard biscuit not only holds the ice cream together, it gives it substance and meaning. The trouble with you is that you just want to have your cake and eat it, too.

STUDENT 1: You've got a thing about desserts today – that 'Foodscapes' lecture in Media Arts this morning must have really affected you.

STUDENT 2: Nah, I wasn't there. I've decided to drop it.

STUDENT 1: I saw you there, in the back row.

PASER-BY 2: Well, you were seeing things. I hadn't even left home by then.

STUDENT 1: You sure?

STUDENT 2: Of course, I'm sure *[they push each other jokingly]*. Anyway, the way to stay happy is to have contrast. If all you do is swim around in the cream, you won't appreciate it for long. You need contrast and comparisons.

STUDENT 1: Comparisons! I compare all the time: one good thing with another. If something isn't up to scratch, I stop doing it. I don't think we should put up with any of that 'life wasn't meant to be easy' crap – that's what spoils the good times. How can you feel good if you're thinking about how painful things can be? And that's the problem with thinking: it makes life unpleasant and causes bad things to happen. I want pure cream.

STUDENT 2: So what's your solution – burying your head in the sand wearing blinkers?

STUDENT 1: Why not? *[Slight pause]* Hey, that reminds me, you know what I find bizarre? We were talking about The Myth of Sisyphus in Literature this afternoon–

STUDENT 2: *[interrupting]* I know. I was there.

STUDENT 1: I thought you dropped it?

STUDENT 2: I was in the back row. It was all about Sisyphus and his fate: condemned by the gods to roll that boulder up the hill.

STUDENT 1: *[pointing through the window into the room]* Hey, what about through there?

Both peer in through the window and look around.

STUDENT 2: Yeah, why not.

They climb through the window, look around further, left and right, like two criminals. They remove their shoulder bags, take out home-made stencils and begin taping them to the rear wall, making a long sign.

STUDENT 2: Never-ending rolling: pushing it all the way to the top where it comes tumbling down again, but he has his moments . . . he keeps trying.

STUDENT 1: Too much hoping for tomorrow and not enough living for today, that's the problem. And the irony – the big bloody side-splitting clown-faced joking irony – is that every tomorrow takes us one step closer to our death.

STUDENT 2: I agree. It's absurd. Everything we do is absurd. But if you'd listened today, you'd have heard the bit about realising that absurdity, how it can set you free. That's the key: keep on trying, no matter how futile it all seems. Otherwise, you're lost, lost to some moribund lifelessness. Stagnation.

STUDENT 1: *[questioning]* Hmmm, I still think what's really absurd is that we even *try* to understand.

They place masks on their faces and remove cans of spray paint from their bags. They begin to spray their sign, working quickly and systematically. As they reach the end of their spraying, WRITER, attempting to make himself more comfortable, begins to reposition his pillows and bedding. With difficulty, he only barely succeeds.

WRITER: Sisyphus and his fate – condemned by the gods to an eternal struggle. That's one way to look at fate, but that's too simple, too clean. We always want a dust-free explanation.

Hearing WRITER'S voice, the two STUDENTS are startled. Removing their masks, they spin to face the bed.

STUDENT 1: Who's that?

STUDENT 2: *[only mildly concerned]* Ah, just some old guy.

STUDENT 1: You frightened us, old feller.

WRITER: A feller is someone who chops down trees. I prefer to see myself as a sower of seeds.

STUDENT 1: I think he followed us from the pub.

STUDENT 2: *[peering closely]* Hey, Professor, is that you? *[Brief pause]* I'm in Comparative Literature 101.

STUDENT 1: *[now also scrutinising WRITER]* Hey, haven't I seen you on YouTube – doing that interview? You walked out. You were really pissed off. The questions really got to you. *[Turning to STUDENT 2]* Yeah, it's him, for sure. He was discussing one of his novels – the one that was . . . the one that caused all that commotion. A whole heap of people – parents – wanted it banned.

STUDENT 2: *[lowering his voice]* And he teaches me Comparative Literature, so cool it.

WRITER: Don't mind me, boys – just passing through.

STUDENT 1: Ain't we all, Professor!

After a quiet moment, WRITER raises his hand and tears open an envelope to read a letter. The two STUDENTS, turning back to their work, begin peeling off the stencils. After skimming through the letter, WRITER lets his hand drop. He speaks aloud to himself.

WRITER: Invited to speak, yet again. One of the staff members must have read 'The Writing Game' or seen the title perhaps and presumed I had something to say about the business of writing. Timely, I suppose, given that I've been lying here, in this bed, trying to forget the pain caused by all those years of fighting for one cause or another. What is it this time? *[He raises his hands and straightens the page to read.]* Oh, yes, 'The Desirability and Sustainability of the Creative Market'. *[He lets the letter drop to the ground.]* Hmm, what is this quagmire that I seem to have strayed into? *[His tone becomes that of a poet or lecturer reciting the classics.]* Fate has twisted its tentacles around my feeble limbs and dragged me into a hostile place without light. But the landscape is not unfamiliar to me, that is for sure. I should be writing with a flurry of creativity, succumbing to the intoxicating Muse. Instead, I have been relegated to the role of scribe. I am a note-taker, a spectator of other people's lives. But survival must come first. Yes, and what a horrid and bitter scavenger survival makes of us.

A brief trumpet call is heard echoing from the distance.

WRITER: Ah! Duty calls.

WRITER carefully reaches to a side table and takes his glasses and puts them on. Slowly, he reaches for a cup and drinks through a straw. He looks up towards the two STUDENTS as the last part of the stencil is removed and the words are revealed. The audience sees clearly the graphic work: there is a phrase, 'Death to the Audience', followed by an image, a cartoon-like depiction of a bomb with a burning fuse. As the two STUDENTS begin packing up, WRITER takes a small notepad and pencil and begins to write.

WRITER: Guests, students, and fellow academics and writers ... *[frustrated]* No, no, that won't do. *[Using the pencil, he scratches out the words on the pad.]*
It is an honour to be amongst ... No! *[He also crosses out these lines.]*
[Spoken without writing now.] Straight into it – that is best. Dispense with the preliminaries. *[A thoughtful pause before, again, writing.]* This paper is titled: Entering the Fictitious.

Writing enthusiastically to begin with, he soon becomes lost in his words, gradually writing less and less.

WRITER: I believe that we kill off a little piece of ourselves each time we write. That is our job, our business, at least, when we are doing it well. We have a need to exorcise things that niggle at us, sometimes some very personal issues, other times, more global concerns, but all very human in the end. I believe strongly in the cathartic benefits of writing. A colleague of mine once said to me, 'If I didn't write, I think I would go completely mad'.

As he speaks the next few lines, slowly his hands and the pad begin to come to rest on his chest. The lights dim to a soft, warm glow.

WRITER: In this bed, my thoughts drift; it is difficult to keep track of their skittish and giddy antics. Before they escape like naughty imps, I catch what I can of them, jotting down snippets onto this pad and onto scraps of paper that I hold in my palm at arm's length before tired eyes. I'm forced to lie flat on my back to minimise the chance of haemorrhaging, I am told. My thoughts slip into the past; somehow a connection exists between the then and now – past, present and future merge like three-coloured jelly in a warm pot, dancing in a colourful swirl.

As the two STUDENTS begin to leave via the window, STUDENT 2 turns and looks at WRITER'S desk. He hands his bag to his friend, who is now outside the window, and goes to the desk and sits.

WRITER: I spiral into the memory of a time not long ago, a time I prefer to forget. I was still developing the craft of writing. I am still developing the craft of writing. Back then, I hadn't even earned the title of scribe, let alone author.

Two moments – then and now – locked in a kindred exchange. The passing of time: inconsequential. Moments alive, extensions of my flesh, of my mind – they are symbiotic; they feed into each other, one nourishing the other.

A tightness in my chest, fear and insurmountable challenges, trying to distract and diffract and envelope, but unable to curb my desire to write. The will to write is a powerful force.

My arms on my chest, my eyelids heavy – a gentle synthesis. I see myself 15 or 20 years ago, sitting at my desk, my makeshift desk – that old, round, weather-beaten pine table found in a shed. Books are stacked as a leg under one side to keep it aloft. Pens and pencils roll conveniently into my lap, the table rocking and swaying to the rhythm of the words. I recede with the rhythm, going back, going all the way back there.

Lights fade to black on the bed as lights fade to bright on the desk.

STUDENT 2 picks up a pencil and shifts pages on the desk carefully, becoming WRITER AS A YOUNG MAN. He takes a match and lights a candle before beginning to type into his computer as he speaks. He stops at times, pondering, with a look of despair, sorts a few papers and continues.

WRITER AS A YOUNG MAN: The electricity to my apartment was cut off today; the gas will soon follow. I managed to get power restored, otherwise I wouldn't be writing this now. The rent is, again, another month overdue. Everything is going down, closing down.

Over in his bed, WRITER begins snoring.

WRITER AS A YOUNG MAN: Hey, Professor, wake up!
WRITER: *[grunting as he wakes]* Who ... who is it?
WRITER AS A YOUNG MAN: You.

WRITER AS A YOUNG MAN leans forward and blows out the candle on the desk. The desk immediately plunges into darkness. He stands, turns and walks out through the window. Lights go on over the bed.

WRITER: Where was I? Yes, in this bed. *[He looks down.]* In this hospital bed. What is this hospital bed doing here? Never mind. The more dissatisfied I get, the more I write and the more I need to tell my story and the stories of injustice. *[His head rolls gently to one side on the pillow, his voice softens.]*

The swirling jelly of youth – so much of what I used to write was born of a need to communicate. My writing was by no means memoir, but it was autobiographical, how could it not be? Every time I was touched, I had the desire to touch others.

[Speaking more sprightly and searching for pad and pencil.] I wrote in the hope that my work would reach an audience, engaging others in an interactive experience and maybe, just maybe, that it would help nudge some miniscule aspect of human thought in an alternative direction.

A female NURSE enters. She begins fixing WRITER'S bed, straightening sheets and pillows and generally interfering. He is indifferent at first, but eventually becomes annoyed.

WRITER: What are you doing? Stop pestering me.

NURSE: My, you're testy today.

WRITER: And why shouldn't I be? You come in here, uninvited, and start interfering. What are you doing in here anyway?

NURSE: My job. What else would I be doing?

WRITER: But I left the hospital days ago.

NURSE: I'm not from the hospital. I'm from the university.

WRITER: The university? Why would the university send a nurse?

NURSE: I'm not a nurse. I'm from accounting. You lost a lot of blood. We want to make sure you don't start haemorrhaging again.

WRITER: I don't understand.

NURSE: There's no need to worry, just leave it up to us. Try and get some rest now.

WRITER: [huffing and muttering, mainly to himself] I don't need to rest. I need to write. I need to be in control.

The NURSE steps over to the desk. She begins to unzip her uniform, then stops. She picks up a block – of a size comfortable to hold in one hand – and tosses it to WRITER. He flinches, but manages to catch the block.

WRITER: What the hell is this?

NURSE: It's your writer's block. You might need it. [She continues unzipping her uniform.]

WRITER: [drifting back into a more contemplative, dream-like state] Writer's block, yes, we tremble at the thought of writer's block and drying out. The fear is more debilitating than the condition itself. She's right, no need to worry.

The NURSE lets her uniform drop to the floor; underneath she is wearing more casual attire – a blouse and skirt. She unties her hair, swaying her head from side to side. She bends forward and takes off her nurse's shoes. Under the table is a pair of high-heeled shoes; she puts them on. She is now no longer the NURSE. She is WRITER'S WIFE.

WIFE: Playing with your block as usual, I see.

WIFE picks up a mirror and lipstick from the table and begins coating her lips as WRITER looks up.

WRITER: *[suddenly aware of his surroundings again]* Who are you?
WIFE: Don't you recognise me? I'm your wife.
WRITER: *[nonchalantly]* Oh.
WIFE: Yes, it's me, Academia.
WRITER: Academia? Sounds like a Greek tragedy.
WIFE: The only tragedy is that you're laid up in bed, and I'm all alone and missing you. *[She walks over to his bed seductively and raises one foot onto the sheets, her heel digging in.]*
WRITER: So, I'm married to Academia. How much more clichéd can this get?
WIFE: Well, you'll just have to do better, won't you? You're the writer, after all. *[She leans her elbow on her knee.]*
WRITER: Haven't I done enough? I've even bled internally.
WIFE: You're not the only one who has bled. *[She begins pacing around the bed.]* But I'm not here to undermine you or your feelings. I understand your agony. I only want to say that maybe you've suffered for the wrong causes.
WRITER: Well, it's a bit late now.
WIFE: Is it?
WRITER: I've spent my life . . . fighting for knowledge, for the education of myself and of others. And I'm fighting right now to keep my job.
WIFE: Exactly. Restructuring, redundancy – it's all caving in on you.
WRITER: I've done my best. Anyway, the situation will improve. It always does.
WIFE: Then why are you complaining?
WRITER: I'm not. I'm just engaging with the situation. Call it discourse or dialectic or the search for truth – call it what you like – but not 'complaining'. Anyway, none of it is my fault.
WIFE: Then whose is it?

WRITER: You know as well as I do – the university, bureaucracy, the money-crunchers.

WIFE: It runs deeper than that. Don't forget, I've worked on both sides of the fence.

WRITER: Yes, and it never bothered you.

WIFE: That's nasty.

WRITER: *[apologetically]* I know. I'm sorry. You were good. You still are. And you're right – it does run deeper.

WIFE: We're both just a little tired, that's all.

WRITER: I just want to help people get to where they want to be.

WIFE: Does anybody really know where they want to be?

WRITER: Does it matter, as long as we're all doing and learning?

WIFE: Perhaps not. But it reminds me of something you used to say. Have you forgotten? 'To learn, you have to be like a sponge. The only problem is that a sponge adsorbs whatever it comes in contact with.' *[Before he can respond, she cuts him off.]* I have to go. Look after yourself and rest. I'll phone you.

WRITER: Before you go, tell me, can you see anything on the wall, anything written? *[He points.]*

WIFE: On the wall? No, nothing.

WRITER: Are you sure? You can't see anything?

WIFE: I'm sure. *[Suddenly, she looks closer – out through the window – as she takes a few steps.]* Wait a minute, what's that? Out there in the lane? That's new. It wasn't there yesterday.

WRITER: What does it say?

WIFE: It's spray-painted, across the wall opposite. It says, 'The truth is: truth is just a lie'.

WRITER: Are you sure? Nothing else? Nothing about death or audiences? Nothing in here on the wall?

WIFE: No. Why?

WRITER: Just looking for answers.

WIFE: Try and get some rest.

WRITER: You've already said that.

WIFE: Have I? Well, it's true. I must go. Rest – the answers will come.

His head falls to one side. After a moment, snoring is heard. Lights fade to black, curtain closes.

End of Act One

Entering the Fictitious

Act Two

It is the day of the presentation of WRITER'S paper on the importance of fiction. He is standing behind a lectern, front-centre stage, facing the audience. Only the window frame remains from Act One. A single spotlight illuminates him. A glass of water and his notes are in front of him. He is well presented, is wearing glasses and appears to have recuperated well enough from his medical procedure only days before. He stares straight ahead, motionless, paused with a finger in the air. After a moment's silence, he jolts into life, addressing the audience.

WRITER: So, I was saying, I'm still waiting on the test results that will determine my future. But while I was lying in bed, recovering from the procedure, my mind drifted – dream-like in thought, planning the future one minute, reflecting on the past the next – thinking that perhaps so much dreaming can take you away from the task at hand.

But what is the task at hand? *[He takes a sip from a glass of water.]*

The task, for me, is the pursuit of authenticity – authenticity without exception and without excuses. If I change the way I write, there may well be rewards, such as commercial gain, but authenticity? Would authenticity not be compromised? If authenticity is compromised, does the happiness that comes from self-fulfilment and self-esteem not suffer? Perhaps not, if commercial rewards are the desired end.

But even if that were the case, if commercial gain was the desired end, would there be anything left of the art outside of imitation and commodification? The creative act – if one still exists in such instances – would be imposed and external. And if that were so, where would be the authenticity?

A preoccupation of our modern consumer-based society is the demand for truth, but what truth? It is certainly not to be confused with authenticity, not as I have intended today. It is a superficial truth, a manufactured, sugar-coated truth.

I have always found the terms fiction and non-fiction to be inadequate. One implies truthfulness, while the other fantasy. I ask myself: is Lacan any more truthful than Joyce? Does Foucault tell us anything more about the human condition than Dostoevsky? The many volumes of religious beliefs that have influenced and informed generations for thousands of years utilise parables, as do the works of Plato, providing a blueprint for our democratic society, our philosophy and moral codes. Stories, yes, stories are a staple of our education. We communicate and pass on tradition and ideas through fictional narrative.

For me, nothing speaks more honestly than fiction, because fiction does away with pretences. Without pretence, we are able to explore concepts without the resistance and bias of preconception. Fiction can reach into the spiritual and the emotional. And fiction has always been comfortable moving about in the metaphysical and the psychological, reaching deep into the realm of the human psyche. Fiction works in a world where there are no promises, yet many solutions. If we lose fiction – if we allow it to be overrun, commodified – we run the risk of losing an innate part of what it means to be human. The fictitious is where we are able to enter a world of creativity and autonomy – a place without lies, without propaganda.

At this point, WRITER stops, a concerned expression on his face. He touches his right shoulder before continuing.

WRITER: I'm sorry to say this, but I feel I must cut my presentation short. There is an intense jabbing pain in my right shoulder. I have been warned that it is a sign that blood is still seeping from the hole in my liver where the sample was taken from. *[He pauses, and when he continues, he seems more composed, even smiles briefly.]* The registering of pain associated with the procedure is quite fascinating, and no one is certain exactly what is happening. The best explanation suggests that because there are so few nerve endings near the liver, a direct response is not felt when it is damaged or after a biopsy. Instead, as blood seeps into the abdominal cavity, it places pressure on the diaphragm and other organs. Nerves in this region lead along the spine and to the neck as part of a more complex neural network where they connect with other nerves leading to the right shoulder. The brain is deceived into thinking that pain is being experienced in the shoulder. Like fiction, it is a little confusing at times: something is happening, but no one is absolutely certain of the how and why. I am reminded of my Chinese acupuncturist who can put a needle in your toe to relieve an itchy ear. The fictional novel uses a different logic to non-fiction, as Eastern medicine uses a different logic to Western, like the paths of invisible meridian lines. Fiction is unusual, less tangible, for the purely academic mind, but it succeeds.

His presentation appears to have ended, but his bowed head and his hands still grasping the pages suggest there may be more to come. After an extended silence, he folds the pages, removes his glasses and turns to walk away. He takes a few steps before stopping. Suddenly, with determination, he replaces his glasses and returns to the lectern.

WRITER: No, no, that is not how I want to finish; not with rusty ideology. I have tried to talk about honour and duty and honesty, but all I have done is reposition a few makeshift boundaries. I have cordoned off and categorised one theory after another, each time taking the same old stale and contrived course, merely to be confronted with a cul-de-sac. With my mind conditioned to incessant partitioning, this way and that, I have managed nothing more than a few cursory chalk-lines on a dusty blackboard.

Something must happen to those lines. *[He begins taking a sheet at a time of his notes, screwing them into balls and tossing them around the stage as he speaks.]* And while I have tried to ignore the obvious, from the corner of my eye, I have sensed it when I write – a slight curve at first, a subtle bend then a gentle opening up – until finally I am forced to confront the truth. I am no longer comfortable with the luxury of being able to sit on whichever side of the fence I choose.

The reason for my reluctance all these years has been fear – a deep-seated dread of being torn in two, of being forced to choose between the fiction of a novelist and the pure reason of an academic. But it has dawned on me that I have no choice, merely acceptance. I am a hybrid – part author, part academic. And in that amalgamation, lies the key: an appreciation that spans from the most abstract art forms to the densest academic discourse. *[A declaration]* I am an authodemic. My work is authodemic. And I live in the world of authodemia.

As an author of fiction, my characters can speak the truth at any time without hesitation, without limitation. As a researcher, historian or memoirist, I am condemned to the annals of libraries or the clouds of electronic depositories waiting for an event to happen, for the words to come forth, or sifting through catalogues and records for an account that fits, or fits close enough. So I ask myself, if factual writing is so often adapted to suit, if even our own personal recollections are frayed at the edges and deceive us, how is the truth ever really the truth? *[He continues screwing his notes into balls and tossing them about.]*

Perhaps, in the end, it is all fiction. Many of us accept that. The difference, however, is that the fiction writer looks for truth through, and within, fiction, without limitations and, therefore, so often delivers truth. Whereas the factual writer is disadvantaged by self-imposed limitations, narrowing the field – eliminating, dissecting and categorising – trying to fashion truth from that which is thought to be tangible and real, but is so often unreliable.

We believe politicians when they tell us lies, yet we question fiction when most of it is the truth.

WRITER clicks his fingers, turning his head to the right as he does so. Immediately, from the darkness, a chair comes sliding towards him, stopping just by his side.

WRITER: As academics, we've been trying to kill the author for some time. What has that achieved? In our rush to usurp the author, we have empowered the critic, the analyst and the audience; we have played into the hands of commodification. The author has been stripped of responsibility, relegated to nothing more than a vehicle – a conduit for the flow of creativity that is ultimately interpreted and levied by others.

The author has become nothing more than a storyteller of other people's lives. The lives of others have overshadowed the essence of the story and of truth. We buy and sell each other's stories and lives and are obsessed with ourselves in terms of the other. And all the while, we strive for fame and freedom. We are told that fame is our right, so our egos have become overfed and swollen. We are told that freedom comes by way of the clothes we wear, the cars we drive, and the hand-held devices we caress. We are caught in an upward spiral of consumerism and self-importance where the difference between object and the individual is blurred. In fact, in this side-show spectacle, the individual has become a commodity.

So how does the author survive in a commercially driven environment where even the audience is willing to abandon them? To compete, the author has also become a commodity. The author has turned celebrity. And while we are all busy parading on the stage, playing into the hands of consumerism and commerciality, the artistry continues to be subjugated. Artistry has been consumed by commodification, and everyone has become an authority on art. Everyone knows better than the artist. *[He looks around studying his audience.]* As I stand at this lectern, I see only the eyes of vultures – dry and unblinking – with an unrelenting hunger.

At this point, WRITER climbs onto the chair beside him. He stands on one leg, sideways to the audience and brings his outstretched arms together in front of him. Turning his head towards the audience, he pokes out his tongue. After a brief moment, he climbs down.

WRITER: I don't know why I did that. I was suddenly taken over by an impulse. Perhaps you know the answer. *[Beckoning the audience]* Anyone? Indeed, you must, surely! After all, I am merely a conduit, a messenger.

The stencil sprayed by the two students, 'Death to the Audience' with the depiction of a bomb with a burning fuse, is illuminated in the background. WRITER turns to it briefly.

WRITER: *[in a quieter, more dulcet tone]* Sometimes, on my way home from engagements like this, I stop to sit on a bench in a park, waiting for the dry tears that I weep to turn into moist, saline droplets. At the very moment that they form wells in the palms of my hand, I have a choice: I can renounce those tears, wiping and sniffling until all is forgotten (and all too often I do) or I can curl my fingers over to hold on to those tears, carrying them with me as I rush home to let them spill onto the page. Those tears are a reminder of a pledge I made to myself a long time ago, 'to be true to myself'. And whenever I'm true, I break the chain of imitation that pervades my existence. Imitation is a pecking vulture.

A STAGE TECHNICIAN enters stage right and methodically and efficiently unplugs the microphone, takes the glass of water – putting a lid on it and placing it in his jacket pocket – picks up the lectern and leaves the stage.

WRITER: *[both amused and confused]* What is going on? Sabotage? Is my time up? *[He looks once more to the window, to the writing on the wall and back to the audience. He steps forward to make sure he is heard without having to raise his voice.]* Since my first, perhaps accidental, smudge on the page, the fictitious has existed as a place of understanding and creation for me, a place where even those two old adversaries – life and death – can be made sense of. The conflict between them, perpetuated in the real world, is ultimately resolved in the fictitious, because the fictitious guides us, while reality is contrived by us. It is time for me to go now, to enter the fictitious.

WRITER turns. Curtains begin to close, lights fade, as we see him exit centre stage, stepping through the window frame.

The End

11 Using the Spectrum to Theorise Apparent Opposition in Creative Writing Doctorates

Vahri McKenzie

Introduction

Creative production doctorates may be considered a hybrid form: a single thesis composed of two different elements. Creative writing doctorates, because both assessable components use the medium of text, are a better fit in this analogy, like comparing red apples with green apples. To speak of colour is a useful introduction: though red and green are different, indeed, opposites, they are connected through a spectrum. But where does red end and green begin? How do we examine yellow and orange apples in a red/green field? Through two case studies, this essay investigates some examples of how, and why, we might ask not 'yes or no', but 'to what degree', when considering creative writing doctoral courses. Creative writing works will be my primary focus here, but I will consider these within a broader array of doctoral degree-based creative productions and will use the latter term, creative production.

A recent and timely article by Carey *et al.* (2009), based on a thorough survey of examination policies for creative higher degrees by research (HDRs) in Australia, reveals the variety of policies currently in place. A positive spin on this situation might point to an opportunity for the savvy candidate to exploit the ambiguity and select a course that accords with her needs, but an awareness of the dynamics involved is unlikely to precede course selection. Anecdotal evidence suggests that most applicants consider course choice based on personnel, location and reputation, not university policies.[1] Yet such is the variety of policies governing the examination of creative writing doctorates – a candidate may unwittingly choose a course that, though conveniently located and amiably supervised, does not serve the creative and research needs of the thesis.

The nuanced objectivity required for examination across this policy range may be achieved by particular examiners, but the likelihood of this is reduced, as the variety and complexity of policies increases. Carey *et al.* point out that the amount of 'openness regarding the shape of a creative HDR thesis places additional demands on examiners' (2009: 4). Part of their answer to this potentially punishing situation (for examiners and candidates) suggests that supervisors:

> ... should be helping the candidate to: clarify the breadth of the project; consider which elements are committed to aesthetics, and which to the generation of knowledge; be clear about which parts need artistic review, and which require close attention to evidence, argument and conjecture. (2009: 4)

This discussion comes under the authors' subheading – 'The Creative Element' – but seems to apply to a description of the whole thesis. Their suggestions can be considered in terms of a continuum, where the spectrum is 'the breadth of the project'; one end is 'committed to aesthetics' and the other, 'the generation of knowledge'. The aesthetics end 'needs artistic review' and the knowledge end 'requires close attention to evidence'. The terms are descriptive, but the information they yield is interdependent: how to frame and position those elements and parts of the thesis that seem committed to aesthetics *and* the generation of knowledge? Attempting either/or discrimination in a field that involves incremental variation might be considered a fundamental problem of the creative writing doctoral project.

Regardless of how the questions are resolved, the hypothetical discussion between supervisor and candidate is a useful one. However, this does not always take place, and a candidate may have insufficient awareness of the policies under which the thesis will be examined, even as the terms of the policies influence the 'success' of the writing produced within them. When the discussion does take place, a candidate will understand that the two assessable parts of her thesis are in dialogue not just with each other, but also with her interpretation of the obligations these policies entail.

Despite significant efforts to institutionalise and standardise creative writing doctoral courses, inconsistencies persist in the course documents considered in this study. This raises significant concerns, as Carey *et al.* warn:

Unless examiners are offered very precise information, it is possible that candidates are not tested sufficiently on what, throughout their candidature, may have been an important element; or that they are critically judged over an aspect that, in fact, is not particularly important for their university. (2009: 5)

To this concern, I would add that even when detailed policies do exist, as in the courses considered in this study, the fact that inconsistencies remain in course documents over time[2] suggests that examiners apply the spirit of the institutions' policies, rather than the letter of the policies, where they attempt to apply institutionally guided examination at all.

The various policies regarding the examination of creative writing doctorates are concerned with interpretation of terms such as 'creative' and 'research', 'context' and 'commentary'. Frequently, the terms are dealt with as antithetical, yet they are defined with reference to each other. The oppositions are linked through a continuum that suggests a set of spectra can be used to rethink these and other terms that dominate examination policies and other course documentation: one spectrum indicates a course's vocational emphasis; another demonstrates the proportional size of the examined components; one signals the approach to 'academic' and 'author', and so on. Certainly, the breadth of the writing disciplines' field is one of its strengths. But creative writing doctoral candidates, as well as their supervisors and examiners, need tools to navigate the broad field.

Case Studies: Curtin University of Technology and Edith Cowan University

Through a detailed case study of two creative writing doctorates and the discourses within which they sit, I will illustrate the use of these spectra to re-imagine the description and examination of creative writing doctorates. The two degrees are those offered at Curtin University of Technology and Edith Cowan University, both in Perth, Australia. There are pragmatic reasons for my choice, but, significantly, both universities provide a strong discipline-based identity for creative writing. This would suggest that some thought has gone into the policies, rather than transferring the policy of an imperfectly matched neighbouring discipline. I've chosen two universities that sit at the 'strong identity' end of a 'disciplinary identity within institution' spectrum, as I'd like strong cases to work with in the assessment of my other areas of interest, which will mainly focus on vocational emphasis. Also, both courses have a variety of interpretive materials in the public domain.

Curtin University of Technology (CUT)

Curtin University began as an institute of technology and restructured as a university in 1987. This history fostered humanities disciplines, with a focus on technique and craft, as well as gradually assuming more traditional areas of study. CUT recognises Creative Writing in its Regulations and places it in a strong disciplinary position alongside Professional Writing in the Department of Communication and Cultural Studies. Although this is the same department to host Literary and Cultural Studies, wherein a higher degree is a PhD, postgraduate creative writers will undertake the Master or Doctor of Creative Arts (DCA). This aligns its creative writing courses with the technique and craft of visual and performing art courses, particularly with regard to their focus on practice in a given medium, where creative writing's medium is text. Just as in other institutions that offer a DCA, CUT stipulates their highest degree in creative research is equivalent in standing and status to other institutions' PhDs and that they are all research-based postgraduate degrees (CUT, 2010a).

CUT's choice of DCA is based upon discipline area; areas 'with a focus on creative practice as a mode of research' (2010a) include Professional Writing and Performance Studies, while Literary and Cultural Studies is included among the broad array of discipline areas that 'should uncover new knowledge either by the discovery of new facts, the formulation of theories or the innovative re-interpretation of known data and established ideas' (CUT, 2010b). Other Australian universities offering a DCA have different rationales for division. At University of Wollongong (UW), a candidate's background determines the choice of course: 'The Doctor of Creative Arts is for those individuals with a track record of high level professional experience, who wish to extend their practice within a scholarly context' (UW, 2010a).[3] The PhD:

> ... is intended for scholars or artist-scholars who have a solid academic and/or artistic background and who wish to develop either or both fields to a doctorate level. Such candidates may have limited artistic experience, but should demonstrate high levels of promise and an appropriate standard of preparation. (UW, 2010b)

The University of Technology, Sydney (UTS) and the University of Western Sydney (UWS) offer PhD, as well as DCA, courses and have creative writing completions of both types; at UTS, most completions are DCAs; at UWS, most are PhDs (Boyd, 2009: 7).

Nicola Boyd draws interesting connections between the universities I've mentioned here, specifically concerning a common pioneering history and

prodigious output: 'These four universities have awarded nearly thirty percent ... of the total qualifications and were among the first universities to
award any type of creative writing doctorate' (2009: 7–8). Three of the four
courses (excluding CUT) have been around for a long time, and it is likely
that they attracted many students because they offered academic, as well as
professional, doctorates, suggests Boyd. Three of the four (excluding UW)
share a history as Colleges of Advanced Education 'at which "second-tier"
level of education much early development of undergraduate creative writing teaching occurred' (2009: 8). Boyd concludes that DCA candidates often
have a writing industry, as opposed to academic, background and may feel
the need to compensate for that background (2009: 16). Her inclusion of
CUT in the discussion suggests that, given time, its course will tend to follow the patterns laid down by other universities offering a DCA. Boyd is a
professional statistician, so, presumably, we can trust her conclusions, but
it ought to be pointed out that very small numbers are being assessed. For
the period of her census (1993–2008), CUT is among more than 40% of
universities with two or fewer completions (generally, this reflects how long
the course has been available (2009: 7)), and the survey's submissions total
199. However, testing her conclusion against CUT's case, it appears to hold
true for the course and its elements.

CUT's choice of highest degree – Doctor of Creative Arts – would seem
to esteem creative production above all, but the degree structure is at pains
to maintain high standards of contextual academic discourse. CUT's degree
offers coursework 'to assist candidates in contextualising their researchques-
tion [sic] and devising appropriate research methodologies by providing
study in relevant history, methodology, theory and criticism' (CUT, 2010a).
Rather than perpetuate a dichotomy between DCA and PhD courses in
a discipline area so fraught with oppositions, however, I wish to draw
attention to the range of approaches to the DCA presented in my short
analysis, which is in keeping with the vast array of policies concerning the
production and examination of creative writing doctoral courses. Given this
diversity, it is useful to consider the array along a spectrum of vocational
emphasis, rather than assuming the either/or categorisation is sufficient
information: one end is 'professional writer' and the other 'academic'.
Although DCAs tend to focus on the professional, CUT's course has a more
academic focus than the other DCAs discussed.

Regardless of whether a university offers a PhD or a DCA creative
writing doctorate, all institutions share the problem of assessing the thesis
in terms of its two constituent parts. The meaningful differences between
the institutions' degrees come down to how they answer two questions:
How does the creative writing thesis fit within the university's definition of
research? And what is the relationship between the creative product and

the essay? CUT attempts to define some terms in its *Courses Handbook*: the thesis is 'a creative body of work and a written exegesis, which together form complementary responses to a clearly defined research question' (CUT, 2010a). This goes some way towards answering the key questions, in that the parts of the thesis can be seen to relate through the research question. But what is a research question in this context?

Extra interpretive information for CUT's degree includes the 2004 article by Barbara Milech and Ann Schilo regarding the relationship between the creative product and critical exegesis in CUT's DCA. They frame their discussion around various approaches to the exegesis: CUT's Research Question Model and its alternatives and the Context and Commentary Models. The Context Model takes a broad approach that recognises creative production *can* be a research thesis in itself, and the exegesis 'accommodates normative university definitions of research as work that deals with theoretical, historical and disciplinary matters in a fashion that contributes to knowledge in the discipline' (Milech & Schilo, 2004: 5). The Context Model is limited, they argue, by its failure to articulate the way the exegesis is to relate to the creative work and leads to the question, in a creative writing doctorate, what is the exegesis for? This model undermines the status of the creative work as a research thesis in its own right by shoring it up with conventional research. Institutions using this model have a bet both ways: by offering doctorates in creative writing, they suggest creative production is itself research, but by failing to articulate the role of and reason for the essay, the creative work's status as research is undermined. The Context Model thus falls back on conventional university expectations of what constitutes research.

The exegesis, within the frame of the Commentary Model, might be defined as the story of the creative work. There are strong and weak versions of this model, where the strong version tends towards the traditional research thesis in its commentary on the creative work, placing it in its disciplinary and intellectual context. The weak version might tell how the creative work came to be written, but with insufficient demonstration of various research skills expected of a postgraduate thesis. Both versions of the Commentary approach, say Milech and Schilo, treat the essay as secondary to the creative work, as an explanation of the creative work. This approach treats *all* creative works as research theses in themselves; the difference between the strong and weak versions of the Commentary Model is that the stronger version 'offers a more cogent means of demonstrating' that the creative work fulfils the normative university requirements for research (2004: 6).

Comparing the two, Milech and Schilo show that, unlike the Context Model, the Commentary Model offers a clear relationship between the creative work and the essay, where the essay proceeds from the creative work. However, the Commentary Model could be described as an uncritical inversion: where the Context Model implies the creative work needs advocacy, the Commentary Model implies the creative work is sufficient unto itself, regardless of what the creative work consists of. Milech and Schilo's main objection is:

> ... that the Commentary Model, in both its weak and strong versions, like the Context Model, preserves the theory-practice divide. Certainly, there is an advance – the binaries of theory and practice ... are reversed, so that creative and production practices are the primary terms and academic writing is the supplement. Still, the binary remains in place. As a result ... the creative work [does not stand] independently as research. (2004: 7)

But there is a problem here. If the Commentary Model frames *all creative production as research,* how can the opposition between creative production and research be said to be preserved? Thus, Milech and Schilo's 'answer' to the 'problem' of the dichotomy is weakened.

Milech and Schilo offer an alternative – the Research Question Model – which they claim mediates a solution, a middle road, that 'undertake[s] to honour two masters – the disciplinary forms and languages of fields of study relatively new to Australian universities and the understanding of research embodied in the genre of the traditional written thesis' (2004: 7). In this model, 'Both the written and creative component[s] of the thesis are conceptualised as *independent answers to the same research question'* (2004: 7 [original emphasis]).

It seems to me that the Commentary Model can be continuous with the Context Model, which is itself not significantly different from the Research Question Model, neither of which deems all creative works as necessarily valid research theses in themselves. Milech and Schilo claim that the Context Model does not adequately describe the relationship between the two parts and that this implies the essay's role is to guarantee the validity of the research thesis. The Research Question Model only avoids these objections through its ambiguous concept of the research question, which appears to perform the same act of implicit value judgement:

> To be research, a creative work or production piece must meet an 'entry' condition – it must be practice conceived and reflected upon in

the interests of answering a carefully and clearly defined research question framed on the basis of a sound working knowledge of a particular field, and in the interests of contributing new understandings to it. (Milech & Schilo, 2004: 7)

What, then, is the purpose of the new model? The Research Question Model relies on a set of circular definitions revolving around 'research'.

Often, a hermeneutic circle haunts theories offering a synthesis regarding creative writing in the institutional setting, but remains largely unacknowledged, evading the paradoxical nature of the creative writing doctorate. Two years after Milech and Schilo, Brian Dibble explained the research question approach in implicit comparison with the commentary and context approaches: 'rather than encouraging the student . . . to explain the actual genesis of the novel or to offer a technical comparison/contrast of it with some other novel, the research question directs the student toward some pre-existing body of information/theory relevant to both' (Dibble, 2006: 113). This explanation retains a diversion: Dibble doesn't say how the candidate is to write up the research, once directed towards it, if not in a commentary or contextual argument. The fundamental paradox of the writing doctorate remains obscured, despite Dibble's partial recognition, when he writes that the research question 'has heuristic use when conceptualising and building the novel and hermeneutic use when informing an exegesis' (2006: 113). That is, the model is both investigative and interpretative: investigative research is always understood from within an interpretative framework, which rests on investigative research – a hermeneutic circle. Nevertheless, Dibble's explanation is an improvement on that already seen, inasmuch as it suggests the research question motivates writing through movement: 'the process is usually an iterative one of moving back and forth between the two modes, production and exegesis' (2006: 113). I think this is the real contribution of the research question model.

When Milech and Schilo wrote their paper, they claimed the context model was the most commonly used in Australian postgraduate writing courses, probably because of its ambiguity. Since that time, things have shifted; in their 2009 survey of creative HDR courses in Australia, Carey *et al.* write:

> . . . of the 20 universities for which we found sufficient information to attempt a classification, six (less than one third) describe their exegetical requirements in context-model terms. With the exception of Curtin University, the remaining two thirds require an exegesis along the lines of what Milech and Schilo define as 'the strong version' of the commentary model. (2009: 7)

I contend that it is more useful to arrange the courses along a spectrum, than to put them in either a commentary or context box, where the 'professional writer' is reflected in the commentary model and the 'academic' is reflected in the context model.

University of New South Wales (UNSW) offers an example of the permeability of the research model divide. Although designated a 'strong version' of the commentary model by Carey *et al.*, UNSW denies a supplementary and explanatory role for the exegesis and instead encourages a dialogical relationship between the parts (UNSW, n.d.). The Royal Melbourne Institute of Technology (RMIT) is a similar case – Carey *et al.* designate it a 'strong version' of the commentary model, probably basing their judgement on the following: 'An exegesis is essentially an "exposition". It is distinguished from a thesis ... [in that] there is greater flexibility about the way the "exposition" may be developed and presented' (RMIT, n.d.: 4). But in the same document, the notion of 'research questions' is used to connect the components of the thesis and draw attention to the process, suggesting a dialogic relationship between the parts. Carey *et al.* put 'Curtin alone ... under the research question model because of the prominence they assign to a question-driven process' (2009: 8), but I contest this on two counts: as I've argued already, the research question approach is not significantly different from the context model; and approaches are so varied as to be misleading when classified in this dichotomous manner. Carey *et al.* themselves acknowledge that research questions can be usefully deployed under any exegetical model (2009: 8).

Milech and Schilo hint that where other institutions mandate a writing-professional response to an academic starting point, CUT formalises an academic response to an arts praxis starting point. In other words, there is an awareness of the need to compensate for an actual, or perceived, disadvantage amongst creative writing doctoral candidates. This is revealed in their final paragraph, when they write, 'the "novelty" of creative and production-based research theses ... requires an array of support mechanisms for both students and supervisors in those areas' (2004: 11). As mentioned previously, CUT's postgraduate writing programme is supported by coursework in context and methodology, though the exact amount is unclear: 25% in one reference and one-third in another (CUT, 2010a). My conclusion is that whilst it is academic in focus, CUT's course may appeal more to writing-professional candidates. This somewhat misleading over-compensation might be summed up by a comment from a current candidate:

I felt (perhaps wrongly) that a DCA was more about creative writing and the focus would be more on that component ... I now feel differently about this as I know more about the possibilities available for PhD students (at Curtin) and I love the academic work.[4]

Edith Cowan University (ECU)

Edith Cowan University is a 1991 amalgamation of teachers' colleges and art schools, and its writing programme was among the first in Western Australia. Writing has a strong identity, with recognition in the Regulations and its own disciplinary area, alongside other humanities in the School of Communications and Arts. Performance arts are located in the Western Australian Academy of Performing Arts (WAAPA), which is worth mentioning, because higher degrees in this school also involve the production of a creative and a critical work. Although the adjacent schools (WAAPA and C&A) both offer PhDs, the differences between them are analogous to the distinction between the PhD and the DCA at CUT. In fact, there was an era, ending in 2007, in which visual and performing arts doctoral candidates would complete a DCA, rather than a PhD. ECU's Pro-Vice-Chancellor of Teaching and Learning is unequivocal in his assertion that ECU's DCAs were equally demanding, but lacked the prestige of PhDs and so the era of flexible DCA programmes came to an end (Oliver, 2009, personal communication).

The contrast between the Schools' PhDs is indicated within their examination guidelines. While originality and a contribution to the discipline remain the focus of the WAAPA courses, students 'will also be expected to provide an appropriate record of their research through a written thesis or exegesis based on their research activities, their artistic ideas and the exploratory processes' (ECU, n.d. b). In effect, candidates are to provide a commentary on the main event – the creative work – where the essay is secondary to the creative product. In addition, courses in context and methodology are offered to supplement what primarily remains work '*in the practice* of the chosen discipline' (ECU, n.d. a[emphasis in original]).

At ECU, the discipline of Writing is clearly different from the Performing Arts, that focus on craft and technique; the Writing degree has greater concern for academic context within its basically creative production-led framework. Although the PhD in Writing is positioned alongside other humanities study areas, it gets a special mention within all Communications and Arts higher degree policy documents. In the course information, a sense remains that the postgraduate writing essay exists to supplement the creative product, which itself:

... will be a substantial, original work which is publishable.

> Included in the assessment of the thesis is an essay (approximately 20% of marks), or set of essays (25,000–30,000 words) which may involve one or more of the following in relation to the writing project: relevant theoretical issues; its conceptual and/or cultural contexts; its aims and methods; its relation to other writers or writing within the genre. (ECU, 2011)

That is, discussions of the *creative work's* context and methodology, or comparison with other creative works of the same genre. The essay comments upon the creative work, but both are concerned with context: literary context in the case of the creative work, theoretical context in the case of the essay. This sets it apart from WAAPA's PhD, where students are vaguely required to 'provide an appropriate record of their research'. But it is not *too* far from WAAPA's PhD, in that it values the creative work over the critical: a difference of degree, not kind.

ECU's Doctor of Philosophy (Writing) would seem to empower 'writing about writing', but guidelines provided to examiners spell out criteria and distribution of marks that clearly value creative production first and foremost. ECU's *Handbook 2011* indicates that the essay should be 25,000 to 30,000 words in length. This is about the same as other creative writing doctorates in Australia, where the most frequently cited figure for the length of the critical component is 30,000 words, often with clarifiers such as 'at least' or 'no more than'. In ECU's *Guidelines for Examination of PhD (Writing)*, however, the instruction is an 'essay or set of essays (15–30,000 words)' (ECU, n.d. c), making this the shortest exegesis of its kind in Australia.

Both the handbook and guidelines stipulate that the essay is worth 20% of the marks and the creative component, 80%. The guidelines also include some interpretive information developed especially for the course, e.g. 'Content of Examiners' Report' [*sic*] (ECU, n.d. c), which details ECU's concerns for the creative project and the essay independently. The two sets of information are somewhat the same, both focusing on conventional university expectations for research, such as originality, significance and cogency. Whereas the creative work ought to be concerned with readership and publishing, the essay ought to be concerned with methodological issues and the link with the creative project. Publishing and readership are not considered in regards to the essay, which supplements the creative work: the essay looks back to the creative product, but not the other way around. ECU is unusual in the heavy weighting it gives the creative component and, also, in the way it stipulates the percentage of marks to be considered for each part. Few other institutions stipulate the division of marks, and those that do, usually give each component equal weight. Other institutions are also more likely to point out that the thesis is assessed as a single work, despite its dual nature.

ECU's examination guidelines are an important contribution to a considered position on how to examine the thesis and can be seen to avoid the pitfall noted by Carey *et al.*, who claim that 'not all universities are clear in their notes to examiners about whether the principal issue at stake is the original contribution to knowledge, publication standard, quality of experiment (innovation) or another imperative' (2009: 5). Yet it is not enough to offer examiners clear guidelines if the candidates are not aware of the principal issue at stake. The potential contribution of ECU's examination guidelines is undermined by the fact that they are provided to examiners, not to candidates.[5] This document can be freely sought, but it is not considered part of the necessary information a candidate requires to produce a thesis.

Carey *et al.* classify ECU's approach to the essay as a context model, and the passage quoted above would seem to align with the context model's concern for conventional university definitions of research. Yet, the essay clearly supplements the creative work and, in this respect, matches a commentary approach. Carey *et al.* hone in on ECU's handbook and guidelines, regarding the critical element of the thesis, stating that the course is 'distinctive in that it explicitly allows the possibility that the exegesis be constructed as "an essay or set of essays", rather than a monolithic entity. It also offers a smorgasbord of content options' (2009: 7). Whilst uncritical, these comments do not conjure the rigour of academia, but, rather, suggest choice and delight. Their analysis suggests that ECU's course emphasises the writing professional over the academic.

Nicola Boyd discusses the rapidly increasing popularity of creative writing courses in Australia, a trend led by ECU: 'Edith Cowan University only began awarding these qualifications in . . . 2003 and [has] now awarded the . . . third largest number overall' (2009: 7). Two ECU academics offer Boyd their versions of the history of the PhD at ECU and both point to professional, rather than academic, concerns. Associate Professor Glen Phillips suggests reasons for the popularity of ECU's course include a writer-in-residence programme, a writer's centre and networks with publishers (Phillips cited in Boyd, 2009: 8–9). Emeritus Professor Andrew Taylor states, '[T]he creative writing degree at ECU was slipped under the radar' because 'other disciplines . . . would have objected to it being classed as a "research" degree since it did not conform to the traditional definitions of university research' (Taylor cited in Boyd, 2009: 9).

ECU's professional focus on readership and publication of the creative work might sit uncomfortably next to the institution's or examiner's understanding of what constitutes an original contribution to knowledge.

'Publishability' is conflated with market concerns and could be interpreted as 'commercial appeal', thus working against originality. Boyd considers this a general problem: 'There continues to be an academic focus on the publishability of creative works as the primary assessment benchmark. Ironically, universities appear to encourage less publishable literary creative works to form part of the creative writing doctorate' (2009: 25). Her conclusion, that writing doctoral courses ought to develop new regard for literary works in popular genres, is logically consistent, but this doesn't address the problem faced by those not writing in popular genres, yet facing examination by publishability.

Conclusions

The case studies reveal considerable variation between courses and indicate that markers such as DCA/PhD are not necessarily useful guides to the course focus. Curtin University of Technology and Edith Cowan University sit at opposite ends of a vocational emphasis spectrum: CUT is more academic; ECU is more concerned with the writing professional. It is interesting that CUT has the most theorised guidelines and rules for creative writing doctorates (as specified in their course documents and supplementary published materials, such as those by Milech and Schilo and Dibble), leading to the inclusion of creative writing with those disciplines that offer a DCA, which remains a less academically prestigious degree. ECU's professionally focused course favours a cause-and-effect relationship between creative and critical work, implicitly encouraging safer writing options, with clarity of genre. Just as CUT's research question focus may inhibit a project, ECU's professional focus may cut off the cyclical movement between boundaries that binds the thesis into a single academic document.

For candidates, examiners and policy writers, how the critical component of the thesis is approached is key to the success of the endeavour. This framing gives an indication of institutional attitudes to the discipline. Not necessarily how important it considers the discipline to be, but certainly whether it considers the discipline to be more concerned with creative production or with contextualising research. The critical aspect of the creative doctorate might be presented as a space for candidates to probe the grey areas of the discipline: taking advantage of the ambiguity of the creative research form offers candidates the freedom to tailor a degree to the needs of a particular thesis, but requires an awareness of the dynamics involved. A highly professional approach will anticipate marketing categorisation for the creative work, while a highly academic approach will assure significant research. My assumption is that the writing discipline's strength – its strategic edge – is found in negotiating a way through apparent opposites, rather than settling into one or the other. This drawing closer, then away – submitting and questioning – charts a territory and creates a dialogic space where oppositions draw closer together. An oscillating, or iterative, approach to writing the creative thesis can reconcile the apparently paradoxical relationship between the parts.

Changes I envisage to creative writing doctorates will recognise that they are one work composed of two parts, one of which tends toward narrative, the other toward criticism. Displacing this distinction onto a different binary, such as context/commentary, doesn't address the fundamental and important contradiction encapsulated in the examination of a single thesis. Another spectrum is called for: on one side sits critical prose or evidence, chronology and the like; on the other side sits fiction, narrative and the imaginary. I would like to position the creative writing thesis in the middle – a pivot point between 'creative' and 'critical'. Ideally, doctorates will offer a sliding scale, proportioning word length and assessment values. Unless this form of research is recognised as an interdependent one, however, movement between the modes is lost, and the discipline's strategic advantage in making an original contribution to knowledge is lost in the constraints of normative university definitions of research.

Notes

(1) In personal communications with 10 candidates and graduates of creative writing doctoral courses at ECU and CUT, the leading factors influencing choice of course were: personnel (feelings towards the likely principal supervisor), location and perception of course reputation. No one I communicated with raised the issue of a course's examination policy; where administrative aspects were considered, they concerned personnel (e.g. administrative staff were 'exceptionally easy to deal with').

(2) See, for example, ECU's 'Guidelines for Examination of PhD (Writing)', in which the critical component is to be 15–30,000 words in length, compared with the *Handbook* entry, in which the critical component is to be 25–30,000 words in length. This discrepancy appears in *Handbooks 2005–2011*. The Guidelines are undated, but have remained unchanged since 2007.

(3) I am indebted to Janene Carey for her 'Information on Creative Writing Programs' (2008) that formed the basis for my broader comparisons between creative writing doctoral courses.

(4) Personal communication with anonymous candidate of DCA (CUT), 2 June 2009.

(5) Patricia Brown of ECU's Postgraduate Student Support Office confirms that the Examination Guidelines document is intended for examiners, not candidates: 'This document is for the examiners and I am not sure if the supervisor bases their supervision on the guidelines i.e. . . . ensures that all components are met . . . I would imagine they would though' (personal communication, 22 June 2009).

References

Boyd, N. (2009) Describing the Creative Writing thesis: A census of creative Writing Doctorates, 1993–2008. *TEXT* 13 (1), . Online at http://www.textjournal.com.au/april09/boyd.htm

Carey, J. (2008) Information on Creative Writing programs, *Writing Network,* online webpage, accessed 10 January 2011. http://www.writingnetwork.edu.au/files/CW%20Policy%20Data.pdf

Carey, J., Webb, J. and Brien, D.L. (2009) A plethora of policies: examining creative research higher degrees in Australia. In D.L. Brien and L. Neave (eds) *The Creativity and Uncertainty Papers: The Refereed Proceedings of the 13th Conference of the Australian Association of Writing Programs, 2008,* accessed 10 January 2011. http://aawp.org.au/files/CareyWebbBrien.pdf

Curtin University of Technology (2010a) Doctor of Creative Arts (Communication and Cultural Studies), *Courses Handbook 2010,* online webpage, accessed 10 January 2011. http://student.handbook.curtin.edu.au/courses/30/300891.html

Curtin University of Technology (2010b) Doctor of Philosophy, *Courses Handbook 2010,* online webpage, accessed 10 January 2011. http://student.handbook.curtin.edu.au/courses/19/198902.html

Dibble, B. (2006) Disinterested passion: Creative Writing and the arts of love and teaching. In N. Krauth and T. Brady (eds) *Creative Writing: Theory Beyond Practice* (pp. 102–120). Teneriffe: Post Pressed.

Edith Cowan University (2011) Course Information: Doctor of Philosophy, *Handbook 2011,* online webpage, accessed 10 January 2011. http://handbook.ecu.edu.au/Course Structure.asp?disyear=2011&CID=83&USID=0&UCID=0&UID=0&Ver=3&HB=HB&SC=PG

Edith Cowan University (n.d. a) *Guidelines for Examination of the Master of Arts (Creative Arts),* online webpage, accessed 10 January 2011. http://www.research.ecu.edu.au/grs/data/tmp/ma_creative_arts_exam_guidelines.pdf

Edith Cowan University (n.d. b) *Guidelines on the Examination of the PhD (Performing Arts),* online webpage, accessed 10 January 2011. http://www.research.ecu.edu.au/grs/data/tmp/phd_performing_arts_exam_guideli.pdf

Edith Cowan University (n.d. c) *Guidelines on the Examination of the PhD (Writing),* online webpage, accessed 10 January 2011. http://www.research.ecu.edu.au/grs/data/tmp/phd_writing_exam_guidelines.pdf

Milech, B. and Schilo, A. (2004) 'Exit Jesus': Relating the exegesis and creative/production components of a research thesis. *TEXT Special Issue:* Illuminating the Exegesis, online journal, accessed 10 January 2011. http://www.textjournal.com.au/speciss/issue3/milechschilo.htm

Oliver, R. (2009) The DCA at ECU, personal telephone conversation with V McKenzie, 8 June 2009.

RMIT University (n.d.) *DSC Portfolio Guidelines for Project-based Higher Degrees by Research,* online webpage, accessed 10 January 2011. http://www.mams.rmit.edu.au/brojw5py8o4qz.pdf

University of New South Wales (n.d.) *Creative Writing at UNSW,* online webpage, accessed 10 January 2011. http://empa.arts.unsw.edu.au/creative-writing-resources/creative-writing-at-unsw/

University of Wollongong (2010a) Doctor of Creative Arts, *Course Handbook for 2010,* online webpage, accessed 10 January 2011. http://www.uow.edu.au/handbook/yr2010/pg/crearts/H10006009.html

University of Wollongong (2010b) Doctor of Philosophy, *Course Handbook for 2010,* online webpage, accessed 10 January 2011. http://www.uow.edu.au/handbook/yr2010/pg/crearts/H10006007.html

12 Outlying the Point that Tips: Bridging Academia and Business

Pavlina Radia

Success stories and manuals about creativity and professional leadership flood the shelves of Canadian bookstores and corporate mega-chains, such as Indigo and Chapters. The rise of interest in creativity as a road to success pervades the new millennial consciousness, propelling us towards radical paradigm shifts that redefine our understanding of education. Consequently, Canadian universities are under pressure to go with the times and embrace a corporate organisational model in which students, as customers, define or contribute to the shaping of university agendas. As the push towards the corporate model of university education is creeping its way into the university rhetoric of Canadian universities, so too is the language of 'creative leadership' pervading the official planning documents of universities. The rhetoric, however, is often in conflict with the administrative expectations of strategic expansion and the day-to-day operations of individual departments that are tasked with transforming the rhetoric into proper learning outcomes – all of which is invariably linked to a strategic approach that will increase future revenue. Not surprisingly, many departments balk at this 'creative' commodification of education. This reaction inevitably poses questions about how we define *creativity* and, consequently, how we perceive *change*.

In many North American universities, creativity tends to be commonly associated with the Frankfurt School conceptualisation of art as high culture, where the true creative potential is distinguished from its sublimation in the low culture of mass commodification. From Max Horkheimer, Theodor Adorno to Walter Benjamin, the notion that the capitalist culture annihilates the ability to think critically is what distinguishes high art from mass-produced, commercialised art. In *The Dialectics of Enlightenment*, Horkheimer and Adorno (2002) develop this notion by deploying the rise of what they call 'culture industry' as a threat to art, hence to *culture*. Adorno's defence of modernist art as an attempt to transcend the kind of dialectics of negation advocated by Plato is grounded specifically in the Expressionist emphasis on pure abstraction that surpasses commodification by highlighting the potentiality of ideas as pure *ideals*. For example, for modernists like Wassily Kandinsky, Kurt Switters, T.S. Eliot or H.D., abstraction is a mode of higher thinking, whereby the non-ethics of 'culture industry' are transformed into the ethics of pure art. As Benjamin (1968) emphasises in his *Illuminations: Essays and Reflections*, in the age of mechanical reproduction, art has lost its aura – to put it differently, it has ceased to 'illuminate' us; by contrast, it participates in stimulating desire and, thus, consequently, consumption (221).

In the closing of his essay, Benjamin (1968), however, warns of separating aesthetics entirely from politics. To some extent, he concedes that isolating the two might be impossible. Adorno (1990) comes to a similar conclusion in his introduction to *Negative Dialectics*. In his terms, thinking that creativity as high culture art can transcend the world of commodity and its economic enslavement is not only illusory, but can potentially revert to a form of totalitarianism that is based in elitist segregation and extirpation of lower ideas in the name of some higher ideal. As he puts it, 'No theory [or art] today escapes the marketplace. Each one is offered as a possibility among competing opinions; all are put up for choice; all are swallowed. There are no blinders for thought to don against this, and the self-righteous conviction that my own theory is spared that fate will surely deteriorate into self-advertising' (Adorno, 1990: 4). To delve into Adorno's dialectics and Benjamin's luminous ideas is to open a can of worms: it is to acknowledge that no matter how much the Frankfurt School philosophers lamented against the culture industry, it is the economic drive of the culture industry that ultimately turns art and creativity into a force of social action. While the resulting social action can revert to a form of ideology, as both Adorno and Benjamin have bemoaned, it can also pave the road towards a new way of thinking that questions and, by means of questioning, challenges the impact that the culture industry has on creative potential and the impetus to encourage change.

Sidonie Smith's article on the inevitability of change, published in the 2010 issue of the MLA journal *Profession*, is a salient case in point. In her article, Smith discusses the 'daunting crises' underpinning most universities' push towards a more corporate model, a model instigating a radical rethinking of education, as well as individual programmes and their course offerings (196). In her view, the rise of 'integrative majors' in English departments challenges the idea of a high culture understanding of education and art as *culture*, since integrative majors encourage interdisciplinary shopping by offering 'heterogeneous courses as scattered opportunities' (198).

Nonetheless, as Smith (2010) emphasises, with the rise of digital humanities and popular culture programmes, resistance to change might be futile, if not counter-productive. To put it differently, even though creativity constitutes the bread and butter of the Humanities, the idea that it should be kept separate from its practical and potentially corporate applications is perhaps slightly obsolete and deserves further inquiry. The inquiry begs the question whether the insistence to keep the corporate 'barbarians' at the gates does not (if only partly) stem from the anxiety of change associated with the concern that the world of commodity would transform our ivory towers into malls of 'fast' consumable learning. Although the anxiety is not unfounded, it often derives from the fear of radical change. This fear can be best illustrated through the tensions pervading the rather ambiguous position of creative writing programmes in both Canada and the United States.

While in Canada and the United States creative writing programmes retain their appeal, creativity as artistic production, or creativity broadly applied as a commitment to change in both private and public sectors that builds bridges between business and academia, continues to be viewed with suspicion, if not derision. Most creative writing programmes define themselves as separate from professional writing: journalism, in particular. Moreover, there is a sense that collaboration of this kind trivialises writing as an inauthentic discipline that is driven by the market, rather than rigor and ideas. The notion that creative writing, if paired up with its more practice and market-driven soul sister, would somehow lose 'intellectual substance' pervades the academy (Lim, 2003: 158). Such a view, however, only reinforces the high culture versus low culture paradigm by endorsing *creativity* as a hegemonic, rather than a democratic, tool of enhancing students' future success and marketability in and outside academia.

The recent popularity of Malcolm Gladwell's non-fiction books *Outliers* (2008) and *The Tipping Point* (2002) suggest that creative writing is gaining respect among the public. And yet, his books hardly ever graze the pages of academic course syllabi. Why the resistance to include a creative work that is commercially successful? For literary studies programmes, Gladwell's success philosophy does not fare well in contrast to the elitist notions of the valued top 40 (canonical) writers. And yet, it is a life philosophy – the ability to apply one's creative and critical ideas successfully to future career, be it academic or corporate – that Canadian universities aspire to teach. Hence, why the discrepancy? This paper argues that although the existing gap between academia and the corporate world in Canada (be it the publishing market or business in general) is partly a defensive response to what Walter Benjamin (1968: 217) called 'the age of mechanical reproduction', it is important to acknowledge that such a response is based on out-dated assumptions about the value of art and creativity that hamper, rather than instigate, 'creative' ways of thinking about disciplinary boundaries and the riches that lie at their possible intersections.

First, it might be worthwhile to contextualise the position of creative writing programmes in North American universities. Shirley Geok-lin Lim's (2003) article, 'The Strangeness of Creative Writing: An Institutional Query', provides salient cues into the liminal space to which applied creativity is often castigated. As Lim (2003) notes, in most universities in the United States, creative writing occupies an 'anomalous position' (151). In spite of the statistical evidence noting the rise of creative programmes across the United States and Canada, creativity is scorned by many English Studies programmes as marginal to the discipline and often paired up with popular culture courses. While some universities turn to professionalising creative writing in order to 'remain distinct from schools of journalism in its emphasis on literary journalism and training for publishing industry' (Lim, 2003: 162), the integration of the practical application and professionalisation of creativity as not only a part of, but, rather, as a full-standing discipline, is lagging. This lag can be explained partly in reference to the ways in which English departments endorse the notion of the canonical approach to literature, in spite of the increasing push towards transnational approaches to literature/s. Another reason for the lag is the tendency to see creativity as simply secondary to the courses on Shakespeare, modernism, history of genre or postcolonial literature, rather than as an essential part of critical agency that drives the discipline, but also expands its influence outside the academy into other professions (Lim, 2003).

Lim's argument opens doors to further inquiry: particularly, to how creativity is defined in relation to change in an age of mechanical reproduction, not so much in isolation to other disciplines and non-academic professions, the market-place included, but also, more importantly, in relation to change. While for the ancient Greeks, the *agora* was a place of education where the private and public spheres were brought into communication (Bauman, 2000), Western education since the Enlightenment has privileged the separation of the two. As Jackson (2006) notes, the 19th century revamping of the North American curriculum towards disciplinary divisions and anti-professionalism established a clear divide between academia and other professions. In spite of the recent emphasis on interdisciplinary approaches and popular culture streams, departments remain locked in what are still mostly canonical approaches to the humanities (Jackson, 2006: 31). Although most English departments offer popular culture courses, there is a reluctance to include works of commercial success in courses that are viewed as 'mainstream', genre or survey courses, respectively. This reluctance is particularly ironic in the wake of the increasing emphasis on creative leadership, strategy and success, notions that pervade university action plans, as I have mentioned above.

The argument that universities are slowly giving in to the pressure of the mass market clearly needs to be re-evaluated. Historically, humanities consisted of a combination of disciplines, including the arts, philosophy, moral ethics, literature and rhetoric, to name a few (Jackson, 2006: 30). The arts also traditionally relied on the generosity of sympathetic, fiscally-endowed patrons. Indeed, the English Renaissance would not have been the artistic rebirth it had been without the passionate patronage of the rich, as Jackson (2006) notes. Correspondingly, the shift towards specialisation stemmed from the 19th century shift towards the commercial model of education, not its renunciation (Jackson, 2006).

Therefore, the question is not so much whether the encouragement of creative thinking as a preamble to critical analysis and academic savoir-faire is a way of submitting to the culture of greed, but, rather, it is a matter of whether the resistance to embrace trans-academic crossings, including its market or business-driven applications, is to 'deteriorate into self-advertising', to use Adorno's words, a gesture restricting our ability to think creatively; or, in other words, to 'use imagination to create something', as the meaning of the word *creative* suggests (*Oxford English Dictionary*). As Malcolm Gladwell (2008) suggests, thinking can be contagious. Its contagiousness does not have to be necessarily negative; by contrast, it can instigate change, or what he calls a 'tipping point', whereby the 'unexpected becomes expected, where radical change is more than possibility' (14).

Based in New York, Gladwell was born and educated in Canada. In his 2010 article, Patrick Brethour cheekily called Gladwell 'the quiet Canadian', highlighting Gladwell's celebrity status as grounded in his Canadian origin. Gladwell's background invokes the typical Canadian hybridity that spans national boundaries, but also pervades his philosophy of success and creativity as an impetus to pursue change in spite of its challenges and downfalls. His recent best-sellers, *The Tipping Point: How Little Things Can Make a Big Difference* and *Outliers: The Story of Success*, celebrate creativity as an ability to embrace hybridity not as a postmodern curio, but rather as an ethical approach to professional success: be it outside or within academia. His best-sellers are based on the same mantra: success does not stem entirely from an innate talent, but requires dedication, commitment and, most importantly, the ability to think creatively; in other words, the ability to think outside the box.

Gladwell (2008) aligns this way of thinking with what he calls 'outliers' – people who are willing to devote their time to something that 'is markedly different in value from others' and who are able to turn adversity into an opportunity (3: 128). Analysing success stories from Bill Gates to Brooklyn immigrants and victims of globalisation, Gladwell's works combine critical analysis with research by simultaneously addressing subjects that span popular and professional realms. What can creative writers, undergraduate and graduate students learn from Gladwell's texts? First and foremost, they will learn that success is hard work that translates into hours of practice and preparation. As Gladwell (2002) notes, 'practice isn't the thing you do once you're good. It's the thing you do that makes you good' (41). Gladwell's conceptualisation of quality work can be aligned with such canonical works as Homer's *Odyssey,* Benjamin Franklin's *Poor Richard*, Henry Fielding's *The History of the Adventures of Joseph Andrews* or Virginia Woolf's *A Room of One's Own* – all texts that highlight the importance of tenacity, coupled with *creative* thinking; thinking that instigates change. It is not a generalisation to say that successful writers know that quality writing is about practice and endless hours of commitment to the craft. As Alice Munro (1993) once said, to write a short story that touches the human heart, the writer needs to understand that '[e]very final draft, every published story, is still only an attempt, an approach to the story' (826).

Like Homer's *Odyssey,* Gladwell's pop culture approach to life as *Bildungs* – a narrative about the protagonist's complex journey – provides insight into human ontology, but also teaches us about the value of ethics. By exploring both positive and negative aspects of historical events that have shaped our lives, Gladwell encourages his readers to think critically, to formulate arguments that are grounded in evidence, but, more importantly, he highlights the importance of a pluralistic, democratic vision that refuses to pander to hegemonic models of thinking. How is this encouragement different from T. S. Eliot's emphasis on poetry as a medium of ideas – a prompt for achieving higher ideals, as indicated in his famous essay, 'Tradition and the Individual Talent' (Eliot, 1953: 37–44); or the feminist call for equality, as opposed to pandering to patriarchal models of hegemonic thinking? Is not the presumption of the top 40 canonical writers lodged in what Gramsci (1994) refers to as hegemonic power? Such an assumption endorses, rather than subverts, the kind of institutionalisation of censorship that goes against freedom of speech – a notion that is supposed to be the heart of university education. If creativity is seen as a trans-disciplinary 'outlying tipping point', to evoke Gladwell's philosophy, then academia and the market place might find commonalities that benefit both; commonalities that allow academics to foster a new, content-based culture, while remaining vigilant to the potential dangers of unbridled consumption.

Nonetheless, the Canadian resistance to providing bridges between academy and other professions is not solely limited to the university populace; in fact, a similar apprehension pervades the world of business and politics. Even though recent research by Philip A. Titus (2007) confirms that creativity instruction is slowly making its way into marketing classes, it continues to be viewed with suspicion (262). It becomes particularly problematic when applied to the crossover between business and politics. The recent political scandal of the Minister of Status of Women, Helena Guergis, whose 'creative' politics included seeking new avenues of encouraging women's professional and creative development through involvement with a diverse range of corporate and professional sectors, not surprisingly, became a thorn in the eye of Canadian politics. Guergis' not-so-recent expulsion from her ministerial duties merely confirmed that unfettered creativity is to be punished. As a representative of the Status of Women in Canada, Guergis joined a longstanding tradition in women's organisations advocating for women's rights and equality across gender, racial and class divides.

It is, therefore, ironic that her expulsion from the conservative caucus stemmed primarily from the serious allegations of her alleged involvement in her husband's (Rahim Jaffer) overpublicised scandal, rather than her tantrum at the Charlotte airport in February 2010.[1] The circumstances surrounding Guergis' expulsion and her husband's shady politics are not entirely clear, in spite of Guergis' public apology on national television. Her CBC interview with Peter Mansbridge circled around what perhaps lurks underneath the veneer of the most blatant of accusations: the sexism pervading Canadian politics.[2] Whether or not Guergis' case required the kind of scrutiny it was given is debatable. However, the fact that the allegations surrounding her husband's activities overshadowed her achievements as a Minister of State serving women in her caucus points to the hegemonic distribution of power that continues to plague Canadian institutions. If, as Gramsci (1994) suggests, the role of the State and government is to educate and 'create a new type or level of civilisation' (p. 90), then *creativity* is the glue of an ethical society, glue which connects different areas of expertise, levels of government and echelons of power.

Although cleared of all the allegations by the RCMP investigation in July 2010, Guergis' political career remains in doubt. Her once-celebrated feminist platform – encouraging women's professional success, fighting domestic violence and organising women-to-women round tables – is now a source of sensationalism and critique. Although Guergis began her political career in 2004 and worked her way up the government ladder slowly, yet tenaciously, as the Minister of State,[3] her political savvy and dedication did not seem to matter, although, given the fact that she was the Minister of the Status of Women, her downfall speaks volumes about what happens to women who attempt to break with social paradigms (Kennedy, 2010). Guergis' scandal brings to light the suspicion that *creativity*, in its essence, is a criminal activity threatening the *status quo*.

The point of this argument is not to defend Guergis or her politics, but to suggest that the kind of anxiety shared by academics – when it comes to the danger of creativity as an intellectual ability versus consumable activity, which threatens to mistake quantity for quality – underpins both the world of politics and the world of business. However, what lies at the heart of this anxiety is not so much the fear of commodification, as the fear of change. Indeed, creativity, as we have seen over the centuries, can have both positive and negative outcomes: it can be used to promote peace and/or violence. To evoke Walter Benjamin's 'Theses on the Philosophy of History' (1968: 253–264), creativity is like the Paul Klee painting *Angelus Novus,* whose wings are caught in the 'storm [that] irresistibly propels him into the future to which his back is turned, while the pile of debris before him grows skyward' (Benjamin, 1968: 258). As Benjamin says, 'This storm is what we call progress' (258). Creativity is such a storm; to make sure that this storm is more of a medium facilitating change, rather than a destructive force, it is essential to encourage a dialogic exchange of ideas.

As Linda Hutcheon (2001), a well-known Canadian scholar and theorist, emphasised in her 2000 MLA Presidential Address, the rise of women's writing and women's rights movements in North America stemmed from their 'creative' ability to see beyond the scope of the everyday. It would have been impossible without 'mak[ing] sure that those channels of communication were open' (518). Highlighting Canada's success throughout history, Hutcheon (2001) constantly draws attention to the links that transcend boundaries – be they disciplinary, national, gender, racial or class boundaries – that remain ex-centric and facilitate participation in a 'creative and constructive critique' (528). What Hutcheon draws attention to is the notion that without a participatory dialogue, proper communication remains difficult, if not impossible. Indeed, if creativity is to be a productive, ethical means of enhancing the sense of cultural ideals that we are increasingly losing, then instigating viable links between the academy and the market is imperative. The stories of Gladwell and Guergis serve as an interesting counterpoint to the traditional creative arc, revealing that in the age of digital media, the bridges between the academic and business world are not only inevitable, but also essential to cultural development and its sustainability in the era of plenty.

If change represents progress, then building creative bridges between the academy and the market allows for the outlying of the tipping point, whereby 'something that is situated away from or classed differently from a main or related body [read discipline]' ushers in the possibility of a paradigm shift (Gladwell, 2002: 3). While creative thinking is essential to the academy, the ability to translate its potential riches into reality through practical applications paves the way towards what, hopefully, one day, we will be able to call an informed, educated marketplace that, in turn, stimulates the arts by promoting creative humanities as the engine that could.

Notes

(1) The Guergis scandal received extensive media coverage. See, for example, Joanna Smith's article, 'Guergis Resigns, Now Faces RCMP Probe' in *The Star* or Peter Mansbridge's (2010) CBC interview with Guergis.

(2) See CBC documentary, *Guergis Breaks Silence on Scandal*, May 12, 2010 from http://www.cbc.ca/canada/story/2010/05/10/helena-guergis-exclusive-mansbridge.html

(3) See, House of Common Members, Helena Guergis. Retrieved February 1 2011 from: http://webinfo.parl.gc.ca/MembersOfParliament/ProfileMP.aspx?Key=128818&Language=E

References

Adorno, T. (1990) *Negative Dialectics*. London: Routledge.

Bauman, Z. (2000) *Liquid Modernity*. New York, NY: Blackwell.

Benjamin, W. (1968) *Illuminations: Essays and Reflections* (H. Arendt, ed.) (H. Zohn, trans.). New York, NY: Schocken.

Brethour, P. (2010) Malcolm Gladwell: The Quiet Canadian. *The Globe and Mail*, 4 April, accessed 10 September 2010. http://www.theglobeandmail.com/news/technology/malcolm-gladwell-the-quiet-canadian/article1522656/

CBC Documentary (2010) Guergis Breaks Silence on Scandal. [Interview]. Interview with P. Mansbridge, 11 May 2010. Online at http://www.cbc.ca/canada/story/2010/05/10/helena-guergis-exclusive-mansbridge.html

Eliot, T.S. (1953) Tradition and the individual talent. In F. Kermode (ed.) *Selected Prose of T.S. Eliot* (pp. 37–44). London: Penguin.

Gladwell, M. (2002) *The Tipping Point: How Little Things Can Make a Big Difference*. New York, NY: Little, Brown, and Company.

Gladwell, M (2008) *Outliers: The Story of Success*. New York, NY: Little, Brown, and Company.

Gramsci, A. (1994) Hegemony, intellectuals, and the state. In J. Storey (ed.) *Cultural Theory and Popular Culture Reader* (pp. 85–91). Toronto: Pearson.

Guergis, H. (2011) Hon. Helena Guergis P.C., M.P., M.B.A., personal website, accessed 1 Feb 2011. www.helenaguergis.com

Horkheimer, M. and Adorno, T. (2002) *The Dialectics of Enlightenment* (E. Jephcott, trans.). Frankfurt am Mein: Verlag.

House of Commons, Ottawa, Ontario (2011) Member of Parliament Profile: Helena Guergis, webpage, accessed 1 February 2011. http://webinfo.parl.gc.ca/Members OfParliament/ProfileMP.aspx?Key=128818&Language=E

Hutcheon, L. (2001) Presidential Address 2000: She do the president in different voices. *PMLA* 116 (3), 518–530.

Jackson, S. (2006) *Professing Performance: Theatre in the Academy from Philology to Performativity.* London: Cambridge.

Kennedy, J. (2010) Scarlet letters and scapegoats. *Ottawa Citizen*, 13 May. Online at http://www2.canada.com/ottawacitizen/columnists/story.html?id=c41f7f16-1c3c-4336-b4e1-e1b585d1e999&p=2

Lim, S.G. (2003) The strangeness of Creative Writing: An institutional writing. *Pedagogy: Critical Approaches to Teaching Literature, Language, Composition, and Culture* 3 (2), 151–169.

Munro, A. (1993) What is real? In G. Gedes (ed.) *The Art of Short Fiction: An International Anthology* (pp. 824–826). Toronto: HarperCollins.

Oxford English Dictionary. E-Resource, accessed 1 Feb 2011.

Smith, J. (2010) Guergis Resigns, Now Faces RCMP Probe,' *The Star* (April 9, 2010). E-source. Accessed on Feb. 1, 2011. http://www.thestar.com/news/canada/article/792861--guergis-resigns-faces-rcmp-probe

Smith, S. (2010) The English major as social action. *Profession* (2010), 196–206.

Titus, P.A. (2007) Applied creativity: The creative marketing breakthrough model. *Journal of Marketing Education* 29 (3), 262–272.

13 Selling It: Creative Writing and the Public Good

Thom Vernon

Introduction: Piss Christ & 35 years On

The same year that I booked my first TV commercial as an actor, Americans were becoming familiar with *fatwas*, crucifixes swimming in urine and bullwhips stuck in Robert Mapplethorpe's ass. The novel *The Satanic Verses* (Rushdie, 1989) and the artworks *Piss Christ* (Serrano, 1987) and *Self-Portrait with a Bull-Whip* (Mapplethorpe, 1978) captured imaginations and vitriol. 'Piss' and 'Bull-Whip' were supported by the National Endowment for the Arts (NEA) and used as rallying points for various groups, pro- and con-. That period became seminal in my understanding of the arts in society. Also, in 1989, there were shrill calls to halt funding of the NEA *and* the National Endowment for the Humanities. These events were synchronous with a larger shift to policy strategies of lower taxes, less regulation and less social spending in the United States and Canada.

This neo-liberal approach to policy-making has not fulfilled its promise to ensure democratic rights and freedoms, while expanding access to economic and personal self-determination. Simpson (2011) comments that, 'Canadian Conservatives and U.S. Republicans have spent at least three decades pledging three things: lower taxes, smaller government and a balanced budget. Their record has been so dismal, and the gap between promise and fulfilment so large, that citizens have to wonder what's been going on'. Simpson, unfortunately, does not acknowledge that Canadian Liberals and American Democrats have also wholeheartedly signed onto the neo-liberal project. President Clinton, after all, largely eliminated social welfare in the United States.

But, in addition to economic failure, the neo-liberal project has eroded many of the social ties that bind. As we work in jobs we hate, to repay students loans we borrowed to earn the economic freedom promised by higher education, we are watched, tracked and censored. There are, since the 1970s, far fewer people doing far better than everyone else. In 2000, the wealthiest 50% of Canadian families controlled 94.4% of wealth, with the

Figure 13.1 *Piss Christ*, Andres Serrano (1989). Source: reproduced by permission of the artist

other 50% holding 5.6% (Brownlee, 2005: 7). In the United States, the Walmart family holds as much wealth as the bottom 40% of the population (Judt, 2010: 14). Consequently, we are bound to our surveillance states and the meanings they deploy, perpetuate and reproduce. 'The problem with market economies', writes Terry Eagleton (2010: 78), 'is that they erode the symbolic, affective dimensions of social existence'. The assertions and arguments that follow could be applied, arguably, to the entire North American arts and humanities project, which I will reference. However, my focus is creative writing. In a culture where meaning is being collapsed and narrowed to the bottom-line, the demand and hunger for the indeterminacy of authoring has, as we shall see, risen.

As I began to poke around the question, *what good is creative writing?* correlations and trends showed themselves. For example, this era of self-determined freedom has seen incarceration rates skyrocket (especially among youth and non-whites) to over 7.2 million in 2009 (USDOJ, 2010: 2). It has witnessed formidable expansions of state surveillance, a chemically poisoned food supply, dramatic decreases in social spending (and the values they inure), the vilification of teachers and the arts and humanities and an explosion of post-secondary creative writing programmes. It is the rise in enrolment in such programmes, often at great personal cost, that motivated me to see if I could articulate 'what good is creative writing?' In particular, how it nourishes the public good in the neo-liberal context.

Thirty-five years on, the North American neo-liberal shift is in full swing. Neo-liberalism has transferred public wealth to private interests (e.g. the Walmart family), as it has interrogated public spending. Social mobility has decreased, while the social ills associated with economic disadvantage – alcoholism, obesity, minor crime etc. – have increased (Judt, 2010: 14). At this point, after a decade of United States and Canadian military interventions abroad, a financial collapse caused by the rollback of effective regulation of banking rules (e.g. the *Gramm-Leach-Bliley Act* of 1999) and a dramatic concentration of media outlets (e.g. Time-Warner, Viacom-CBS, GE-NBC, News Corp, Wall Street Journal, Fox News etc.), questions of public spending on social democratic projects could be described as red herrings. In other words, the interrogation of public initiatives that inure socially cohesive values masks the transfer of wealth in the form of government bail-outs, military expenditures, Wall Street bonuses and a relaxed regulatory environment.

Public spending on redistributive policies (e.g. programmes to assist the poor) is ideologically framed as untrustworthy (Rudolph & Evans, 2005), even though cash-strapped and unhealthy consumers and workers are hardly the components of economic growth and stability. For instance, the United States pays 17% of its Gross Domestic Product (GDP) for healthcare, while other countries with universal healthcare pay between 7–10% (Bartlett, 2009). The United States has fewer doctors, fewer overall office visits and fewer acute hospital beds than any other comparable nation. Rhetorically, in a climate of *pull-yourself-up-by-your-bootstraps*, these shifts also feed negative beliefs about ourselves and the people around us. As under-regulated self-interest has increased, the anxiety and stress associated with the gross inequality contribute to our mutual *mis*trustfulness and the highest rate of mental illness (25%) of any similar industrialised nation (Judt, 2010: 19).

Countries, such as Canada, with universal access to health care are roundly and solidly demonised in the United States. This demonisation, usually by demagogic entertainers cloaked as policy experts, is perpetuated by the concentrated corporate media. Arguably, that media has a vested interest (higher ratings = higher advertising rates) in social divisiveness and crisis that result from inequalities of wealth and opportunity. Spending on public initiatives that would lend social cohesiveness, such as universal healthcare, are demonised as contributing to the weakening of the nation.

Devaluing and Defunding the Public Good

Rhetorical platitudes from the bully pulpit supported the devaluing of public goods, such as healthcare and education. Margaret Thatcher and Ronald Reagan shot opening rhetorical salvos that questioned the notion of *society* altogether, while proclaiming that public funds had no business supporting 'intellectual curiosity' (in education, for example) (Clabaugh, 2004: 256). Yet, the Centres for Disease Control and Prevention (2010) provides evidence demonstrating, for instance, a correspondence between weak educational performance and social ills, such as alcoholism, violence and obesity. Denying this, the Reagan Education Secretary called such correlations 'sociological flimflammery' (Clabaugh, 2004: 257–258), while the President called university campuses havens for 'brats' and 'fascists'. This has culminated in hardly any public discourse around educational pedagogy, but plenty around teacher performance. Gary K. Clabaugh (2004) of the New Foundations educational advocacy group points out that it was claimed that teacher performance was the main factor in low student scores on standardised tests. These scores then justified defunding public education. This overlay of political ideology resulted in a reallocation of resources away from public education into private charter schools. Charter schools today compete with public schools for public dollars and students (Ross, n.d.).

But it is not that public spending has decreased overall, rather, it has shifted from social democratic projects to the private sector. By the time he left office, Reagan had successfully halved the federal budget for the Department of Education (Clabaugh, 2004: 256), but increased military spending by over 39% (Rogers & Ferguson, 1986). Canadian funding for public education was also halved in the same period (Munt, 2010), while military expenditures matched Korean War levels (Robinson & Ibbot, 2003). These trends continue. In 2009, 43% of global military spending was United States based (Defence Talk, 2009). There is more and more money for military adventurism, but less and less for social-democratic projects, such as income assistance. During his two administrations, Reagan reduced social spending by 10%. 'Morning in America', Reagan's 1984 campaign slogan (Reagan-Bush, 1984), culminated with the *end of welfare as we know it*, President Clinton's *Personal Responsibility and Work Opportunity Reconciliation Act of 1996* (US Congress, 1996). Clinton collapsed the meanings of public income assistance into an individual character flaws (Vobejda, 1996). Not surprisingly, too, after *Piss Christ* and other controversies, the combined NEA and National Endowment for the Humanities funding dropped from around $300 million to $124 million by 2006 (NEA, 2007a: 5). The de-valuing of education and social investment nourished and justified defunding.

In a pluralistic society, rightly, definitions of the social good run the gamut from universal healthcare to generous defence spending. That said, it is not too far-fetched to say that the good refers to those *qualities* of public and private life which are generally accepted as reasonably beneficial to all or most people: mutual cooperation, respect and so on. Civil society is a fair system of cooperation, as John Rawls (2003: 20) argues, which is not tied to any particular conception of the good. But what collective goods do we lose in public life when meanings are collapsed into the bottom-line?

Neo-liberalism's reduction of 'society' to a thin membrane of interactions between private individuals is presented today as the ambition of libertarians and free marketers. 'But we should never forget', argues Tony Judt (2010: 119–120) in *Ill Fares the Land*, 'that it was first and above all the dream of Jacobins, Bolsheviks and Nazis'. Over the last 35 years, neo-liberal values (low taxes, less waste, government effectiveness and efficiency, etc.) have increasingly transplanted the traditional social democratic values fostered by, say, literature. A little further on, we shall see exactly how art and literature helped victims of the Nazis, such as Walter Benjamin and Paul Klee, to articulate the collapse of meaning and the rise of fascism.

The *Good* of Creative Writing

If we think of pieces of literature as purpose-built spaces, we may gain a better understanding of exactly how it serves those qualities we call the public good. We enter an author's literary spaces in order to transform raw perception and sensation into experiences of qualities that also happen to nourish the public good: recognition, trust, empathy, etc. When we read a book or a story and have an aha moment – it is very similar to walking into any new space, such as a cathedral, art gallery or even a new friend's living room. Our senses register patterns, colours, smells, and our brains organise this sensory data into what we call 'experience'. The construction of these spaces is, I would argue, a principle *raison d'etre* of authoring. It is an activity that links private imagination to the communities in which we live.

Engagement with literature has a private side: we read and write alone. In these constructed literary spaces, our imaginations take flight. Our imaginative capacities, research has shown, are positively correlated with the reading of literature, for instance. Invariably, then, we bring our private neurological, psychological and emotional apparatus and experience back into the public sphere. One consequence of this private-public exchange among writers and readers is that our creative capacities increase our employment prospects. In fact, our creative capacities will soon provide our only economic security. Ours, the NEA (2007b: 77) advises, 'is a world in which comfort with ideas and abstractions is the passport to a good job, in which creativity and innovation are the key to the good life, in which high levels of education – a very different kind of education than most of us have had – are going to be the only security there is'. Not surprisingly, then, reading rates are also positively correlated with social engagement (NEA, 2007b), as well as a sense of belonging. Hence, our private literary engagements dialectically shape, and expand, our public ones.

If one insists on understanding the value of the arts through its econom-ics, then the arts make a very strong case for themselves. In Canada, the Conference Board (2008, i) informs us that the contribution of the cultural sector to the nation's GDP is over 7% annually, with publishing leading the way in exports; and for every dollar invested in the arts, specifically, $1.84 is value-added to the economy (Arts Research Monitor, 2008: 29). For its part, globally, the United States is one of the top three producers and exporters of cultural goods (UNESCO, 2005). Even in the 2008–2010 economic downturn, book sales declined only slightly (Millet, 2011). So the case for the economic benefits of the arts betrays their demonisation.

But even with all of the revenue-generation and employment (1.1 million in 2007) (Conference Board of Canada, 2008: 29), there is some-thing inherently valuable in the practice of, and engagement with, the arts, specifically, literature. Roland Barthes (1985: 93) asserts that we are born into a system of symbols of which language is integral, and it is this 'symbolic which constitutes the man.' Literature allows us to engage meaningfully with this symbolic order, because it resists the collapse of meaning through amplification and refraction. 'We become', Charles Taylor (1994: 32) writes, 'full human agents, capable of understanding ourselves, and hence of defining our identity, through our acquisition of rich human languages of expression'. Because our self-conception is inherently formed through dialogue and struggle with the society and symbols in which we live, we depend upon engagement with language to communicate and traffic socially.

If our values do not bind us to each other, then we can only look to the state for meaning. Judt (2010: 118) contends that the neo-liberal shift has 'eviscerated society'; the privatisation and bottom-line thinking in regards to public goods, such as education, leaves 'nothing except authority and obedience binding the citizen to the state'. With the squeezing-out of public discourse of meanings, other than those relevant to the bottom-line and the state, we also diminish our capacity to recognise our unique self-conceptions and those of others. This is where fascism enters. But the arts – such as creative writing – could enter here too.

In the following sections, I would like to demonstrate some of the philosophy and a few of the mechanics behind all of this construction to which I refer. Creative writing weaves self-interest (and exploration) into the public good through its construction of literary structures. It does this by positioning and deploying correspondences between the private experiences, perceptions and sensations of author and reader. These privacies then reverberate as *experience* for the reader.

The middle section of the final volume of Proust's *In Search of Lost Time*, for instance, offers one way to position such correspondences.

> One can list indefinitely in a description all the objects that figured in the place described, but the truth will begin only when the writer takes two different objects, establishes their relationship, the analogue in the world of art of the unique relation created in the world of science by the laws of causality, and encloses them within the necessary armature of a beautiful style. (2002: 198)

Proust, of course, is the master of these deployments. Very early in the first volume of 'Search', there is one example – a description of the reflections from 'a magic lantern' placed in his room by his mother or grandmother to soothe the boy:

> . . . Golo would come out of the small triangular forest that velveted the hillside with dark green and advance jolting toward the castle of poor Genevieve de Brabant. This castle was cut off along a curved line that was actually the edge of one of the glass ovals arranged in the frame which you slipped between the grooves of the lantern. It was only a section of the castle and it had a moor in front of it . . . (2003: 8)

The author's memories (real or imagined) prepare a scaffolding, bound together by emotion, upon which the reader's imagination can climb. Reading just this section could allow a reader to experience ancient forests inhabited by a mysterious Lady, the frustration one can encounter as a child trying to make a mechanical thing work properly, remote castles to be conquered (and all things yet to conquer) and the soggy moors full of dangerous traps, pitfalls and missteps. One can imagine being a frustrated and lonely boy, such as the narrator, put to bed too early and awaiting his mother's kiss. The very purpose of placing such pillars is not to choose one or the other as correct, but rather to erect a structure into which a reader's imagination may enter.

As authors create these spaces, readers practice those values that cohere us, normatively. Editor Alana Wilcox (2010) puts it this way: 'Reading and writing hone the imagination like nothing else, and imagination is the key to empathy, which is key to a successful, compassionate society. It's here, in this empathy, that literature contributes most to the public good'. Recognition, empathy and trust are the foundations of civil society. But more precisely, Taylor (1994: 35) holds that what has 'come about with the modern age is not the need for recognition but the conditions in which the attempt to be recognised can fail'. Provocatively, in this same era, where public support of the arts and humanities and of education has been drastically reduced, more and more people have turned to creative writing. For example, in 1977, there were 77 post-secondary creative writing programmes in North America, while today, there are almost 900 (AWP). Perhaps because of the dialectical structures it employs, creative writing (for either producer or consumer) provides the spaces for empathy and recognition, upon which our social cohesion depends. It is the dialectical impact of these structures to which I turn now.

Architectures of Empathy

Elsewhere (Vernon, 2010a), I have located the site of literary creation – metaphorically – in the debris pile in Paul Klee's *Angelus Novus* (1920). *Angelus* helped Walter Benjamin and Klee understand the distortions of the collective good, in their time, as fascism gripped the national German imagination. The angel can help us here, too, as we flesh out exactly *how* literature contributes to the public good through the multiplication of meaning.

For Benjamin and Klee, *Angelus* represented the progress of history. In it, an angel is caught in a storm. He beats his wings furiously, his curls wild, his eyes riveted on the right – the past. A 'pile of debris before him grows towards the sky. What we call progress is *this* storm' (Benjamin, 2003b: 392). The storm is the storm of history, and the debris is potent wreckage waiting for resurrection. The wreckage is composed of *trace*: memories, experiences, perceptions and sensations. Each 'trace', and so the debris pile, too, is organised by original, organic impulses to desire, love, empathise, recognise or trust (Kristeva, 1995: 17–19). It is the foundation of the *organic* formalism that Klee offers, in response to Martin Heidegger's *technological* formalism (Watson, 2006). 'Organic' because each perception or sensation, noticed by our awareness or not, organises itself into what Freud (1999: 351) called 'memory-traces', Benjamin called (2003a: 316) 'trace', and we now call *neural networks*. Perceptions or sensations, and, so traces', carry with them original impulses and authenticities (auras), which makes them ripe for the author's picking. Benjamin (2003c: 254) advised that it is 'the authenticity of a thing … that is transmissible in it from its origin on, ranging from its physical duration to the historical testimony relating to it'.

We authors, then, brood over 'trace' in a psychological/emotional state of melancholy, and then craft that debris (some conscious, some not) into auratic vessels, such as allegories, narrative lines, short stories or novels. Seemingly long-gone memories and experiences are revived and refracted through literary techniques, such as multiple perspectives, tmesis, discontinuities, metaphor and metonymy. Our melancholic engagement displaces aura into different points of view so that new meanings can surface. This

Figure 13.2 *Angelus Novus,* Paul Klee (1920). Source: public domain

dialectical relationship between past and present in a literary context casts the reader and author as messiahs.

The past is reified as humans narrate their lives into stories. When I tell you of my experience, organised from perception and sensation, it becomes your own. For example, my Aunt Sarah confessed to me, at 90, that she still felt very guilty for setting the schoolhouse on fire in the little Arkansas hamlet where she was being courted by her future husband, Uncle Joe. Even at that age, she swore me to secrecy. Sarah's guilt rears its head, sometimes more or less consciously, every time I make an absent-minded misstep. The circumstances of my missteps are different than Sarah's, but her original impulses and auras traverse the decades and inform my contemporary

Figure 13.3 *My Brother Son Tomey (sic) + Aunt Sarah* (1959).
Source: Private collection of the author

experience and my literature. So, when in *The Drifts* (Vernon, 2010b), Julie abandons Pity, a nine-year old girl, in a storm-swept parking lot, I experience Sarah and her arson.

In *On Some Motifs on Baudelaire*, Benjamin (2003a: 316) puts it this way:

> Story does not aim to convey an event per se, which is the purpose of information; rather, it embeds the event in the life of the audience in order to pass it on as experience to those listening. It thus bears the 'trace' of the storyteller, much the way an earthen vessel bears the 'trace' of the potter's hand.

Our novels and allegories become these earth-bound, auratic vessels.

These perceptions *qua* experience can be measured as electrically charged exchanges of sodium and potassium in brain cells. The charge is produced as brain cells (and other neuro-elements) emit energy, measured by frequency and amplitude (Hz and μV, respectively). Such *Aha!* moments are the brain's electrophysiological response to environmental stimuli, and it is a response that can be measured and recorded as *event-related potentials* (ERPs) (Moran, 2004). This energy emits, like the pulse of aura, when we have *experiences*. The sodium-potassium transfer reifies the past as it reconstructs it as the structures of allegory, metaphor and experience.

Like neuroscience, chaos theory has something to offer this discussion. Allegories, as auratic vessels, cobble 'trace' into story, much like subatomic particles create *strange attractors*: the unique, seemingly chaotic formations made by the collusion of subatomic particles moving over time (Bradley, 2010). Because the movement of subatomic particles seems so random and fleeting, they do not, it seems, leave traces'. But tracked over time, elaborate structures are found to have been erected and organised as the particles are pulled towards, and driven from, one another. These are forces akin to the 'love' that Kristeva (1995) cites. These attractive forces, acting as love, empathy, recognition, trust, etc. are the material ties that bind when it comes to trace (Benjamin, 2003: 389–90).

'Traces' are inscribed, disrupted and deployed like magic spells by writers. It is authenticity that sustains 'trace' over time. And if clustered into neural networks, or 'trace', original authority becomes food for the progress of history, but not so fast. There is a whore who casts the spell called 'Once upon a time', according to Benjamin (2003: 396). Hitler and his followers, for instance, invoked the mythical *Volk,* in order to embody Germany's past in himself and the Third Reich. 'The Fuhrer himself and he alone *is* the German reality', Heidegger told his students (Evans, 2005: 421).

Figure 13.4 *Strange Attractor* (TBD).
Source: Baudoin, P. (2011). Boring. New Media Blog. Accessed 12 December 2011.
http://blog.philipbaudoin.com/?p=135&cpage=1#comment-436

This embodiment was deployed by Nazi culture as an instrument of historical and philological paralysis. In his *On the Concept of History* (2003b), Benjamin works out how, if we can cut loose from the spell of 'once upon a time' (p. 390), the past endows us with a 'weak' (p. 390) messianic power. We must, through dialectical engagements (such as authoring, reading, baking) 'wrest tradition away from the conformism that is working to overpower it' (p. 391). The love, empathy and trust that become our own experience during, and after, our engagement with these traces', erect the ceiling and walls of what we come to recognise as our experience (Kristeva, 1995: 21). These impulses also act as the organising and motivational principle for our social behaviour, according to Jane Jacobs and others (cited in Judt, 2010: 67).

The difference between writing and authoring is the 'good' of writing. In *The Grain of the Voice* (1985: 94), Barthes distinguishes between *writing* (writing without polyvalence) and *authoring* (writing that provokes a multiplicity of meanings); between *matte* (*sans* echo) and textured writing. If a piece of work lacks dimension (i.e. echo), it risks its ability to resonate as literature. Authoring, though, is a deliberate placing of trace on the margins of linear time so that 'a logical framework for the countless flashes, condensations, plots, and meditations' moves the reader beyond into a grand cathedral (Kristeva, 1995: 189) of her own making. These 'trace's then interrupt chronological story-time so that a reader's imagination can enter' (Chatman, 1992: 406). Here, socially cohesive qualities can be experienced and practiced. The reader steps inside the literary space and into the pulsing, textured vibration emitting from each, her senses perceive the pulse of authenticity and then she, herself, becomes an encoder (Kristeva, 1995: 232). An east Los Angeles university fiction student emailed me that, 'creative writing helps us learn what it means to be human from a variety of perspectives in time and place' (Ariel, 2010). She is alluding, I presume, to the multiplication of meaning that comes from engaging with creative writing. Our allegories enslave objects in meaning as they disturb aura, and so meaning, into new codes and meanings (Eagleton, 1981: 20). The virtue of this authoring, then, is that these codes are situated in the text, without instruction; the word, liberated, disrupts signs into a new architecture of meaning(s) and *experience* and so, empathy, trust etc. This sort of writing is the blood of our literary *Ahas* and our liberation.

And so, perhaps, here lies the reason that so many creative writers are enrolling in post-secondary programmes. Authoring has the ability to interrupt the chronological temporality of a story so that a reader can expand the picture imaginatively (Chatman, 1992: 406). Barthes' organic accidents of meaning take guidance, practice and skill. The whole literary project is passed from generation to generation, writer to writer. In the neo-liberal era, these hand-offs are happening more and more in post-secondary creative writing programmes.

Why Study Creative Writing?

The question – *what good is creative writing?* – takes on personal, political and public urgency in the neo-liberal context. When most of our lives are reduced to the bottom-line, to its dollar value, we begin to hunger for our stories and the meanings pulsing in them. The reaction to the failures of neo-liberalism has been widespread and deep. Recently, during a screening of *Inside Job* (Representational Pictures, 2010), a documentary about the 2008 global financial crisis, one person shouted 'F#@K YOU!' to the now-billionaire financiers onscreen. Her shout was full of rage and obvious personal suffering. This frustration is increasing, supplying provocation to the American Tea Party movement, for example. But these experiences get channelled into creative writing, also.

Although tuition is expensive, the Association of Writers and Writing Programs (AWP) confirm what was certainly true in my case: writing classes demonstrate the desire to direct energies towards what is aesthetically, socially and politically positive (AWP). Her experiences with literature provoked Karen McD., a creative writing graduate student, to give a battered woman client Stephen King's *Rose Madder* (1995). 'It had changed her life . . . . The novel had helped her more than the legal process . . .' (2010). Karen then began to study creative writing. Tuition for post-secondary writing programmes run from approximately $1,500 at a community college to upwards of $40,000 (or more) for some private graduate-school programmes. Adult creative writing classes are big money-makers, while creative writing classes for traditional students are regularly the most popular classes, supporting a variety of less well-attended programmes (Comparative Literature, etc.) (AWP). Since there are, it seems, fewer and fewer public avenues to form or reform the world, the AWP writes, enrolment become justifiable. We will pay big bucks to learn to contribute positively to other people's experience.

Studying creative writing allows students to become more astute thinkers, producers and consumers. As writers, we are constantly interrogating our thoughts and beliefs and those of our characters. We must become minor experts in quantum physics, neuroscience, credit-default swaps – you name it. We learn the difference between gamma grass and crab apple, elm and poplar and alexandrine and slug lines; between Barthes' texts of pleasure and texts of bliss (1975: 21). Objective correlatives emerge from our once *matte* texts. 'The making and exchange of literary talents and gifts is, of course, a highly civilised and humane act; and appropriately, academe has accepted the practice and making of the literary arts along with study and scholarship in the literary arts' (AWP). Karen continued, 'the post-secondary setting creates a different kind of incentive and more 'real' deadlines for writing projects. 'Also,' she added, 'feedback from a university professor tends to be more objective (and therefore useful) than feedback from a writing group member' (McD., 2010). The study of creative writing puts students in direct contact with literary masters. For example, in what other context would Hubert 'Cubby' Selby, Jr. (*Last Exit to Brooklyn, Requiem for a Dream* etc.) have pointed out to me that I was alternating between 14 and 16 syllable lines in my writing? It took a master to notice this raw, organic formalism emerging.

Poet and critic R.M. Vaughn advised me, 'Perhaps in the larger sense, even if most of the students will never end up getting published or have careers as writers, they will be more literate, more media savvy, and more prone to think independently, and thus be better consumers. On the other hand, I think knowledge sharing ought to be assessed for its innate value, not on an economic level. A more creative populace makes for a more creative world, and that obviously includes economic prosperity' (2010).

We, North Americans, are 'well aware that something is seriously amiss' (Judt, 2010: 29). It is inspiring to see that so many of us have taken up our pens quietly and doggedly to earn our keep, but also to contribute to the collective good. The architectures of empathy that we create allow readers to have their own experiences, of themselves and the rest of us. We hunger for the textured intermittences of a Proust or Alice Munro. There, in the drawing rooms of *fin de siècle* Paris or the fox farms of south-western Ontario, we are recalled and revived in the symbolic world that literature erects. The author's skill at crafting these structures and qualities can be practiced in class so that we can then deploy them publically in our writing. As we have seen, these contributions contribute enormously to civil society, the economy and our own well-being. In an era where neo-liberal policies have decimated savings, eliminated jobs and grossly exaggerated the income gap, creative writing offers the means to contribute our suffering, loss and triumph to the public good.

References

Arts Research Monitor (2010) *Culture Goods Trade (2008)* 8 (8), Hills Strategies Research: Hamilton.

Arts Research Monitor (2008) *Valuing Culture: Measuring and Understanding Canada's Creative Economy*, 7 (5), Hills Strategies Research: Hamilton.

Association of Writers and Writing Programs (AWP) 'About AWP'. In *The Association of Writers and Writing Programs*, online document, accessed 12 December 2010. http://www.awpwriter.org/aboutawp/index.htm

Barlett, B. (2009) Health Care: Costs and Reform. *Forbes.com*, 03 July, online article, accessed 08 January 2011. http://www.forbes.com/2009/07/02/health-care-costs-opinions-columnists-reform.html

Barthes, Roland (1975). The Pleasure of the Text, Hill and Wang.

Barthes, R. (1985) *The Grain of the Voice: Interviews 1962–1980*. New York, NY: Hill and Wang.

Baudoin, P. (2011). *Boring*. New Media Blog. Accessed 12 December 2011. http://blog.philipbaudoin.com/?p=135&cpage=1#comment-436

Benjamin, W. (2003a) On some motifs in Baudelaire. In H. Eiland (ed.) *Walter Benjamin: Selected Writings, Volume 4, 1938–1940*. Cambridge: Belknap.

Benjamin, W. (2003b) On the concept of history. In H. Eiland (ed.) *Walter Benjamin: Selected Writings, Volume 4, 1938–1940*. Cambridge: Belknap.

Benjamin, W. (2003c) Work of art in the age of reproducibility. In H. Eiland (ed.) *Walter Benjamin: Selected Writings, Volume 4, 1938–1940*. Cambridge: Belknap.

Bradley, L. (2010) *Chaos and Fractals*, seminar website, Department of Physics and Astronomy, Johns Hopkins University, accessed 02 January 2011. http://www.stsci.edu/~lbradley/seminar/attractors.html

Brownlee, J. (2005) *Ruling Canada: Corporate Cohesion and Democracy*. Halifax: Fernwood Publishing.

Centres for Disease Control and Prevention (2010) *Healthy Youth! Student Health and Academic Achievement*, online document, accessed 18 April 2011. http://www.cdc.gov/HealthyYouth/health_and_academics/#2

Chatman, S. (1992) What novels can do that films can't (and vice versa). In G. Mast, M. Cohen and L. Braudy (eds) *Film Theory and Criticism* (pp. 405–419). Oxford: Oxford University Press.

Clabaugh, G. (2004) *The Educational Legacy of Ronald Reagan*, essay reprinted online, accessed 25 November 2010. http://www.newfoundations.com/Clabaugh/Cutting Edge/Reagan.html#_edn7

Conference Board of Canada (2008) *Valuing Culture: Measuring and Understanding Canada's Creative Economy,* online document, accessed 18 April 2011. http://www.conference board.ca/temp/ebe998fe-d627-4e7f-b3dc-dd2b204d7e42/08_152%20Canada%27s% 20Creative%20Economy_RPT_WEB.pdf

Defence Talk (2009) *Global Military Spending Soars Despite Crisis: Report,* online document, accessed 09 January 2011. http://www.defencetalk.com/global-military-spending-soars-despite-crisis-report-26731/

Eagleton, T. (1981) *Walter Benjamin, or Towards a Revolutionary Criticism.* Brooklyn, NY: Verso.

Eagleton, T. (2010) Reappraisals: What is the worth of social democracy? *Harper's Magazine* 321 (1925), 77–80.

Evans, R. (2005) *The Coming of the Third Reich.* New York, NY: Penguin.

Fenza, D. (2010). About AWP. *The Association of Writers and Writing Programs,* accessed 12 December 2010. http://www.awpwriter.org/aboutawp/index.htm

Ferguson, C. (2010). *Inside Job.* Representational Pictures and Sony Classics (2010). USA. Documentary Film.

Freud, S. (1999) *The Interpretation of Dreams* (Joyce Crick, trans.). New York, NY: Oxford University Press.

Gramm-Leach-Bliley Act 1999 (United States Senate) Washington DC: Library of Congress. Online at http://thomas.loc.gov/cgi-bin/query/z?c106:S.900.ENR:

Judt, T. (2010) *Ill Fares the Land.* New York, NY: Penguin.

King, S. (1995) *Rose Madder.* New York, NY: Signet.

Klee, P. (1920) Angelus Novus. *Israel Museum,* Jerusalem.

Kristeva, J. (1995) *Time and Sense.* New York, NY: Columbia University Press.

Mapplethorpe, R. (1978). *Self-Portrait with Bull-Whip,* online image, accessed 5 April 2011. http://artportraiture.blogspot.com/2010/05/robert-mapplethorpe-self-portrait-with.html

Millet, J. (2011) Units had modest decline in 2010. *Publishers Weekly,* 10 January. Online at http://www.publishersweekly.com/pw/by-topic/industry-news/financial-reporting/article/45716-units-had-modest-decline-in-2010.html

Moran, M.A. (2004) Brain fingerprinting: Is the science there? *Neurology Today* 4 (11), 74–78. Online at http://journals.lww.com/neurotodayonline/Fulltext/2004/11000/Brain_Fingerprinting__Is_the_Science_There_.21.aspx

Munt, G. (2010) Financial and funding trends in Canadian universities. *Strategic and Budgetary Priorites,* online document, accessed 11 January 2011. http://www.uwinnipeg.ca/index/cms-filesystem-action/pdfs/fac-arts/money-woes.pdf

National Endowment for the Arts (NEA) (2007a) *How the United States Funds the Arts,* online document, accessed 12 December 2011. http://www.nea.gov/pub/how.pdf

National Endowment for the Arts (NEA) (2007b) *To Read or Not to Read: a Question of National Consequence* (Report 47), online document, accessed 12 December 2011. http://www.nea.gov/research/toread.pdf

Northern Illinois University. *Right Turn,* online document, accessed 25 November 2010. http://www3.niu.edu/~td0raf1/history468/apr0401.htm

Personal Responsibility and Work Opportunity Reconciliation Act of 1996 (United States Congress). Washington DC: Library of Congress. Online at: http://thomas.loc.gov/cgi-bin/query/z?c104:H.R.3734.ENR:

Rawls, J. (2003) *Justice as Fairness.* Cambridge: Belknap Press.

Proust, Marcel (2002). *Finding Time Again.* Trans. Ian Patterson. New York: Penguin Books. 198.

Proust, Marcel (2003). *Swann's Way*. Trans. Lydia Davis. New York: Penguin Books. 8.

Pytka Productions (1984). *It's Morning in America*. Television Commercial, accessed 06 April 2011. http://www.youtube.com/watch?v=EU-IBF8nwSY

Reagan, B. (1984) Television Commercial, accessed 06 April 2011. http://www.youtube.com/watch?v=EU-IBF8nwSY (2010). *Inside Job* [Documentary Film]. Representational Pictures and Sony Classics.

Robinson, B. and Ibbot, P. (2003) Canadian Military Spending: How Does the Current Level Compare to Historical Levels? . . . To Allied Spending? . . . To Potential Threats? *Project Ploughshares Working Papers*, online document, accessed 15 December 2010. http://www.ploughshares.ca/libraries/WorkingPapers/wp031.pdf

Rogers, J. and Ferguson, T. (1986) *Right Turn,* online document, accessed 25 November 2010. http://www3.niu.edu/~td0raf1/history468/apr0401.htm

Ross, B. (n.d.) Charter Schools on the Rise: What You Need to Know, *Education.com*, blog post, accessed 12 January 2011. http://www.education.com/magazine/article/parents-charter-schools/

Rudolph, T.J. and Evans, J. (2005) Political trust, ideology, and public support for government spending. *American Journal of Political Science*, 49 (3), 661. Online at http://www.jstor.org/stable/3647738

Rushdie, S. (1989) *The Satanic Verses*. London: Penguin.

Serrano, A. (1987) Piss Christ. New York.

Simpson, J. (2011) Whistlin' Past the Graveyard of Conservative Vows. *The Globe & Mail*, 14 January. Online at http://www.theglobeandmail.com/news/opinions/opinion/whistlin-past-the-graveyard-of-conservative-vows/article1869229/

Statistics Canada (2008) *Culture Goods Trade: Data Tables*, online document, accessed 18 April 2011. http://www.statcan.gc.ca/pub/87-007-x/87-007-x2009001-eng.pdf

Taylor, C. (1994) The politics of recognition. In A. Gutmann (ed.) *Multiculturalism*. Princeton: Princeton University Press.

Tea Party (2010). Core Beliefs, *Tea Party,* website, accessed 5 January 2010. http://teaparty.org/about.php#beliefs

United States Congress (1996) *Personal Responsibility and Work Opportunity Reconciliation Act of 1996*, Bill of United States Congress. Online at http://thomas.loc.gov/cgi-bin/query/z?c104:H.R.3734.ENR:

United States Department of Justice (USDOJ) (2010) *Correctional Populations in the United States, 2009*. Washington, DC: Bureau of Justice Statistics. Online at http://bjs.ojp.usdoj.gov/index.cfm?ty=pbdetail&iid=2316

UNESCO (2005) *International Flows of Selected Cultural Goods and Services, 1994–2003*. Montreal: UNESCO Institute for Statistics. Online at http://www.uis.unesco.org/template/pdf/cscl/IntlFlows_EN.pdf

Vernon, T. (2005) *My Brother Son Tomey (sic) + Aunt Sarah*. Author's private collection.

Vernon, T. (2010a) *The Angel at Our Table*. Unpublished manuscript.

Vernon, T. (2010b) *The Drifts*. Toronto: Coach House Books.

Vobejda, B. (1996) Clinton Signs Welfare Bill Amid Division. *Washington Post*, 23 August. Online at http://www.washingtonpost.com/wp-srv/politics/special/welfare/stories/wf082396.htm.

Watson, S.H. (2006) Heidegger, Paul Klee, and the origin of the work of art. *Review of Metaphysics* 60 (2), 327–357.

14 On the Commercialisation of Creativity in the Merlion State

Eric Tinsay Valles

The Merlion is an icon, with the head of a lion and the body of a fish, which has come to represent the affluent island nation of Singapore. The original 8.6m statue is at Merlion Park, situated close to the Fullerton Hotel and linked by a bridge to the premier performing arts centres that are the Espalanade Theatres on Marina Bay. On 12 March 2011, the latest creative interpretation of the Merlion was unveiled. A foreigner – the Japanese artist Tatsuro Nishino (who sometimes uses the alias Tatzu Nishi) – became the first guest at his own installation artwork, the Merlion Hotel, which enclosed the icon in a 100sqm five-star, full-service suite. This artwork could be the result of an observation of the Merlion's vaunted role in national life, as a magnet for high-spending tourists. Nishino says, 'It is an international Merlion so I hope it will attract international guests as well, Singaporeans, Japanese and . . . people from Hong Kong and Thailand' (Nanda, 2011). It might also be a judgment of Singaporean life and creativity: government patronage of the arts has brought on some smugness, but state-created myths do generate vibrant creative arts. This Merlion Hotel art project is part of the Singapore Biennale – a showcase of both local and international artworks.

The image of the Merlion has become a touchstone for Singaporeans and permanent residents alike to elucidate their identification with the island and to account for their different approaches to creativity. This is so because Singapore's relatively short history has not yielded any more significant or enduring icon. But people in Singapore have taken the limitation of their island's history as a challenge to generate their own icons and stories. Their relationship with the Merlion is complicated. The icon elicits, on different occasions, various feelings, from anxiety to consternation, but it has also been a site of inspiration and a window to their viewers' experience of themselves as creative producers. As such, it may signify the tension between the individual artist and state policy and the nature of creative expression in a postcolonial society.

Far from being a break from the past, the Merlion is a creative revision of legendary stories about Singapore's past. A foreigner, Prince Sang Nila Utama, supposedly landed on the island's shores after a stormy boat ride. He saw a lion, which he took to be a good omen. He then established a colony on the island, which he called Singapura, meaning 'lion city'. This story is retold and performed in schools and public celebrations. During the island's 40th annual National Day Parade on 9 August 2005, for instance, a float featuring the image of Sang Nila Utama with a lion preceded the image of Sir Stamford Raffles, who claimed Singapore for the British crown in 1819. The performance highlighted the key role that Western influence has played in the evolution of modern Singapore and its characteristic prosperity as a regional trading hub and creator of literary and other art works. British writer and theatre maker Paul Rae suggested that the 'meaning-making processes that have accompanied infrastructural development in much postcolonial nation-building have had a particular cast' for the inhabitants of the island state (2007: 120). The impact of the Merlion, however, goes beyond officially sanctioned events.

The Merlion itself is the result of the island's long-standing, state-directed pragmatism and creative practice of engagement with the West. It was the creation of another foreigner, Fraser Brunner – a member of the Souvenir Committee of the Singapore Tourism Board (STB) – in 1964. The icon was adopted and henceforth promoted by the STB. Its target audience was, no doubt, foreign tourists 'who may come across this emblem and arouse ... a desire to visit Singapore' (Rae, 2007: 121). In 1972, the first statue of the Merlion, constantly spitting into the Singapore River, was installed at the spot where Raffles stepped ashore for the first time in 1819 (Rae, 2007: 121). Over time, the Merlion has successfully supplanted other island state symbols, such as the tiger (which appears on the logo of a local beer and a globally-recognised medicinal balm) and Singa the Courtesy Lion. The Merlion's likeness has appeared as souvenir sculptures, chocolates, even a wind instrument (Rae, 2007: 122).

Indeed, the half-lion half-fish icon has exceeded its tourism function and has come to represent the Singapore brand more generally. The Merlion is also seen as a symbol of the island's aspiration to become a cultural hub of Southeast Asia and, even, of the whole world (Talib, 2004; Chin, 2006; Poon et al., 2009; Gwee, 2005). The cultural hub plan aims to bolster political stability, social harmony and perceived national values among cosmopolitan

Singaporeans who are 'familiar with global trends and lifestyles and . . . [feel] comfortable working and living in Singapore as well as overseas' (Tan & Yeoh, 2006: 150; see also, Gwee, 2005; Wong, 2009). By promoting global awareness and a willingness to appropriate the best that the world has to offer, the government hopes to expand the conceptual basis of creative production and enable the island state to be comfortable in its place among developed nations.

Given the central role it plays in Singapore's iconography, the Merlion has become a fixture of the local artistic landscape, especially of poetry. It has become almost a rite of passage for aspiring authors to write about the national icon. The island's unofficial poet laureate, Edwin Thumboo, transformed the icon into a personification of Singapore with his landmark poem 'Ulysses by the Merlion' in 1979. Since then, the Merlion has become a trope that has yielded its own body of poetry. This has been collected in a volume and, as is typical in many local literary and creative arts projects, published with state funding through the National Arts Council (NAC). This volume, entitled *Reflecting on the Merlion: An Anthology of Poems* (Thumboo *et al.*, 2009), illustrates the Singaporean approach to creativity: it is the result of interplay (usually a complementarity) between private initiative, which is growing, and continued government funding and support (or tolerance). The anthology is the outcome of a project initiated and co-edited by Thumboo. It involved writers Yeow Kai Chai, Enoch Ng, Isa Kamari and Seetha Lakshmi as co-editors. Finally, it was designed, as well as printed, by a leading literary publisher, First Fruits.

This chapter aims to clarify the nature of creative in(ter)vention (Pope, 2005: 62) in Singapore, as exemplified through poetry inspired by the image of the Merlion. By in(ter)vention, I refer to the combination of the words 'inventive' and 'interventive' to signify that creative productions 'introduce some [profound] change into life' (Pope, 2005: 62).

Icon as Muse

The ways in which Singapore's writers have appropriated the icon reveal the various socio-cultural concerns and literary conventions of their respective eras. The Merlion poems exemplify the second and third of three types of creative activity in the local scene, as summed up by critic Koh Tai Ann: '(1) that which is seen as a "luxury we cannot afford"; (2) culturally symbolic expressions of communal identity; and (3) the pop culture of Westernised cosmopolitan youth' (cited in Patke, 1999: 52). The first type, as defined by Singapore's first Prime Minister and now Mentor Minister, Lee

Kuan Yew, soon after the island's independence, comprises Anglo-American inspired artworks that are beyond the experience and understanding of the Singapore masses. From the 1960s to the early 1970s, these works sought and failed to gain a mass-based readership (Gwee, 2009: 237). Thumboo and the early Merlion poets, whether identifying with or ironically questioning the symbol, represented the second type. They recognised that Merlion had the capacity to represent cultural symbolism and collective activity. Subsequent poets represented the third. They engaged with the Merlion using tools and techniques drawn from Western pop culture. These types of appropriations demonstrate how Singapore-based writers negotiate tensions between their desire for individual expression and the limitations imposed by the state and the Western market.

It is not surprising that Thumboo, who continues to champion Singaporean literature as a dean and academic at the National University of Singapore, initiated the poetic groundwork for the Merlion as a personfication of the young republic. He has worked for the government in various capacities, beginning with a stint at the Department of Inland Revenue and the Central Provident Fund Board. As an accountant at the latter, he was involved in the establishment of the Singapore Tourism Board, which created the Merlion as a mascot. Thumboo's most notable work, especially in *Gods Can Die* and *Ulysses by the Merlion*, exemplifies his public role as poet. Even his mature poetry reinforces a national literary identity. A few critics, such as J.K. Watson, claim that his work is 'based on the government's developmental path' (Watson, 2008: 688). But Thumboo, in an interview, pointed out that in a *Youth* magazine editorial, as early as 1952, he already stressed the importance of forging a national literature. That was two years before the ruling People's Action Party was founded and seven years before Singapore became self-governing.

Thumboo embraces the artist's role as an instrument of social cohesion and nation building. He demonstrated this nationalist sentiment, even during British rule. It is a little known fact that he was one of eight charged with sedition, that is, bringing the then-colonial government to disrepute and contempt. The academic and critic Rajeev Patke characterised this role as 'an ideational poetic function, done symbolically and unironically' (Patke, 1999: 51). Part of this function was to effect a change in creative orientation from what Thumboo called 'exile to native' for Singaporean literature, in the context of literature in English (cited in Patke, 1999: 46). Thumboo aimed to represent the views of his compatriots. At the same time, he transmuted the narrative about the Merlion into high art. He did so by positing continuity between Singapore's colonial past and postcolonial present, which alludes to classical figures and stories:

> I have sailed many waters,
> Skirted islands of fire,
> Contended with Circe
> Who loved the squeal of pigs
> Passed Scylla and Charybdis
> To seven years with Calypso,
> Heaved in battle against the gods. (Thumboo *et al.*, 2009: 18)

The dramatic speaker, like his subject matter, taps many sources. He is, apparently, Ulysses – the Roman equivalent of the Homeric epic hero, Odysseus. But the speaker could also be creative, icon-making Singapore: 'made myths myself' (Thumboo *et al.*, 2009: 18). This speaker suggests that the old symbols of Singapore's various ethnic groups are inadequate for conveying the boundless ambition of his young people. He, thus, creates a hybrid discourse on a national identity:

> Perhaps having dealt in things,
> Surfeited on them,
> Their spirits yearn again for images,
> Adding to the dragon, phoenix,
> Garuda, naga those horses of the sun,
> This lion of the sea,
> This image of themselves. (Thumboo *et al.*, 2009: 19)

What Thumboo achieves in this poem is the 'construct[ion of] a ... community called Singapore', whose constitutive peoples work toward 'social harmony' (Watson, 2008: 698). He does so with the use of a foreign tongue, English, which he used as his main language from age nine. The ethnic groups in Singapore speak various Chinese dialects, Tamil or Malay. Thumboo also draws poetic lines and techniques from Western sources, such as Homer, Keats, Marlowe and Yeats. Thumboo, for instance, deliberately incorporates elements of Marlowe's Doctor Faustus. Literature student Christine Chong (2010: 6) identifies borrowings from Marlowe's *Doctor Faustus* ('The bounty of these seas / Built towers topless as Ilium's') and, more significantly, Tennyson's 'Ulysses':

> Despite unequal ways,
> together they mutate.
> Explore the edges of harmony,
> Search for a centre;
> Have changed their gods,
> Kept some memory of their race. (Tennyson, 1996: 897)

In so doing, Thumboo posits a body of Singaporean literature, written in English, within the Western literary tradition. It is also significant that 'Ulysses by the Merlion' – the quintessential Singaporean poem – is dedicated to Maurice Baker, the son of an English migrant father and a Tamil mother. Though himself the site of liminal existence, Baker had no difficulty in leading a fully integrated life and had a rich personality.

Just as the physical Merlion has spawned physical copies in its current site in front of the Fullerton Hotel, in the nearby island resort of Sentosa and even in distant Kaohsiung, Taiwan (Thumboo *et al.*, 2009: 10), 'Ulysses by the Merlion' has become a Singaporean hypotext, or source text, that has generated multiple hypertexts (Chong, 2010: 5). These Merlion hypertexts derive meaning from the image, whilst imaginatively reflecting on and revising it. They ultimately illustrate strategies of creative production in the island state.

The first poetic response to Thumboo's poem comes from Lee Tzu Pheng, a fellow academic and another poet from the first generation of Singaporean writers. Locating Lee's 'The Merlion to Ulysses' in the landscape established by Thumboo, she champions the icon as a symbol of communal and cultural identity. Her poem is a strident, postcolonial apology for a pragmatic Singapore: 'I am the instant brainchild of a practical people' (Lee, 2009: 22). She makes the icon, her dramatic speaker, put on battle vestments: 'I wear the silver armour of my moneyed people' (Lee, 2009: 22). She also berates the foreign traveller, Ulysses, as a nanny would a mischievous ward. She writes, 'Before you leave, O feckless wanderer, / remember to respect my creators' (Lee, 2009: 23). This rhetoric, with the aim of instilling discipline, is reminiscent of the language used by the island's ruling party, the People's Action Party (Chong, 2010: 7). By letting the Merlion stand its ground and provide a poetic exegesis of itself in a monologue with the classical Western hero Ulysses as audience, Lee privileges Singaporean poetry. She establishes the latter as an equal to the Western canon.

Alfian Sa'at – a member of the third generation of Singaporean writers whose poetic reaction to Thumboo was published earlier than that of Felix Cheong – questions the symbol's long-term significance. In 'The Merlion' he writes:

It spews continually if only to ruffle
its own reflection in the water; such reminders
will only scare a creature so eager to reinvent itself. (Sa'at, 2009: 25)

Sa'at demonstrates resistance to the hold of the Merlion, now a communal symbol, on the Singapore artist's imagination and creative efforts. In contrast with Thumboo and Lee, Sa'at does so through dialogue. Sa'at, in fact, ingeniously dramatises the conflict between Thumboo's Western literary orientation and Lee's foregrounding of the Singaporean one. Sa'at also adds to this mixture, symbols of Western pop culture adopted by Singaporean youth:

> 'I know exactly what you mean,' I said,
> Eyeing the blond highlights in your black hair
> And your blue lenses the shadow of a foreign sky. (Sa'at, 2009: 25)

Sa'at valorises the poet as an individual who does not subscribe to an official narrative about his role in society. He sensationalises the hype that has been heaped on the icon 'to provoke domestic attention to the scandal of art' (Gwee, 2009: 238). Sa'at's work marks a shift toward greater self-reflexivity and maturity of creative development in the local scene.

Other writers have contributed to the debate over the Merlion's relevance and its legitimacy as an inspiration for creativity by interpreting the icon according to the prevailing mood of their times. Felix Cheong – a member of the second generation of Singapore writers, but writing in response to Sa'at – questions the Merlion's relevance. Nonetheless, he feels it a poetic duty to add a work to this literary corpus, as expressed in his poem's title, 'The Obligatory Merlion Poem'. Cheong thus exemplifies what may be considered the 'double bind' of postcolonial writing and creativity: 'a veiled neomodernism hostile to its origins in the early anti-colonial movements' and a '. . . [rejection] and [departure] from the libratory language of national emancipation' (Brennan, 2005: 102). This hostility is manifested in the poem with irreverence at the iconic landscape that Thumboo and Lee so meticulously built. Cheong writes:

> But what would you have done
> Given the freak of history
> And the quirk of circumstance,
> With this half-fucked city
> That was at once a meeting point
> And a point of contention. (Cheong, 2009: 43)

He concludes that the need for celebrating nationhood has been unduly privileged over the dignity of the individual artist:

> . . . mitigating
> our need to put on a brave face

with the migratory urgency
to be freed. (Cheong, 2009: 43)

More recently published poets have written about the reception of the
Merlion and Singapore poetry. In the anthology's second section, performance poet Marc Daniel Nair, for instance, uses the national icon to voice
a complaint about the anonymity of local poets. In 'Confessions of an
Ambivalion', he writes:

Forgive me citizen, for I have doubted who I am;
Uniquely Singaporean, Merl the ambivalion,
Unseen by my countrymen. (Nair, 2009: 60)

This writer – a permanent resident – in turn, adopts the Merlion trope as a
migrant's strategy to assimilate the culture and language of his adopted
society (Mendoza, 2002: 140–1). In 'Putting on the Merlion', his dramatic
speaker – a migrant – learns to speak the language of his new neighbours,
while retaining his accent:

Art as tool, without excuses;
A batik of metaphors
Carved from the same sandstone I now call home. (Valles, 2009: 66)

This same speaker thus chooses a life that is settled and yet marked by
otherness.

The anthology *Reflecting on the Merlion* presents a literary canon that,
like the Merlion iconography and the Singaporean cultural identity, is
fragmented and cosmopolitan. The anthology includes works in Chinese
and Tamil, as to be expected in a multiethnic society that boasts the 'oldest
multicultural policy in the region' (Wee, 2004: 773). Local poets and their
readers thus had an opportunity to do what the anthology title prescribes
in their own respective mother tongues. This same multilingual and multicultural nature of creativity in the island state has generated many other
cultural projects, which illustrate the widening reach of Singapore's artists.
Notable among them are: an intercultural Asian *King Lear* theatrical project
funded by the Japan Foundation Asia Centre (JFAC) in 1997 and 1999; the
love poetry anthology *Love Gathers All*, a collaboration with Filipino writers,
in 2002; the poetry anthology, *Double Skin: New Poetic Voices from Italy and
Singapore*, in 2009; and a soon-to-be-released poetic collaboration with South
African writers that is edited by Gwee Li Sui.

The publication of *Reflecting on the Merlion* itself was aimed at a broad Singapore readership comprising various age and socio-economic groups. Its launch was timed during the 2009 Singapore Writers Festival which featured popular authors, such as fantasy and science fiction writer Neil Gaiman. The Merlion book launch, in fact, coincided with an autograph signing session with Gaiman that drew hundreds to the Arts House. The anthology challenged readers to consider a wide array of issues that cut across generations, from 'systems of effort like Thumboo's or of nomadism ...' (Gwee, 2005: 252) to '... [digesting] and ... [being invigorated] by the quotidian of ... everyday Singaporean life into the subjective consciousness of ... [the] poetic imagination' (Wong, 2009: 233).

Finally, the anthology serves as a historical chronicle detailing, not only the creative production of three generations of published writers, but also the first published works of what could turn out to be a fourth generation, which includes permanent residents. *Reflecting on the Merlion* features, after all, alumni of the Ministry of Education's Creative Arts Programme (CAP). That programme was established by Thumboo. Though no full-length study of the impact of CAP on the island's artistic life has been made, the fact that the works of two of its graduates, Alfian Sa'at and Ng Yi-Sheng, almost form bookends in the anthology's first section and the work of another prize-winning alumnus, Aaron Maniam, is showcased in the second section, indicates that the high hopes for the anthologised CAP participants are not entirely misplaced. It is also noteworthy that the anthology reaches out to a pan-Asian audience by including permanent residents such as this writer.

Site of Fissures

The Merlion-inspired canon suggests some tension in creative production, primarily between the Singapore-based artists' desire for individuality and otherness on the one hand and the drive toward conformity with state policies or Western market expectations on the other. This tension is evident in, and a spur for, Singapore poetry in English, an official language imposed by the government to maintain social harmony. John Kwan-Terry observes, in Singapore poetry in English, a 'sense of a dichotomised world, split between meaning and medium, utterance and message' (Patke, 1999: B1). In this context, he sees Thumboo's 'Ulysses by the Merlion' as a 'problematic hermeneutic of ideation' (Patke, 1999: 51). Like its art source, Merlion poetry thrives in hybridity.

One factor that is often cited as stunting the growth of creativity in Singapore is state control. State policies do tend to propagate singularity, what some concede to be an inescapable 'servitude to the state and to global markets' in the creative arts (Wee, 2004: 773). Another limiting factor is the drive towards a broader audience, usually synonymous with the West. The latter is seen to obscure artists' vision and make them produce a dull aesthetics that is 'less Singaporean than international' and 'less poetry than prose' (Gwee, 2009: 237).

The central role of state planning in Singapore's free-market economy has made the government a major patron to creative artists in the small island state. Tommy Koh, chairman of the National Heritage Board, explains the government's intentions in its first campaign to develop the local arts:

(1) We wanted to raise the social status of artists; (2) We wanted to promote the growth of flagship companies in the arts. Theatreworks [a drama group] and the Singapore Chinese Orchestra became independent and fully professional; (3) We supported young and experimental artists. We gave support to the Substation [an arts centre]; (4) We wanted their audience to grow; (5) We wanted to support the arts colleges. (Koh, 2010)

The same benevolent attitude lies behind the government's support for the Merlion Hotel artwork, the Biennale and the local creative industries. The National Arts Council (NAC), for instance, has earmarked S$3.5 million over five years to bankroll the production of creative artworks from inception to completion (Tan, 2011: C2). In 2010, NAC received 88 proposals and approved 20 (2011: C2). The grant recipients received from S$15,000 to S$50,000 each (2011: C2). The works that received NAC funding ranged from traditional Chinese opera to a play about a puppet master and stop-motion animation (Tan, 2011: C2).

The government's drive to nurture the arts and make them an integral part of people's lives is evident in more grassroots and community events. Michael Koh, chief executive officer of the National Heritage Board, says:

It's all part of the idea of helping Singaporeans be more aware of art in the surroundings. Art is actually everywhere. We want people to appreciate art every day. (cited in Ong, 2011: B2)

To be sure, some government officials are aware of the limitations of a model of creativity that is dependent on government fiat. Khor Kok Wah, deputy chief executive officer of the NAC, says, 'Because we are small, there could be a sense of micro-management and confinement' (Khor, 2010). But he is quick to maintain that local creativity flourishes, despite strictures, because of the diversity of private initiatives. He says:

Creativity is known to thrive in many kinds of environment. Our various schemes at NAC try to help artists progress, but they can only do so much. We need more support for artists and the arts from non-government sources, the other sectors, audiences, and we need more organisations to grow organically to provide mutual support towards a more vibrant scene. (Khor, 2010).

This tension between the individual artist and state policy, though real, could be one expression of the anxieties about the development of creative industries and the nature of creative expression in a postcolonial society. This may not be true only in Singapore, a former British colony. Frantz Fanon (1963) posits, in 'Concerning Violence', that a 'genuine eradication' of the colonial order may result initially in the disappearance of individualism, that is, 'the idea of a society of individuals where each person shuts himself up in his own subjectivity' (Povinelli, 2005: 147). The social embeddedness of the artist thus becomes paramount. The artist is then not so much self-made, as he or she is a 'social determination' (Povinelli, 2005: 149). The artist whose 'projects ... are incompatible with the core values promoted by the [g]overnment and society or disparage the [g]overnment then may be penalised' (Khor, 2010). In 2010, this happened to theatre group Wild Rice, which has staged provocative plays that touch on politics, in the form of a funding cut of between S$20,000 and S$170,000 (Chia, 2010: C7).

Many artists in Singapore take this social determination as a given. Yong Shu Hoong, Singapore Literature Prize winner in 2006 and literary activist, acknowledges that poets and other artists in Singapore practice self-censorship. He says: 'I believe self-censorship still exists. But oftentimes, because poetry tends to bury meanings deeper beneath the surface, poets can get away with a little more (through their poetic license) than reporters who are always reminded to be balanced and objective, and to base their writings on facts' (2011).

These artists look creatively at the givens of their circumscribed existence and generate poetry and other artworks. 'The young poets were dealing with issues that I was keen on', says *Straits Times* book reviewer, Ong Sor Fern. She adds:

Things like growing up in a post-colonial globalised society, the irony o f being a democracy in an authoritarian state, the confidence of our identity as Singaporeans, the confidence in our identity as Singaporeans, the confidence that we have in our system. No matter how much we bitch and moan about it, we actually think that it works, and we don't get why Westerners get so worked up about us being authoritarian. (Ong, 2009: 173)

Many Singaporean artists accept this situation with resignation. Poet, playwright and fiction writer Alfian Sa'at (2010) said, 'Singapore may not be a city. We are so small. The heartlands and suburbs are so enmeshed. The city is bound and the suburbs have anonymity. The city is micromanaged. There is no way to escape'.

As a result, Singaporean writers pitch their work to Western markets as a necessity. This desire to market creative work may be the cause of tension. Sanjay Krishnan says Singapore's 'new challenges need to be seen as the partial consequence of its embrace of the international culture of consumption' (Patke, 1999: 54). Dave Chua, a fiction writer and recipient of the Singapore Literature Prize Commendation Award in 1996, takes this challenge in stride. He contributes to online magazines in Canada and elsewhere. He says: 'Asians tackle universal themes. The bottom line is how good your writing is' (2010).

Working within limits, whether imposed by the self or external forces, yields its own kind of creativity. That is certainly the case of Singapore. Yong says:

> The city is limited by its physical boundaries, but the psychological boundaries are harder to define and may be much wider and wilder than expected. It's the contradictions that make Singapore interesting. And with it being more prominent on the map and in the global consciousness, there could be increasing intrigue in what it stands for. (2011)

Like other economically advanced East Asian societies, Singapore is in a state of hybridity in that it desires to appeal to both a local audience, as well as that of the West. Niu Weihua notes that creativity in these societies tends to develop from adapting practices and techniques from the West, while not veering away from their inherent cultural differences. Niu also maintains that the study of creativity in the East must consider 'the study of culture and its influence on the conception of creativity, a continuous focus on creative education, and the existence of an ongoing indigenous movement' (2006: 656). Projects such as a pan-Asian *King Lear* could be ideal objects of such a study. The *King Lear* producer, Hata Yuki, says that 'although our modern [Asian] theatre is deeply influenced by the West, we also have our own traditions. The theatre in new Asian culture should be searching within its own traditional culture' (Wee, 2004: 797). The Asian King Lear is intra-Asian and contemporary, though it is adapted from a canonical Western play. It thus refashions the old order from the viewpoint of a creative new Asia.

Reflecting on the Merlion, in turn, suggests creative paths that newer Singaporean writers – whose works make up the bulk of the anthology's second section – may take over the next few years. Marc Daniel Nair, whose 'Confessions of an Ambivalion' opens the second section, targets his poetry at a younger audience, with an emphasis on performance and the inclusion of musical elements. He actively participates in poetry slam events in schools. He also recently published two collections of poetry. Creative Arts Programme (CAP) alumni Theophile Kwek Mui Yi and Kylie Goh Jin Ying, still in their teens, have been featured in the new literary print journal *Ceriph*. Despite limitations, the state-funded CAP thus continues to serve as a seedbed for potential artistic talents. The journal *Ceriph* itself is another platform for showcasing new literary works. It is a publishing venture of Math Paper Press, which is linked to bookstore Books Actually, another champion of local literature. Several Merlion poets, namely Kwek, Joy Chee and this writer (also published in the January 2011 issue of *Ceriph*), have been included among established writers, in another literary canon proposed by Thumboo (2010), in a more recent anthology, *& Words: Poems Singapore and Beyond*.

Literary critic and poet Gwee Li Sui sees the mid- to long-term prospects of creativity, especially in the literary arts, in Singapore as being shaped by three critical factors. These are 'media exposure, changes in school education, and [an] emerging healthy bookshop culture' (2005: 253). Indeed, the initial exposure to Singapore literature in schools could be reinforced with news reporting, as well as distribution support from booksellers. Greater affluence in the general population of Singapore has enabled wider access to mass media and has boosted overall book sales. Local literature and the other arts, in turn, are showing greater maturity with many innovative private initiatives influencing their development.

As regards media exposure, though editorial space devoted to literature and the other arts is still inadequate, more pages are already given to reviews of local literature and the other arts in *The Straits Times* and state-owned newspapers and magazines. Also, writers and other artists are collaborating on their own to stimulate media interest in their creative work. In 2009, the publisher First Fruits put together *Wolfnotes* – an exhibit of artworks that interpreted the works of six of its authors at the Art Studio. The state, nonetheless, continues to play the role of patron of the arts in schools. More funding is available for arts education through tote board grants. In early March this year, the NAC funded a literary road show, *Words Go Round*, in several schools and junior colleges to promote the Singapore Writers Festival that is scheduled later this year. More Singaporean texts, both fiction and poetry, have been introduced in the University of Cambridge Advanced-Ordinary Level Literature courses.

Finally, the business of bookstores, such as Japanese retail chain Kinoku-niya and home-grown independent Books Actually, which stock locally published literary work, is growing. In fact, Books Actually moved in March this year closer to the commercial business district. These bookstores regularly host book launches and other literary events.

An increasingly outward-looking Singapore craves greater appreciation of its literature beyond its media, schools and bookstores. Patke says: 'Of course, it is not criticism that can do this for the writing, but it can at least prepare the way for a wider reception of what has been accomplished by the writers, and it can work towards fostering a more propitious climate for the writing of the future' (1999: 57). Singapore literature is gaining wider critical attention. Academic Peter Nazareth teaches works by Thumboo and other Singaporean writers as part of literature courses at the University of Iowa. Refereed journals, such as *The Drama Review* and *Contemporary Literature*, have published articles on the Merlion and Singapore poetry, respectively, over the past five years. Even the anthology *Reflecting on the Merlion* has become the subject of a critical essay in a local journal, *Prism*.

In 1999, Patke, echoing earlier voices, wrote about the need for Singapore to narrate, critically, its own literary history. A decade later, this aspiration was realised with literary publisher Ethos releasing two series of critical studies entitled *Interlogue: Studies in Singapore Literature* and *Sharing Borders: Studies in Contemporary Singaporean-Malaysian Literature*. This ambitious project received a boost from the support of Thumboo, who served as general editor. It also obtained state funding from the National Library Board and, once again, the NAC.

However, creativity in Singapore is appraised. It is far from being in stasis. The study of the literary arts in Singapore, as seen through the microcosm that is Merlion poetry, offers a glimpse of creative practice on the island. Far from offering a monolithic, 'parachuted-down' view (Watson, 2008: 709), the reflections on the national icon offer divergent ways of thinking. Literary pioneer Edwin Thumboo observes that poetry in world Englishes (that is, in English written outside Anglo-Saxon countries) tends to evolve from a stage of imitation to one demonstrating consciousness of nationhood and finally to a stage of negotiating between introspection and their relationship with their milieu (cited in Patke, 1999: 47). Cyril Wong – a new-generation poet who has achieved both critical acclaim and a popular following – thinks that final stage is when poets '. . . [discover] poems both in their surroundings and themselves' (Wong, 2009: 233). This is already happening in Singapore. Wong says Singaporean poets are 'producing a far more urgent and vital poetry' than previous generations. The confidence and assertion of individuality of artists are likely to spur new ways of reflecting and revising the Merlion and the greater landscape of Singapore. Gwee maps out the thematic landscape of this artistic future: 'existential wakefulness, interrogations of privacy, transformations of self, the relation between art and wit, artistic and human influences, multi-lingual connections, the urban condition, the values of the absurd, and spirituality' (2005: 253). Indeed, the dynamic marketing of the Merlion and its many symbolic representations suggest an exciting in(ter)ventive future for both.

References

Brennan, T. (2005) The economic image-function of the periphery. In A. Loomba, S. Kaul, M. Bunzl, A. Burton and J. Esty (eds) *Postcolonial Studies and Beyond* (pp. 101–122). Durham and London: Duke University Press.

Cheong, F. (2009) 'The Obligatory Merlion Poem'. In E. Thumboo, K.C. Yeow, E. Ng, I. Kamari and S. Lakshmi (eds). *Reflecting on the Merlion: an Anthology of Poems* (p. 43). Singapore: First Fruits Publications.

Chia, A. (2010) Benson reveals his plans for the arts. *The Straits Times*. 22 November. Online at http://global.factiva.com.libproxy1.nus.edu.sg/ha/default.aspx

Chin, G.V.S. (2006) The anxieties of authorship in Malaysian and Singaporean writings in English: Locating the English language writer and the question of freedom in the postcolonial era. *Postcolonial Text* 2 (4), 1–24. Online at http://postcolonial.org/index.php/pct/article/view/474/365.

Chong, C. (2010) From Ulysses to the Melion: Hypertextuality and a Singaporean Canon. *Prism* 3 (1), 5–13. Online at http://www.scribd.com/doc/44252241/Hypertextuality-From-Ulysses-to-the-Merlion-Christine-Chong

Chua, D. (2010, November 2) Creativity in Singapore. [Interview]. *Interview at the Arts House*. Singapore.

Fanon, F. (1963) Concerning violence. In R. Philcox (trans.) *The Wretched of the Earth* (pp. 1–52). New York, NY: Grove Press.

Gwee, L.S. (2005) Poetry and the renaissance machine in Singapore. *Harvard Asia Quarterly* 9 (1–2), 33–41.

Gwee, L.S. (2009) The new poetry of Singapore. In L.S. Gwee and E. Thumboo (eds) *Sharing Borders: Studies in Contemporary Singaporean-Malaysian Literature II* (pp. 236–259). Singapore: National Library Board and National Arts Council.

Khor, K.W. (2010, November 19) Creativity in Singapore. [Interview]. *Interview at the National University of Singapore*. Singapore.

Koh, T. (2010, October 29) Singapore: From cultural desert to cultural oasis. [Discussion]. *Talk at the National University of Singapore*. Singapore.

Lee, T.P. (2009) 'The Merlion to Ulysses'. In E. Thumboo, K.C. Yeow, E. Ng, I. Kamari and S. Lakshmi (eds) *Reflecting on the Merlion: an Anthology of Poems* (pp. 22–23). Singapore: First Fruits Publications.

Mendoza, S.L. (2002) *Asian Americans (Reconceptualizing Culture, History and Politics)* (F. Ng, ed.). New York and London: Routledge.

Nair, M.D. (2009) 'Confessions of an Ambivalion'. In E. Thumboo, K.C. Yeow, E. Ng, I. Kamari and S. Lakshmi (eds). *Reflecting on the Merlion: an Anthology of Poems* (p. 60). Singapore: First Fruits Publications.

Nanda, A. (2011) Sleeping in the Merlion's Den. *The Straits Times*, 5 March. Online at http://global.factiva.com.libproxy1.nus.edu.sg/ha/default.aspx

Niu, W. (2006) The meaning of dragon: When yours is different from mine. [Review]. *The American Journal of Psychology* 119 (4), 655–59.

Ong, A. (2011) Roaring trade at Merlion hotel. *The Straits Times,* 12 March. Online at http://global.factiva.com.libproxy1.nus.edu.sg/ha/default.aspx

Ong, S.F. (2009) [Interview] Ong Sor Fern. In R.D. Klein (ed.) *Interlogue: Studies in Singapore Literature Vol. 8: Interviews II* (pp. 163–184). Singapore: National Library Board.

Patke, R.S. (1999) Singapore literature in English. In C.B. Huat (ed.) *Singapore Studies II: Critical Surveys of the Humanities and Social Sciences* (pp. 46–68). Singapore: Singapore University Press.

Poon, A., Holden, P. and Lim, S. (eds) (2009) *Writing Singapore: An Historical Anthology of Singapore Literature.* Singapore: National University of Singapore Press.

Pope, R. (2005) *Creativity: Theory, History, Practice.* New York, NY: Routledge.

Povinelli, E.A. (2005) A flight from freedom. In A. Loomba, S. Kaul, M. Bunzl, A. Burton and J. Esty (eds) *Postcolonial Studies and Beyond* (pp. 145–165). Durham and London: Duke University Press.

Rae, P. (2007) Cat's entertainment: Feline performance in the Lion City. *The Drama Review* 51 (1), 119–137.

Sa'at, A. (2009) 'The Merlion'. In E. Thumboo, K.C. Yeow, E. Ng, I. Kamari and S. Lakshmi (eds) *Reflecting on the Merlion: an Anthology of Poems* (pp. 24–25). Singapore: First Fruits Publications.

Sa'at, A. (2010, November 2) Writing the City. [Discussion]. *Talk at the Arts House.* Singapore.

Talib, I.S. (2004) Malaysia and Singapore. *Journal of Commonwealth Literature* 39 (4), 71–96.

Tan, C. (2011) Cash for Creations. *The Straits Times,* 13 January. Online at http://global.factiva.com.libproxy1.nus.edu.sg/ha/default.aspx

Tan, S. and Yeoh, B. (2006) Negotiating cosmopoltanism in Singapore's fictional landscape. In J. Binnie, J. Holloway, S. Millington and C. Young (eds) *Cosmopolitan Urbanism* (pp. 146–168). London: Routledge.

Tennyson, A. (1996) 'Ulysses'. In M. Ferguson, M.J. Salter and J. Stallworthy (eds) *The Norton Anthology of Poetry* (pp. 896–97). New York and London: W.W. Norton & Company.

Thumboo, E. (1976). Introduction. In E. Thumboo (ed.) *The Second Tongue.* Singapore: Heinemann Asia.

Thumboo, E. (1988) Exile to native in Singapore poetries. In B. Bennett and S. Miller (eds) *A Sense of Exile: Essays in the Literature of the Asia-Pacific Region* (pp. 43–56). Nedlands: Centre for Studies in Australian Literature.

Thumbo, E. (2009) 'Ulysses by the Merlion'. In E. Thumboo, K.C. Yeow, E. Ng, I. Kamari and S. Lakshmi (eds). *Reflecting on the Merlion: an Anthology of Poems* (pp. 18–19). Singapore: First Fruits Publications.

Thumboo, E. (ed.) (2010) *& Words: Poems Singapore and Beyond.* Singapore: Ethos Books.

Thumboo, E., Yeow, K.C., Ng, E., Kamari, I. and Lakshmi. S. (eds) (2009) *Reflecting on the Merlion: an Anthology of Poems.* Singapore: First Fruits Publications.

Valles, E.T. (2009) 'Putting on the Merlion'. In E. Thumboo, K.C. Yeow, E. Ng, I. Kamari and S. Lakshmi (eds). *Reflecting on the Merlion: an Anthology of Poems* (pp. 65–6). Singapore: First Fruits Publications.

Watson, J.K. (2008) The way ahead: The politics and poetics of singapore's developmental landscape. *Contemporary Literature* 49 (4), 683–711.

Wee, C.J.W.-L. (2004) Staging the Asian modern: Cultural fragments, the Singaporean eunuch, and the Asian lear. *Critical Inquiry* 30 (4), 771–99.

Wong, C. (2009) Nationalism and interiority: Reflections on Singaporean poetry from 1980s to 1990s. In L.S. Gwee (ed.) *Sharing Borders: Studies in Contemporary Singaporean-Malaysian Literature II.* Singapore: National Library Board.

Afterword: Creativity, the Market and the Globalisation Challenge

Kirpal Singh

Key issues in this book revolve around the question that if creativity as a human endeavour is dead, creative mutants nonetheless ceaselessly reappear in discourse. What this book, indeed, asks first and foremost is: is creative writing a primarily human action? How do we promote and advertise human creativity? What is the role of governmental policies in influencing how creativity is perceived? In so doing, it reassesses the long history of creative writing in universities, which can be viewed as a history of many parts and many developments, and the role of current technologies in making the contemporary world one in which creative writing and exchanging activities and artefacts of creative writing can occur relatively freely.

To some extent, and justly so, *The Creativity Market* joins the conversation sparked by recent books and newspaper articles which lament the perilous state of the Humanities, including creative writing. The common theme of such literature is money and the globalisation challenge. In *Universities in the Marketplace*, Derek Bok (2003), a former Harvard president, argued that conflicts of interest were ubiquitous in the corporate university worldwide. He argued that if profit-making limits the free exchange of information, conflicts of interest also occur when academics become entrepreneurs. He also contended that 'excessive commercialisation in every part of the university' (Bok, 2003: 8) is harmful to traditional academic values. I suspect that the situation is even worse in Asia, where the new universities bank on business, science and technology.

As I write this, the news that Osama Bin Laden has been killed has just been confirmed by President Barack Obama. Do I take this as ubiquitous? Does death mitigate everything? Perhaps this is as good a place as any to begin an important discussion of the topic and theme which I set myself for this book: to discuss and share, by way of exploration, how creativity (and all its relations under various names, appellations, guises) is understood (or not) across cultures in an age when globalisation has become the one key determining factor for all of us. Sure, there are many who would deny this and others who remain in denial, despite their own awareness of the truth of this reality. And, yes, there are, of course, small parts of the world which have still to encounter and experience globalisation in any significant way. However, we are concerned with the now and, more importantly, the future. And, in this respect, there is no doubt whatsoever that if we refuse to be part of the globalised world, we do ourselves, and those who might be in our charge (such as our students, families, employees) or those who we might be eager to reach out to (such as colleagues, potential employers, buyers of our services etc.), little good. For the world is shrinking, and, in a shrinking environment, survival is going to get that much harder, that much more competitive and that much more onerous for those unwilling to see the light.

I return to the infamous and notorious Osama Bin Laden. There can be no one in the civilised and educated world who does not know what we mean when we mention '9/11'. Here was a drama unfolding right before our eyes, as so many of us stood in utter disbelief. I remember the incident vividly. My wife and I had gone out to watch an evening movie, and as we got into the car afterwards, we heard a report over the radio saying that the World Trade Center Towers in New York had been hit by aeroplanes. The report was confusing. My wife and I listened, not knowing what to make of this. I drove home with fury. As soon as we got home, we turned on the TV, and there it was, no matter which of the six channels we turned in to, they all had the same images, again and again: aeroplanes flying straight into the Twin Towers. Extraordinary, dramatic, unbelievable, horrific, terrible, disastrous, catastrophic – the latter adjectives came as we began to realise and take in the full measure of what we were witnessing. And then came that tragic, sombre knowledge that this was a terrorist attack. An attack like no other the United States – or, for that matter, the world – had ever seen before. This was a tragedy which struck a totally new fear in all of us, because the entire episode unravelled, almost like one of those early movies/films we had been accustomed to. I reflected on this, and Orson Welles' rendition of H.G. Wells' *The War Of The Worlds* (1898) rang in my ears (Welles, 1938). But that was fiction, even if many had not thought so when they first heard Orson Wells' booming voice in narration. Now, on 9/11, the situation seemed reversed. We were gasping for truth, aghast at what we were clearly seeing, but reluctant to admit that this was not fiction, but fact – a bad, terrible, horrible, tragic fact that somehow was going to change the world forever.

Would it be a travesty of judgment, perhaps even of wisdom, understanding and sensitivity to term that remarkable display of defiance as 'creative'? (for no one, till then, had believed, could believe, could even imagine that an aeroplane – a civilian, commercial, passenger plane could fly straight through those strong, tall, powerful buildings). This is a question I ask with plenty of caution and temerity, but ask I must. For it goes right to the very core of what my reflection here is fundamentally concerned with: how do we judge, sense or find creativity? And how, more significantly, is creativity looked at by people of different cultures, values, religious systems? Are there commonalities shared by all across the globe? Or are there serious, major differences in approach, knowledge and understanding? Would an incident like 9/11 be seen as 'creative' by all? Or only by those who acted it out, those who thought about it, planned it and then, to the horror of the entire world, executed it?

Although nearly a decade ago, in a paper I gave at the annual international conference of the ACA – the American Creativity Association – in Philadelphia, Pennsylvania, I still hold today the paradigm vision of creativity which I then sketched. We were then – though we were unaware of it – in the phase of a third globalisation, one that is concerned with preserving national and local identities, in order to avoid a tremendous process of rationalisation and standardisation. I stated that no matter which way we look at it, we do need to ask the important question: where and from which source do we think this creativity (poem, dance, drama, song, invention, attack ...) comes from – the demonic or the divine? These occupy the poles of my paradigm, but there is a continuum with the polarities governing the left to right axes. Most of the creative products, services, entities and experiences we all have can be easily slated on to the continuum along the paradigmatic axes. My paper ignited plenty of fiery discussion and debate. Indeed, though many still remember it, few have ever cited it in their publications. Was I wrong? Was my creativity source paradigm misplaced? A mis-reading of all I had been taught and all I had learnt?

When I gave that paper at the ACA in 2003, I was nearing the end of a book I had been working on, thanks to a research award granted me by my university – The Singapore Management University. That book appeared and was published under the title: *Thinking Hats and Coloured Turbans – Creativity Across Cultures* (Singh, 2004). I shall desist from alluding more than really necessary to the book, but I do need to say that my book explores the very notion of creativity from perspectives which, startlingly, had somehow not been adopted hitherto. And my book also makes quite a few claims, some, as a few reviewers noted, nothing less than sensational in their boldness. But I mention my book more in passing, to provide a context against which my thinking was then identifying and wrestling. For far too long, I knew we had assumed that we all knew and understood what creativity is. But, just as most authors in this book acknowledge, I realised that this was a major mistake, a serious flaw in our apprehension of the global complexity attached to creativity, and, therefore, to those who consider themselves – or are considered so by others – as creative. My four years of hard, and often difficult, research demonstrated amply the need for a greater vigilance when discussing creativity across cultures, across peoples and nations which we now can no longer simply dismiss as being alien or unrelated to our own lives. It was obvious to me – and to the many from whom I sought edification, illustration, advice – that creativity from time immemorial had been problematic and that different cultures, different societies, different tribes had had very different, and often conflicting, ways of treating and handling it and those who saw themselves, or were seen, as 'creatives'. I do not wish to labour my point, but it was quite astonishing to me to find out, note and then be the first in the world to state and claim that language was a key determinant in the shaping of a creative sensibility, outlook, disposition and personality. This claim of mine is still to be scientifically proven, and I am leaving it to those who are better equipped to do this than I. For me, it is sufficient that I know – from extensive conversations and exchanges with many, many individuals around the world – that I am right, that because language is the mainstay of cultures and the transmission of norms and values, it remains fundamental to the presence or absence of creativity in a specific society, community or tribe. By way of extension, I could also say that if we take language as coded, then the codes used by those who may actually speak, read and write the same language (say, English) may, in reality, also offer a good insight into the receptivity or otherwise of creativity. Thus, if an organisation says that 'while we want and need to be creative and innovative we do also need to realise that creativity is a precious and rare commodity . . .', we know that it is basically not supporting, or not proactively seeking, creativity.

Of course, the above may rile some who are now reading this. But more quintessential is the question which my readers, I hope, are also now beginning to ask: so how do we arrive at a consensus? How are we to get on in this new world if there is going to be, on the one hand, such an intense and urgent need for creativity and, on the other, such basic differences in its meanings, acceptances and evaluations? Let me put it another way. We know that in many of the monotheistic cultures it is considered wrong (or arrogant) of man to try and imitate his creator by attempting to create the artificial man. From the golem to the contemporary android, with all manner of progenetive types, our human attempt to try and create life is, mostly, met with consternation – frequently masquerading as a 'lack of resources' at best or as 'this cannot be allowed' at worst. Humans shiver and quake at the very thought that hidden in the deepest chasm of every scientist and/or artist is this need, this yearning, to prove that he/she can come up with something that has never been seen, heard or done before. Fools do indeed tread where angels fear to go, but without someone treading out there, as the wise Bernard Shaw observed, we would still be living in caves and wearing fig leaves (Shaw, 1921: 23).

In recent years, and especially since the publication of my controversial and provocative book, I have been blessed by more invitations than I can actually accept to share my insights and ideas about the nature of creativity and the future of our creative enterprise. And, as before, it amazes me that it is the United States which still leads in this arena of wanting to find out more. Whether or not this structuring coincides with Florida's movements of the creative class (Florida, 2004, 2005), I am not sure, but it does convince me that if the so-called great universities of the world are so described, it is because they do seek, and provide, the right and necessary platforms for problematical discourses. Hence, my visits – frequent, these days – to Yale, MIT, Columbia, UPenn, NYU and College of William & Mary. Hence, also, the numerous invitations to address exciting meetings of CEOs, executives, entrepreneurs and government officials. Hence, too, my being invited to conduct umpteen creativity workshops, particularly those pertaining to creativity across cultures. The vast divides which make the same 'creative' idea or product appear different to different people, stays at the heart of all of these invitations.

Just three weeks ago, I was invited to conduct a workshop on 'creative writing across cultures', as part of the well-established Austin International Poetry Festival, which has, now, been going on for 19 years. I had 16 poets in my workshop. I was humbled by their presence, but was struck by just how much these wonderful and gifted makers of words wanted to know and experience the real meaning of cross-/inter-cultural engagements. Starting with very simple and basic questioning of assumptions (what does the colour black or white mean to you, and for you, and in your community?) to more complicated issues (how do you view university education being conducted in the air via an aeroplane?), we travelled the gamut of realisations, observing when we become sensitive to, and aware of, the fact that not everybody thinks, feels and experiences the same way, even when the same language is utilised. Thus, white means purity, pristineness, in one culture (say, Anglo-Saxon), while it means death, mourning in another (the Chinese, for example). Black is evil to many, but beautiful to many, as well, and so on.

Thus, if we are thinking of creatively using words to communicate, it is vital to know who we are reaching, who we are targeting. Marketing campaigns become silly when the creatives working on the advertisements or jingles or images overlook the cross-cultural dimension of creativity under the false complacency of uniformed understanding or acceptance. I always regale my audiences with the famous example of how a smart young executive, newly arrived in Malaysia (then it was still Malaya), noted that the savings in the bank of which he was an employee had hit rock bottom. This observation started him thinking about developing a new, creative strategy to get people saving money again. After several months of toil, trouble and brainstorming, he arrived at the conclusion that the only way the bank was going to achieve a real measure of success in this arena was to 'go back to basics'. He advised that the bank ought to bring back the good old piggy bank – start with the young and, soon, the adults will follow. Walla! Very quickly, the piggy banks for depositing coins appeared all over the peninsula, being displayed prominently through the bank windows and doors. Advertisements appeared exhorting people to get colourful piggy banks and help their kids save. Shockingly for this young man, the savings declined even more, with more customers of this bank withdrawing their funds and going to other banks. It took a while for him, and for those around him, to discover that proclaiming the piggy bank as a solution to the savings deficit in an environment where the majority of people were Islamic was, perhaps, not the cleverest thing to do. As a side note, this young man also learnt, rather painfully, that when using the colour green, it is always advisable to check what it means or implies to those for whom it may be intended. Thus, green, for Muslims, is the colour of paradise. A little bit of homework can help create wonders, but we do need to work hard at it.

Creativity across cultures demands that we ceaselessly look for hints in order to ascertain whether or not a certain 'creative' thingy on our part will fly. Put this in other terms: if I want to sell a new creation of mine (let's assume this is a new pen), I now would not only need to be sure that my pen is, indeed, new, but also to note, in promoting it, its size (many cultures are very fussy about size) and colour. Furthermore, I would also need to ensure that when images of persons using my pen are displayed, these are done with significant sense of understanding. For example, because age and seniority are integral to respect in most Asian and African cultures, it would be safer and wiser to have the most expensive version of my pen being seen to be used by the elders and not the young, super rich and brash equity bankers. Of course, the young bankers will have a modicum of glamour, but, overall, they are in the minority, and the cultural norm works against them, so the wise marketing guys will know that in promoting my pen, the right user is foregrounded. Of course, if the pen is to be promoted at a specific event where only the super-rich derivative executives are going to be present, then, by all means, take the risk and go for them.

In creative writing, it behooves us to be doubly careful, because not only is the very nature of language use prone to misinterpretation (what exactly do we mean when we say Jane is a pretty, attractive and attention-getting woman?), but also that in different contexts and to different individuals within the *same* culture, the meanings implicit in our works might mean precisely the opposite. I learnt this as one of my first classic lessons more than 50 years ago when, in wanting to impress my teacher (I was then in grade two of primary school) in an English composition class and given the title of My Teacher, I decided to write a poem. I cannot now recall all of the lines I was so silly to write, but I remember the opening two:

> *I have a teacher called Miss Lau*
> *Whose face is like tau sar pau.*

What transpired, still strikes me. In describing my teacher's face as a *tau sar pau* – a bun stuffed with red bean paste – I was trying to tell her just how beautiful she seemed to me, because, like the bun, her face was smooth and round and sweet. But, sadly for me, my teacher misunderstood my good intentions and took my allusion to the bun to mean that she was fat, rotund and, therefore, ugly and unbecoming! Very luckily, I was spared the rod, because, through tears, I convinced her that my aim was noble, though my method was disastrous!

Those of us who are writers, creative writers, know that we have to always try and get the right word in the right order so as to fashion and elicit a meaning, a response, which we want from our readers. When, in July 1998, *Time* magazine interviewed me and asked me to provide an example of what I would proudly call a good, creative Singaporean poem, I offered a few examples, from which *Time* took this for its story (it was doing a story on creativity in Singapore):

'The East Is Red'

> *The East is red*
> *The west is blue*
> *Elvis is dead*
> *Confucius, too.* (Sin, 1998: 18)

These four simple lines, which make the complete poem, are lines from the pen of a well-known Singaporean writer known as Damien Sin (1998). Sin is better known as a writer of ghost stories, but his creativity as a poet shows itself manifestly in this short, simple, but provocative and multilayered poem. For those who don't know, Confucius was the great ancient Chinese sage, whose philosophy of life is followed, still, by millions of Chinese everywhere. In Singapore, the universally acclaimed and internationally respected father of modern Singapore, Mr Lee Kuan Yew (now in his late eighties), has always stood for Confucian values as the cornerstone of a solid, good, progressive, moral society. The traditionalists found – and continue to find – Sin's poem dismaying, indeed, a betrayal of all that the normative nurturing, especially that of a Chinese, embraces. The more modern thinking of Singaporeans, among them, people like the poet himself, believe that Confucian thought is now outmoded and to continue to worship this ancient sage only shows how unrealistic Singaporeans can be. They would like us to accept that, just as another *king* of a major civilisation (the Western) – Elvis – is dead, so, too, Confucius. But critics accuse Sin of near sacrilege when he posits Confucius in the same category as Elvis: how can the good philosopher be on the same platform as the king of pop? Sin's creativity – juxtaposing these controversial life perspectives in lines, which, once read, seem difficult to forget – arouse the ire of many, because they contain an undoubtable punch, one which delivers itself squarely where it hurts – truth.

However, as common wisdom will have it, one man's truth is another man's poison, so the lines quoted above, while stating an obvious 'truth' (both Elvis and Confucius *are* dead), leave millions upset, which may, or may not, have been the poet's intent. What the poet does seem to assert is that perhaps a new philosophy, a new way of looking at things, of guiding behaviour and human conduct for a new world might well be necessary. After all, not many Singaporeans would truly say they are happy and comfortable to accept the teachings of good Confucius, some of which now seem almost anachronistic ('wives must stand in waiting for their husbands and only eat their husband's leftovers', 'children must follow whatever their parents tell them regardless of what they – the children – think'). There are different ways of reading the poem, but one important point it illustrates is that creative writing carries within its creativity its own potential perils of multi-interpretations; readings which may, sometimes, result in extreme responses to what is written and to the writers. And here, to make matters even more tricky, we are not yet discussing the perils of real inter-/cross-cultural creativity, since the focus of the poem just alluded to is, at least, Singapore, where the dominant majority are ethnic Chinese, all of whom were brought up on good, traditional Confucianism values, even if some of them later moved on to become Christians or Buddhists or followers of the lately departed Sai Baba.

To shift from the gravity of traditional masters being taken to task in creative ways to a product which, when it was first created, obviously fulfilled a certain definite desire (and, possibly, need): petticoats. I grew up at a time when most women I knew wore these undergarments, and, for us, young boys and men, to even so much as catch a glimpse of petticoats was considered an erotic achievement. Fast forward 50-plus years and, today, it is rare to find any woman, even those who used to wear them as young brides or young ladies, wearing petticoats. So this creative garment is now, in a sense, put to rest, with the world's top fashion houses coming up with new creations belonging more to the category of lingerie than the simple, basic, traditional petticoats. Of course, there were, and always have been, women for whom the petticoat never existed and probably never will. Women in the Papua New Guinea I lived in between 1980–82 did not bother about petticoats, content to move around simply in their ragged, rugged skirts or long dresses, sometimes with nothing beneath. Cultures and cultural norms vary tremendously, and it is very hard to generalise and decide and judge what is good creatively and what is not, what might fly and what will crash, what creativity will be embraced and what repulsed.

As we move towards even greater inter-connectivity between, among and beyond the world's myriad cultures, our sense of what is creative, and how creativity is going to be received and sit among those beyond our ken and kin, is going to prove awkward, cumbersome, costly and, on occasion, dangerous. Rather than dismissing this as a 'you-learn-as-you-live' thing, or extolling the virtue of daring experimentation, we need, collectively, to recognise diverse modalities and negotiate around them. Thus it is no longer enough, or even advisable, to say that one man's music is another's noise, because these terms polarise, instead of cushion, the realisation that noise is *not* music, full-stop. But full-stops of this kind can easily descend to contempt, condescension, derision and, ultimately, open conflict and war. I am convinced that unless we will ourselves to bring our differences together, we are going to carry on creating and innovating, writing poems, stories, fictions and dramas each in our own way, without any due regard for how others think, feel and act, leading everyone to believe that he, or she, is right and has ownership of what being creative means. Such a state will spell doom, not only for millions of humans, but for our cherished goal and dream of becoming more creative, so as to save a dying world. Forget the volatile market, the struggle has already begun: witness the haphazard developments surrounding the many creative, or innovative, designs and schemes pertaining to the 'green' world debate touched upon in the first two chapters of this book. Further, to me, there does not seem to be too much in sight which lends assurance to a mutual respect for differing approaches and ideas. We need a passionate resolve to understand and experience *the other's* sense of his/her world and the accompanying values and normative systems. And when doing our creative writing, we need to be sensitive and alert, knowing that each and every word we use is nuanced, or will be given a nuance, by those who read and think differently from us.

I began by citing Osama Bin Laden. Perhaps I can also end by referencing him. In one of the very rare interviews this man ever gave a white person, shortly after 9/11, Osama was asked by the journalist: 'Can you please tell me, sir, what exactly is Al Qaeda?' Looking at his interrogator straight in the eye, Osama replied: 'You ask me about Al Qaeda. You want to know, what is Al Qaeda? I will tell you what is Al Qaeda. Al Qaeda is a metaphor'. Now how does the mind fathom a *metaphor* – that touchstone of powerful and embedded memory going deep into our unconscious? As I have tried to tell so many of those who think that terrorism is dead now, that its most-feared advocate is dead, it is easy to kill a man, but it is almost impossible to kill a metaphor. The only way one can destroy metaphor is by creatively coming up with a new and even more forceful metaphor. And this is quite a feat. Though the market is open, the challenge remains.

References

Bok, D. (2003) *Universities in the Marketplace: The Commercialization of Higher Education*. Oxford: Princeton University Press.

Florida, R. (2004) *The Rise of the Creative Class*. New York, NY: Routledge.

Florida, R. (2005) *Cities and the 'Creative Class'*. New York, NY: Routledge.

Shaw, B. (1921) *Back to Methuselah*. New York, Brentano's. Online at http://www.archive.org/details/backtomethusela00shawgoog

Sin, D. (1998) *Saints, Sinners and Singaporeans: A Collection of Poems*. Singapore: Angsana Books.

Singh, K. (2004) *Thinking Hats and Coloured Turbans: Creativity Across Cultures*. London: Prentice Hall.

Welles, O. (1938) The War of the Worlds. *The Mercury Theatre on the Air* [Radio broadcast]. Online at http://www.mercurytheatre.info/

Wells, H.G. (1898) *The War of the Worlds*. London: Heineman.

Index

[Created with the assistance of **TExtract** / www.Texyz.com]

433981